A Father's Divorce

Ryan Alfonso

Table of Contents:

Part I:

Chapter   Title

I	Dedication
II	About the Author
III	Preface
IV	Prologue
1	Introduction
2	Wife & Family History
3	Wife's Control
4	Girlfriends
5	Personal Hygiene & Cleanliness
6	Emotional Issues
7	Children
8	Final Straws
9	Wife's Court Career
10	Work
11	Friends & Family
12	Enter the Angel
13	After the Divorce
14	Support & Advice
15	Fathers' Rights Movement

Part II:

Entry #1:	Pre-Divorce Diary (Quarter 1, 2015)
Entry #2:	Separation Diary (Quarter 2, 2015)
Entry #3:	Divorce Diary (Quarter 3, 2015)
Entry #4:	More Divorce Games (Quarter 4, 2015)
Entry #5:	No End in Sight (Quarter 1, 2016)
Entry #6:	Close to the End (Quarter 2, 2016)
Entry #7:	Post Divorce Games (Quarter 3, 2016)

I
Dedication:

This book is dedicated to the wonderful fathers, husbands, and boyfriends out there which do what they can with their limited resources, and live life to the fullest when they see their children (no matter what length of time).

This book is for those fathers who get their weekly harassment child support payment reminders saying they are criminals before they even send in their checks and continue to fight for equal rights to their children.

But most importantly, this book is dedicated to my own children who have been pulled away from me. I love and miss you all so much! I always have and always will. I have loved you the moment I heard your cries in the delivery room. I am sorry for what happened, but you will always be in my heart and I will never give up fighting for you.

I also want to give my sincere gratitude and thanks to my own Yankee Bell. Without you, I would be lost. I want to thank you and your family for being so supportive and wonderful to me. You are my rock, my world, my joy, I love you.

II
About the Author:

Ryan Alfonso is a veteran of the US Army and the Iraq war. He became a loving, devoted husband at the young age of 23. He became a father three times over in 2009, 2012, & 2014. This story explains how at a blink of an eye that can all go away and a once seemingly perfect life could be destroyed for two simple things: the sense of entitlement & money. Like the main character; he was reduced to see his children only four weeks per year!

III
Preface:

This is a story written by our main character; Mr. Robert Arlotta, a young man who at an early age learned how to fend for himself. A man who always worked; no matter what the pay or hours. A man, who served his country in Iraq, eventually got an education, and a good paying job. This man eventually became a loving, devoted husband at the young age of 23. He became a father three times over in 2009, 2012, & 2014.

This story explains how at a blink of an eye, a once seemingly perfect life can all go away and be destroyed for two simple things: the sense of entitlement & money.

This book is unlike any other. These next few chapters are of the life, the divorce, and the removal of the main character from his children's lives. You can kind of say, this is his diary. He has included his thoughts, feelings, and emotions and tied them all into this.

This book is not to be used in any way as legal assistance or provides any legal advice. Please consult an attorney for your specific case. Due to legality issues; this book is for entertainment purposes only and is considered a fictional novel. The following story is based upon true events. The names, places, and other personal information have been changed to protect the author and publisher of any legal recourse or legal ramifications by the guilty individuals. Some if not all items may or may not have happened.

This novel is a story of one father's journey through a corrupt system. It is based upon the diary of a father seeking justice and fair treatment. The schedule of events in this story has been changed, but the time tables and timeframes remain untouched. Enjoy!

IV
Prologue:

This novel follows a man named Mr. Robert Arlotta. This is a story of the year that changed his life forever. This book is divided into two parts. The first is his story: his background, his ex-wife, their history, issues, and his eventual saving grace.

The second part is a diary of sorts which involves the complete destruction of a man, his constitutional rights, his rights as a father, and an annihilation of a war veteran's military service. All this for one simple thing: Greed. This part is the complete diary of Robert's journey through it all.

It shows how one person can be defeated by Courts, Judges, Lawyers, and the entitlements of money. Where accusations are proof, and evidence is thrown out if it proves you are innocent. You are no longer a father, but a pay check. The same courts, who claim that children are their #1 priority, are the first ones to pull you from your children and leave their "child support" as a fighting coin until the end.

Robert endured a pre-planned divorce which during the first six months of it, he could not keep up. His attorney which employs several attorneys and dozen more paralegals, assistants, and others were all working on my case and could not keep up. The lawyers from his firm, along with others he spoke with explained that this case was premeditated, preplanned, and all the paperwork and made up lies were ready to go and ready to be mailed out.

Robert spoke with multiple attorneys from different states. They could not believe his story, it is wrong at every angle. This severe corruption is unbelievable. Even attorneys within the state of New Jersey could not believe the unethical practices in this case. He has heard everything from, "this is against the law" to "this is malpractice." Luckily, Robert saved every email, every letter, and every court document. Thousands of pages and gigabytes worth of hard drive space.

Many people ask why write a book on this? The answer is simple. This book is for fathers going through similar cases. This book is to let those other fathers know there is hope, there is light, and they are not alone. Others like you have been down that path, the heartbreak, the suicidal thoughts, and the pain. All that can be said is, keep going. There is light, we promise, but it is a long road. Hopefully, you find this book enlightening and perhaps it can help you find your path.

Part I

Chapter 1: Introduction

My name is Robert Arlotta. Before I begin my story of events which will change the course of my life, I would like to tell you a little about me, my wife Natalie, my marriage, my three beautiful children, things that I have done. Afterwards, I will tell you about the beginning of the break down, lies made by people who said they loved me, and tell you about the courts that have lost touch with reality.

I am not famous, nor is this a biography, so I will keep it brief: I am an only child, born to a mother who had severe medical issues. I grew up taking care of her. She had a severe case of Lupus. She had several sets of artificial hips where it made her mobility very difficult, she would break into seizures at a moment's notice (especially in the sun), and overall health was diminished. Though not divorced, she and my father were estranged from each other and he lived in another town. This was the case before I was born.

I was born in the 1980s in Manhattan, New York. Due to my mother's Lupus, I was an only child. She had multiple miscarriages and I was her "miracle." As she always called me.

My family was of standard Irish & Italian heritage. My mother and grandmother took care of me and taught me how to cook, clean, and take care of myself. During my younger years, I saw first-hand my mother and father's relationship.

They were separated before I was born and during many times of my life. My father would come and live with us for short times, but would eventually leave and most of the time lived in different towns.

I have always wanted children. I promised myself I would never be divorced and place my children through such hell. If anything, I would stay in the relationship for the sake of my children.

I grew up with my mother in an area of New Jersey called; Brendon County. This area is extremely democratic and a very affluent area. It is a suburb of New York City, and the majority of the residents work in New York City and maintain six figure incomes. The other residents all come from "old money." The reason we were there was because my mother and father grew up there and my father worked on Wall Street in the city.

I grew up around my mother's family mainly. All of her family that we speak with is up in Massachusetts. I have an Aunt, Uncle, and two cousins which I consider sisters and who are also the God Mothers of two of my children. I have a relationship with my father's side of the family, but not as strong as my mothers.

We are all devout Roman Catholics and my mother along with her family always felt strongly about our religion and attending church. I had a fairly standard childhood. I participated in sports, coached fencing, honor roll, and other activities. During the summers, my mother and I would go camping.

When I was a young child and teenager, I was involved heavily in the Boy Scouts. My mother helped with this hobby and supported it greatly. She was heavily involved with donating her time with helping out the scout troop. I started out in the Tiger Cubs at seven years old and worked all the way up to Eagle Scout. During the summers, I visited a local camp called, "No Be Bo Sco." I spent the majority of my summers there achieving ranks in the scouts along with learning to thrive in new environments on my own and, developed survival skills and personal development. I was able to attain the rank of Eagle Scout (which now, only a few people know what that is).

I was also involved with the sport of fencing. It's that sport where people "fencers" use swords to poke each other. My father was a fencer and started me out young. I fenced with a non-profit fencing club which he was a member of when he was younger, in the 1970s. His coach from back then was also mine.

This coach started the non-profit and was the main instructor. He was an older gentleman, and through the years, I developed a strong relationship with both him and his wife. They gave me great opportunities to include taking over and instructing a high school girl's fencing team while I was in high school myself. The school originally had issues with this, but he was supportive and quelled many of the concerns explaining how professional I am. After that, I became a full instructor and coach with the club for years, teaching both adults and children almost every day of the week at the various schools they operated out of.

Eventually, this man retired and the non-profit members voted me into the position of President of the non-profit. As a hobby and community service, I operated the non-profit which taught fencing to adults and children throughout the county.

While growing up, I took care of my mother, as her Lupus would flare up often, along with the mobility issues and seizures. I would do the household chores, work around the yard, and help her with the day to day activities. I would assist her when she became ill, had severe pain with her hips, or broke out into seizures. It was quite a task and heartbreaking. But growing up with her and her condition, it was second nature to me and all I ever knew.

She eventually died when I was 17, while I was away in basic training for the US Army. I joined the Army at 17 in their early enlistment program. My mother had to sign a parental release form to allow me to join at such an early age. She knew how I always wanted to serve in the military. I served for a total of eight years. The experience was amazing and took me to different areas including a year tour in Iraq.

After she passed away, I completed high school and worked full time at various retailers doing electronic sales and repair to pay for my basic necessities. I worked multiple jobs along with school and I got my first apartment at 17.

After my mother died, I eventually received her inheritance which was processed with the sale of her house. I was to split the difference of the profits of the sale of the house with my father. It was eventually sold at the bottom of the market. I received about $75,000. Natalie, my wife at the time immediately used it to pay off her credit card debt. She blew though $60,000 within two years. Before it was all gone, I was able to use the remaining $15,000 to pay off some of my student loans. She was not happy about this. Rightfully so, as she explained that it was "her money." Eventually she brought this back to court, saying that she is entitled to the $75,000 claiming I still had it (she must have forgotten that it was used on her credit card debt).

From a young age, I wanted to be a pilot. I always had a love for aviation. I went on my first airplane ride from Newark, NJ to Florida on Kiwi Airlines with my family. The flight crew brought me into the cockpit where I saw all sorts of buttons, gauges, and "stuff." I was instantly hooked. Growing up, I wanted to be a pilot. Even my childhood nickname was "Kiwi." So it made sense when it was time to go to college, to choose that field.

After high school, I started college and continued my career in the military. I was stationed down in Florida. While I was in the military, I took college classes in aviation at the local University. I really wanted to stay in Florida. It is a beautiful state. Plus, I hate the cold weather of New Jersey.

In college, I continued my training to become a pilot, but eventually I ran out of money and could no longer afford the training flights. I thought about my skill set and changed my career course. I used my technical skills with computers and became an aircraft mechanic and more specifically an "avionics" technician where I repaired the aircraft communication, navigation, computer, and electrical systems.

During this time, my soon to be wife was just a girlfriend. I begged her to move down with me, but she had us stay in New Jersey, where she grew up. I came back to New Jersey and eventually completed three college degrees though the college campus on the local military base and a certificate to work as an aircraft mechanic.

After the military, I started a career in aviation. I worked midnight shifts in most of the jobs which worked out with watching the children. I would go to work when they went to sleep and I was able to play and take care of them during the day while I was home.

I married young at the age of 23. I got warnings about marrying so young from family and friends. I did not listen or heed their words.

After being married, I had multiple jobs in aviation. My wife was always pushing me to go out and make more money. Each job I got, I made more and more and picked up second jobs teaching at Universities which I was once a student.

Like most people, I've dreamed about leaving behind a legacy, something I would be remembered for. I envisioned inventing something like a flying car, like the Back to the Future DeLorean. As I grew up, I learned that my children are my legacy.

Chapter 2: Wife & Family History

I met my wife through friends in high school and we began dating. She was two years older than me. We began our adventure in my senior year of high school when she was in college. When Natalie and I got together, I remember the hallowed words she explained to me about our relationship, "I am entitled to be happy, and this makes me happy."

We were always on again/off again with our relationship. We were together one moment and broken up the other. Usually it was always my fault (as I was told) and I had to apologize for something which I didn't even know was wrong. We'll get into that stuff later. We eventually got married after my deployment to Iraq in 2006. To save on costs, as New Jersey is extremely expensive, we lived in an apartment complex owned by her father. We lived in a tiny, two bedroom apartment.

Natalie had an odd relationship with her father. He was very controlling and demanded Natalie perform certain things without question. He did this with all of his children. Natalie told me of times which he forced both her and her brothers to play sports or he would not pay for their college, or in other instances would make them walk home and drop them off a few towns away.

Her father made Natalie do various tasks or make life decisions which he was in control of and then would reward her with money. Before our first son was born, Natalie cut a deal with him that if she quit her job, he would provide her $2000-$4000 a month in an allowance for her to have spending cash.

Another example of his control was the naming of our children. He wanted certain names, and when he did not get what he wanted, he would have a temper tantrum and "cut her off" for a period of time.

Natalie's other family members were interesting at best. She had two brothers and a step-sister. Her step sister and cousins were strippers.

Her brothers loved to squabble and lazy. They both lived down in Washington D.C. Her oldest brother required Natalie and her mother to call him to wake him up for work as he did not deal with alarm clocks and at every family get together, she and her two older brothers would constantly squabble with each other about their father's money and their inheritance. They were always fighting over their father's money, his assets, and apartment buildings. He was not even dead yet!

Natalie's mother and father were divorced and her mother had a "very good, unethical, vindictive lawyer" which Natalie was proud of to represent her mother and often boasted how he has the longest running divorce cases in New Jersey history. I would learn later that Natalie retained this same lawyer to represent her.

Natalie's mother was a medicated schizophrenic who was living in a make-shift apartment within her ex-husband's apartment building which we lived in as well. She was in the downstairs unit which looked more like a storage room than an actual apartment. I guess Natalie's father was nice enough to rent it out to his ex-wife and her current husband.

Her mother remarried a few years ago and her current husband's career is still about to take off. As he states, he was never a "9 to 5 type of guy," thus he never worked a real job.

Instead, his music career was always about to take off and make millions of dollars. This was the line that he has used for the past twenty years. This man is a recovering alcoholic, who still drinks. Many occasions, when Natalie's mother was over watching the children and he was present, he would raid my liquor cabinet and take down ¼ bottle of Patron Tequila in a sitting. Despite my objections, my wife allowed him to drink and watch the children alone. Thus, when I found out the days he was going to watch the children and decided to drink his large quantity- normal alcohol consumption, I started to hide my liquor before he came over.

During family occasions, while we were out at one of Natalie's family homes; he would get so drunk; he would fall asleep in one of the family beds for the night. I brought up my concerns about all this, but I was being "mean" there are a lot of recovering alcoholics which drink on a daily basis.

But the worst thing in my mind was that he and Natalie's family had no respect. He frequently explained how he was golden and how I am constantly wrong and how dumb I am. Natalie and her family would concur with him.

He had no respect with items. Not only was he taking alcohol, but special foods, sandwiches and other items. I remember a few times where I had lunch with my name in the fridge wrapped with my name on it and it would be taken with the excuse "I didn't know it was yours." It's in my fridge, with my name on it, packed in my work lunchbox…how did you not know?

Both Natalie's mother and step father went to a quack doctor who was known to be the best doctor for giving medical diagnoses and constructing paperwork to get people medical disability retirements.

They got their disability retirements with her mother only working for a few years and her step father not working at all. It is the classic case of people not putting into system, but reaping its benefits.

What is more unfortunate is that I have been told by Natalie and her family that this "music man" job is more productive to society and more important than anything I have done- including the military and his "financial ideals" are correct and were being followed by Natalie because they are "sound decisions."

These sound decisions left Natalie's mother and stepfather with multiple homes throughout the years. Unfortunately, due to bad spending habits and little income, both of them lost three homes in three years with their spending.

Unfortunately, Natalie's spending was also affected with these financial decisions as she maxed out two credit cards on cruises and trips with her girlfriends along with thousands of dollars in student loans for an education degree she ended up not wanting to utilize.

Eventually, I thought that Natalie would start noticing that the sound financial advice she was receiving was not working, but unfortunately, it was not her spending or the advice she was following. It was because I did not make enough money (according to her).

Chapter 3: Wife's Control

Natalie was always about control. I believe she learned this trait from her parents, especially her father. It began while we were courting and dating. I would submit to her ideas, her thoughts, and her wants. When I brought up an idea, it was either automatically wrong or "stupid;" even if we ended up going with that idea anyway. She would rephrase it as it was her idea in the first place.

It continued even on our wedding day. She told me how I could not drink alcohol during the reception. She didn't want me to have one sip of alcohol because it would ruin "her" wedding. So I didn't. I didn't have time to be honest. I was helping her as she was taking down triple shots of Black House and other alcoholic beverages. She was drunk before the end of the night.

Natalie was tied to the hip of her parents. Natalie saw her mother on a daily basis. If her mother wasn't physically right next to her, she was on the phone with her. She also saw her father as well. Each holiday, we HAD to go to her families. Since her family did not know how to cook, Thanksgiving was with her family at a diner. Christmas and Christmas Eve was with her aunt's house.

Natalie limited my time with my family. My mother's & father's family would get together during the Thanksgiving and Christmas holidays. Natalie did not want us to go, since holidays were to be spent with her family only.

She would always find an excuse to not go, especially with my family up in Massachusetts. Two hours in a car was way too long for her. So seeing my family on a holiday was a rare treat. If we were to see my family, it was normally done with just the boys and I. Natalie would not participate.

If she did go, she would not get dressed or prepared until the very last minute to ensure that we got there late. In the car ride to wherever we were going, both the children and I would hear her screaming having an aggressive temper tantrum in the car; like a teenaged girl who did not want to go. Thus, most of the time, especially non-holidays; my family would have to come to us.

This same behavior was the same for funerals. I was required to go to her family funerals, which I did not have any issues with. That's what husbands and family do. But when I had a death in my family; either I went by myself or if she came, I would get an earful of why she should not have to come.

One of the most important funeral services I remember was my mother's memorial. I held onto my mother's ashes for years. My mother always said she wanted to have grandchildren and she also wanted to be poured out into the Atlantic Ocean. I waited for years until I had children to pour her ashes. I figured that I would fulfill her final two wishes. So after she became a grandmother (post mortem of course), I decided it was time to pour her ashes into the Atlantic Ocean.

My family in Massachusetts helped me pick a spot in Hampton Beach, New Hampshire to perform the memorial service and spread her ashes. After all the planning was completed, I inquired with Natalie if she wanted to attend. At first I met with resistance, but she eventually said she would go, but only if I found a babysitter.

Natalie's mother babysat the children most of the time for her to go out on her social outings, so I asked if she would be able to watch the children so that Natalie could attend this very important moment with me.

Days went by and I asked Natalie if her mother ever responded. She said with a smile that her mother cannot watch the children, thus she cannot go to the memorial service. So, I went with my family to perform the service and drove to New Hampshire and back within a day.

When I got home, I was extremely exhausted from driving all day, wet from rain and snow, and emotionally drained after saying goodbye to my mother. When I went into the apartment, I found Natalie's mother inside with her. They were hanging out in the apartment all day together. I inquired with Natalie that if her mother was available today; why did she not want to watch the children so that Natalie could attend the memorial? Instead of answering the question; Natalie and her mother found it prudent to just leave and left me with the children.

Now on top of being emotionally drained, I was devastated. Finding out that Natalie and her mother lied to me so that she had an excuse not to come and support her husband blew my mind. I guess my mother's memorial and ash burial was not that important. What is even more disturbing is her lack of empathy while she left me in tears when I confronted her about it.

Natalie was also controlling when it came to who I associated with and long-time friends I held dearly. She forced me to end contact with many friends who she found to be "bad influences on us" which included many of my female friends.

According to Natalie; men and women cannot be friends. She claims that there is always a sexual undertone. However, this theory did not apply to her, as she was the exception to the rule. She firmly believed this as I would previously talk with other women about work, current events, school, etc. just to have her accuse me of trying to have an affair with them. Natalie would constantly tell me how men she spoke to on a regular basis had a "thing" for her and would refer to them as "backup husbands."

I alienated so many friends because of her. She even tried to get me to end my relationship with my closest friend and supporter- Harry. Many times she would tell me how she doesn't like him and how is he not good for me. She tried everything in her power to not allow me to see him.

I needed permission to go out with friends. Usually if I asked, she would have a temper-tantrum and leave herself. If I spoke to another woman, even work related, I would get the same temper-tantrum. During these instances, she would leave and wouldn't come home for a few hours, or sometimes a few days.

Natalie would constantly check my phone on a daily basis. She would check text messages, emails, phone call history, etc. I had to submit it to her every day. If I didn't like it, she would threaten divorce. Her excuse was because I "cheated on her once" when I decided to talk to a female friend without her knowledge. This short backstory was when I was talking to a female friend before I left for Iraq and she was wishing me well and I did not tell Natalie about it because I knew speaking to another woman would upset her. We did mention going out for coffee when I got back home though, perhaps that was cheating?

When I was out; whether it was for work, training, etc. Natalie would check an application which tracked me via GPS. I think the program was called "Latitude." She would check to see where I was a lot. It didn't stop there though; she would check the computer, phone, and every electronic piece of equipment, including my work laptop. If I placed a password on one of the devices, I would be greeted with a temper tantrum, lecture, and inquisition about what I am trying to hide from her.

On occasion, my phone or computer would do an update to the software which would prompt a computer password screen. She would become excessively irate and "freak out" about it. She would once again question me on what I was hiding.

When I tried to reverse the roles and requested her to relinquish her phone to me (or computer) I received an outright refusal, her stuff was "off-limits" and another lecture of how dare I ask followed by her storming out for the rest of the day to hang out with girlfriends or her family. It was a double standard.

Professionals I have spoken to have informed me that these behaviors are normally performed when they (the people trying to control) exhibit those unethical behaviors and are usually the ones which are cheating on their significant others.

For work, I am required each year to go into the Midwest for training for one or two weeks. Each time I would get my orders to leave she became irate and explained how it is a vacation for me, which any work training function is not.

She explained that if I go on a two week vacation for "work" she is entitled to the same. So usually, a week before my trip, when I tried to get ready for it, she would leave and the moment the taxi dropped me back home after a trip, she would leave again for her vacation.

But of course after I got home, she did the calculations of my "per diem" monies and said they were hers to spend. In government, "per diem" is a term used for money given to you during travel for food and small expenses. As I would be in a hotel room for one, two, or even three weeks without a kitchen, the per diem money would pay for food. It changes on the area, length of travel time, and other factors; but it is usually $50 a day which usually covered three meals and a snack.

I always had to maximize this number and not go out. Natalie would check each day with me to make sure I didn't spend my "per diem" and if I was to go out with other trainees or coworkers during training, I would get the speech of how going out to a restaurant with friends and not making myself available to her without any noise (i.e. in my hotel room), I was being selfish and should be ashamed. If there was a female trainee in my group, then it would be cheating.

The control over money did not end with the per diem. Natalie demanded full control over the checkbook and monies. Natalie did not allow me to manage the financial accounts. My paycheck began supporting her mother and step-father. Natalie went back to school for degrees and certifications in teaching which she explained she would never utilize.

After the sale of my mother's old house, I received half of the net value of the home as inheritance. Natalie used my inheritance to make lavish purchases, cruises with her family, and on her credit cards. Before it fully ran out, I used a portion of it for some student loan debt I had. She threw me out of the house for using it. I was not allowed to use my mother's inheritance as it was for the "family" or really- her. Later on in my divorce case, Natalie would actually attempt to get the court to force me to pay her my inheritance again.

For years, the majority of my pay went to entertainment costs for her and her girlfriends, Natalie's expensive tastes, and supporting her step-father's music career. If I spent $5 on lunch, I would hear it the moment I got home.

At some certain points in the marriage, I wanted to start saving, especially seeing each one my paychecks being spent within days without anything going towards debt. I knew she was living beyond her means. When I began taking some money out each week and putting the cash aside almost like a "rainy day fund" I was accused of hiding money from her, forced to give it to her and it was spent right away. I remember the words, "How dare I take her well earned money." When I explained where the money comes from and where it should be going, I was told that I am wrong and she contributes more money to the marriage without even working.

When I received additional money, like working a second job, teaching at the Air Force base, doing overtime, or my "Post 9/11" GI Bill Education monies; I had to hand over those funds to her as well. Those moneys went to her credit cards. My credit cards were none of her concern.

Natalie would constantly belittle me: Not only did her family do it, but she would as well. It did not matter if we were in public, with friends, alone, or in front of the children. She would always rave about her high IQ and that if I took a test, I would score extremely low. She would constantly belittle me and explain how I was dumb and an idiot. How her college was the best, and mine was the worst in all academics. How her step father did more for the children then I ever did. She would consistently tell people how she supports her family financially, even though I was the only one that worked. During the divorce process, Natalie would even bolster about her high IQ during mediation sessions in which she informed my attorney how she qualifies for "Mensa" and is more intelligent than him.

Natalie has belittled me in front of others explaining that my cooking is terrible, my cleaning habits are just me being "OCD" and "unnecessary" and that my paycheck (the only one paying the bills) is nothing compared to what she brings in financially (which is zero). She consistently explains that she is a strong, independent woman; and I, a piece of worthless poop.

Natalie's mother would comment that my job is worthless and I must quit it to give her daughter more of a break. I would be compared to her husband and told to emulate him, since his upcoming music career is much more important and exciting.

The question arises though, if I quit my job; and I am the only one working; where does the flow of money come from?

Chapter 4: Girlfriends

Natalie grew up in a wealthy area. When her family sold their home, it was in the millions of dollars. Her friends are all from the same area and demographic. They are all from extremely wealthy families. So both Natalie and her girlfriends are extremely well off. A lot of her friends do not work, or do not have real jobs. Some of her friends have trusts which their family set up for them and their daily job is to "manage their trust." Other friends were told by their families to get jobs to stay busy. Her girlfriends always free during the day.

At one point, Natalie stated that she was going to "work" with a few of them at a local firm. I asked about her hours and pay. It was either making little to no money. It was more of a social thing. It was a club, not a job.

During the day, while I was at work, Natalie's mother would normally watch the children for Natalie to hang out with her friends. When I got home from work, she would leave again. Other days, when she did not leave, she would be on the phone or computer with them for hours. I often wondered how the ones that did work were able to do this, as if I was a boss I would be pissed to have an employee be on the phone constantly with their friends, not getting their work done.

On a daily basis, Natalie would leave for hours on end without explaining where she was. Natalie would leave during the day and night, constantly hanging out with girlfriends all the time and with the birth of each child, I was staying up with the babies the entire night and going to work the next day. She would be too tired to help.

Natalie always was entitled to something or owed by the world. Every holiday including Father's Day, my birthday, and other occasions were all about her; no one else. She was entitled to see her friends on a daily basis. However, when it came to her "equal" which she hated the term, it was not allowed. She would consistently explain how I have no friends and that I am a loner and that is why she needs to go out with her friends instead of me going out on occasion with friends.

To attempt to prove this hypothesis of hers regarding me being a "loner," she went as far as making me take an online questionnaire which consisted of about one hundred questions about my interests, personality, and quirks. She was firm that I had Asperger's syndrome. I took the test to appease her, and when I scored lower than her (far from being a loner, anti-social, or Asperger's syndrome), she began to have a temper tantrum and the now "accurate test" became invalid.

Natalie would continue her control games with her girlfriends throughout the years. Many times, I would have set plans with coworkers and friends and inform her of those plans weeks in advance. When the time came, she would make last minute plans herself and when I would start to get ready for my planned event; she would leave. I got used to the "I forgot" excuse. Luckily, my friend's love children and I would bring them with me.

Other times, I would have last minute plans; usually emergencies. During these times, Natalie would either leave on the spot or call her friends while I was rushing out the door.

During one instance I remember, there was the funeral and wake of a dear friend from the fencing club. I knew this woman for years and she was like a grandmother to me. I desperately wanted to go to the wake to pay my respects. I told Natalie about the death the moment I found out. She did not have any prior plans as she hung out with her girlfriends already that week.

After I told her that I wanted to attend the wake; Natalie's plans changed within seconds. On a whim, she wanted to go out with her girlfriends again. I begged and pleated with her to go to my friend's wake. It was extremely important to me, but she did not care. She began havening a temper tantrum explaining that she wants to go out again with her friends. I tried to explain that in my mind, a funeral takes precedence over seeing friends three times in a row during the week. I was overruled. I was not allowed to go to my friend's wake and funeral unless I got a babysitter. Natalie's mother came up and only gave me one hour to go to my friend's wake. At the wake there were dozens of old members who have not been around (moving, other priorities, etc.) which I grew up with. They were there to pay their respects and later went out for drinks and food afterwards. I was only able to attend all this very briefly, and left quickly as Natalie's mother could only spare an hour since her TV show was coming on.

This was the last time I saw all these individuals in one setting. When Natalie got back from seeing her girlfriends, she berated me again explaining that "how dare I think that going to a friend's funeral is more important that her happiness."

Natalie's social obligations also interfered with my work schedule. My current job is the best one I have ever had. I have a flexible schedule which I can change my hours along with the ability to work from home a few days a month. They call that "telework."

On my telework days, I am supposed to be working on my duties as I do in the office. There should be no difference between working at the office and working at home. Natalie loved these telework days because it was an excuse for her to leave and I would take care of the children. I told her how I needed to get work done and helping out a little is fine, but I cannot watch the children every second as she leaves. I was ignored and was told that it is my job to watch the children while I am at home, telework or not.

Initially, I was working from 8:00AM to 4:30PM. I would go to the gym religiously every morning. It became a little much for me. I asked Natalie if I could go into work at 7:00AM and spend the last hour at the gym. I would still get home at 4:30PM like usual. She originally agreed. So, I took an earlier work schedule shift to perhaps get a run or workout in. Now I got out of work an hour earlier. Within days of changing my schedule, she reversed her "approval" and told me to stop going to the gym and I was expected to be at her front door at 3:30PM. I was expected home (no workout) as it interfered with her newly changed social obligations with her girlfriends. This was odd since that is the time I leave work. I do have a commute time. I was told that if I want to go to the gym, I must do it during work hours according to her.

I work fifteen minutes from my home. Natalie's "job" of watching one child during the day ends at 3:00PM. So when I arrived home at 3:45 (15 minutes after work), I was greeted with screaming and yelling of how horrible I am for leaving her alone with the children. It did not matter if I was late coming home or on time. The moment I got home, it was the same story.

On day, Natalie explained that I do not give her time to go to the gym. I told her I am with the children while she is out from the moment I come home to the moment I leave for work while she is out with her friends. That did not count? If I am with the children and she is out and about each moment I am home from work, how is that not time?

On occasion, I would request to go out with friends, as she did. But if I did not secure a baby sitter for the children or go without her permission, I would find myself locked out of the apartment with the chain locking the door.

Seeing what was going on, my aunt and cousins came down to take the children off our hands for a weekend. They wanted Natalie and me to have a "weekend off" and attempt to repair the strained relationship. Natalie used this opportunity to leave for the weekend. She didn't say where she went. I asked her, but no response. I can only imagine.

Many occasions, when Natalie stated that she was going out with her girlfriends and left, while she was out those same girlfriends would call the house telephone line looking for Natalie. She was supposed to be with them. That's interesting "I thought she was with you?"

As I grew up from my party days and became a responsible adult and father, she regressed. I firmly believe that she never came out of her "rebellious phase." I understand completely what that phase in life is like, but it is over. Once you have a child, let alone three, it's time to grow up and take on a responsible role. Not just for the sake of your child's upbringing and safety, but also for them to become a strong person. If you are a parent, you will understand: children are sponges and learn from you. If you are not a responsible adult and just want to party, that is what they see as the normal thing to do.

Chapter 5: Personal Hygiene & Cleanliness

Natalie is a self-promoted "good person" and a stay at home mother. Natalie's home skills were to be desired. She never learned them growing up. Her mother was too sick to cook and her family was always very wealthy, and she was able to eat out each day and did not have to clean up after herself. So, Natalie never learned how to cook or clean.

It also does not help when she was of the mindset of cooking, cleaning, and raising children are "not her responsibility." My family invited her to learn from them, but she refused. Heating premade chicken tenders and tater-totes in the oven was considered "home-cooked."

Keeping herself and the children clean was a challenge for her. Her cars, each one has been subject to being a disaster. Her old car, a Toyota Corolla and her new one: a Toyota Sienna minivan both had to have professional detailing every six months.

Natalie would go to fast food restaurants multiple times each day. Both the children and she would eat in the car. The car cup holders would become motes with soda and water in them as she left the fountain soda paper cups in the cup holders for days and the condensation from those cups along with them breaking down created a little pool of disgusting mess.

Her cars always contained a mountain of soda bottles, candy wrappers, fast food, and paperwork. It was disgusting. When she opened a door, many of these items fell onto the ground. The children would have to walk on top of this mess to get to their car seats. The car seats themselves were even sticky with old food.

The apartment was also a mess. Natalie had paperwork stacked in areas which I called "vortexes." Important paperwork mixed with junk mail with old food mixed in where inside each one. There were dozens of these.

There was old food, bottles, and just plain "stuff" all over, under beds, just everywhere. There were many times when the apartment became infested with carpet beetles and other pests. We had two cats living with us and there was cat litter and cat pee all over the place which eventually stained the floors.

During the marriage, I would constantly clean the apartment. Before we had children and after. My mother always instilled in me having a clean body and clean home. Plus being in the military made me even more organized. When I got home from work, I would always clean normally to the early morning or late evening. But it was exhausting. I would always be underfoot to Natalie. I felt that she needed a maid just to follow her around.

My concerns are being ignored and dismissed. While I work, cook, clean, and take care of the children, I have Natalie and her family on a daily basis creating more work for me. Natalie and her family leave large messes and wait till I come home from work to clean them. At one time, a full bottle of milk spilled all over the kitchen floor and underneath the refrigerator. It was left for me to clean when I got home.

She would belittle my cleaning saying that my cleaning habits are just me being "OCD" and "unnecessary." Eventually I quit. The messes were getting larger and larger and I was at the brink of exhaustion.

Natalie wanted to hire her step-father's friend (also his drug dealer) to come clean the apartment each week. I said no, as I did not trust this person and really didn't think that we had the money for a maid. I asked that since she is a stay at home mother, why couldn't she pitch in? Both her and her mother screamed at me for this notion. Nonetheless, they hired his friend and not surprising, things went missing and the apartment was never cleaned. But I still had to pay his friend.

Before my divorce began and I was removed from the apartment, I was able to take pictures of this disaster, but it proved useless in court.

On many occasions, Natalie and I were asked by Eric's State Social Workers, friends, and family about the condition of the apartment and the mess. Natalie always had the same excuse, "My husband failed to clean it." Even after my removal from the apartment during the divorce, her apartment mess was my fault and I was questioned by friends, workers, and anyone who saw it.

Natalie's personal hygiene was non-existent. Natalie would wear the same outfits for days at a time and did not shower for days to weeks at a time. Natalie bathed once a week at best. Brushing her curly hair became too much of a hassle, so every six months she would spend about $500 to have it straightened. She did not own a toothbrush, so brushing of teeth was not expected. She was constantly sick due to the apartment being a wreck and her lack of showers and keeping up with herself.

Natalie and children's bathroom habits were non-existent as well. Many times I would find feces left in the toilet without toilet paper. I thought it was my toddler and when I went to potty train him again, he explained that he did not do it. Natalie chimed in and explained it was her. I inquired about the lack of toilet paper and I was yelled at and she explained that "you do not have to wipe every time." During those womanly days, she would not wipe down the toilet from the blood and it eventually made permanent stains on the toilet.

She instilled the same hygiene with the children. No baths, no brushing of teeth, no wiping. If it was to be done, guess who was responsible. Many days I would pick them up for visitation and they would be sticky and not bathed for days.

Natalie did not help with the laundry, as that task is below her. "Why should a stay at home mother do laundry?" That was my answer. So, with my schedule being jammed packed as it was, her father picked up the laundry each week and sent it to a "Wash & Fold" laundromat service.

Chapter 6: Emotional Issues

Natalie claims she has depression which she blames on her genetics. She takes medications for Bi-Polar depression.

These medications sedate her to the couch. She has her good days and has her bad days. It is quite apparent when she is depressed and when she is at a high. One moment, she is extremely nice and offering the world, the next she is screaming and yelling. One instance I remember is when she offered some furniture to me when I was removed from the apartment during the divorce. After she offered it, a few days later she was crying in court how I wanted to dismantle her apartment and it was never offered, I just wanted to steal everything.

These medications make her forget about what she does, what she says, and what she is thinking. Many times, she would produce written items such as an email or letter and not remember writing it. I would show it to her, but I would be lying about it.

Natalie would lie about things and when I questioned them, she was a good person, and I was lying (turning the tables). Other times, she would attempt to get me to spill the beans on anything by asking "do you have something to tell me" or "I know where you have been" or "what have you been doing"

While she sat at the computer for hours, she would consistently look up people on Facebook. When someone "defriended" her on Facebook, she would become irate for days then depressed for others. She would ask me why I thought this random person would "defriend" her and she obsessed about it. She would obsess about her ex-boyfriend which she was reunited with, which you will read about in this book.

Since we have met, Natalie was addicted to pain medication & sleep aids. She takes in 6-10 Excedrin a day; she claims it is for her migraines. She takes Ambien every night. She cannot go to sleep without it. She claims that she gets migraines multiple times a day and requires this amount of pain killers.

To also aid her migraines, she was addicted to Diet Coke. I don't believe a drop of water ever touched her lips. Any time you saw her, she had a Diet Coke in her hand. I really do think that her Bi-Polar medication mixed with the Excedrin and Ambien is interfering with each other and causing an imbalance.

Before I was removed from the apartment during the divorce, I also was able to take pictures of Natalie's medications and dosages. But once again, to no avail. Pictures of medication is not proof and in addition, Natalie's attorney explained through letters and in court how Natalie's depression is too severe for her to ever work, but it is not severe to impact the children and she can be the custodial parent.

I had severe concerns about Natalie, her behavior, and her lack of judgment. She was getting daily advice from her mother (who is a medicated schizophrenic) and an alcoholic step-father.

In 2013, we became pregnant with a third child (before my actual 3rd child), but without my knowledge she took the advice of her mother (a medicated schizophrenic) and aborted the pregnancy. She told me a week after she did it. What is really messed up about it is the fact that she was discussing baby names and the pregnancy with my family over the phone AFTER she already aborted! She told me that I was the reason she aborted. She explained that she knew I wanted the abortion and that why she did it. I still never understood this as she knew what my opinion was and how happy I was about having a baby. Apparently, the medicated schizophrenic in her life spoke with a few imaginary friends and came to the conclusion that it was a good idea.

I left the home for a few weeks. I stayed in hotel & motel rooms for over two months. It cost me a fortune. Eventually I moved back in to attempt to fix the marriage. But Natalie's first words out of her mouth were "she's glad I came to my senses and know that she is right." The months after, I continued to be harassed how everything wrong was my fault.

During the divorce and after it; Natalie's Bi-Polar lows had her telling me that she wanted me in prison, so she can visit me and show me how wonderful a life she is having. She promised me that she would keep me in court, bankrupt, and "ensure my demise."

Chapter 7: Children

After our marriage, Natalie and I eventually had three children: Aaron, Eric, and Wyatt. Aaron was born in 2009, Eric in 2012, and Wyatt in 2014.

Aaron since he was born was always brilliant. He is extremely intelligent and learned things from an early age. She placed Aaron in portable cribs and exo-saucers in front of the television during the day as she lay on the couch. She would turn the television onto either the Sesame Street show or the DVD "Your Baby Can Read" series. Nonetheless, he was being raised by the television with her.

This adversely affected his social skills. When I took him to parks and outside, when he got close to other children, he began screaming uncontrollably. Natalie and I checked with his pediatrician and she explained that he needs more social interactions and keep him away from the electronic babysitter.

Natalie decided to sign up for a Mommy & Me class with Aaron. She attended one session, but said it was too much for her to be with him that one day and the class also interfered with her "social schedule" and she ended up not going again. If I wanted him to go there "I would have to go." Apparently that's what sick time is for.

Natalie discussed this matter with the schizophrenic. They both agreed that the pediatrician was wrong and decided to continue the 24 hour television babysitter. I attempted to voice my opinion, but since I was "stupid" my opinions were dismissed. I was furious.

I was in agreement with what the pediatrician said and saw firsthand what the television was doing to my son. I begged Natalie to turn off the TV and was met with more temper tantrums. I took matters into my hands. At work, we have lock boxes which go over electric plugs. They call them lock-out devices. They are made to lock out equipment which is inoperable and to ensure that no one mistakenly plugs them in. I borrowed one of these devices and installed it on the television electric plug. That morning while I was at work, I think the entire Eastern Coast was able to see Natalie launch. She forced me to come home and remove it or she would get the police to arrest me.

I was logging the children's television viewing times through the Netflix program. In an average day; my four and two year olds would watch anywhere from 8-12 hours of Netflix programing & cable television.

I have attempted on several occasions to cancel the cable and lock out the television power cord. Each occasion resulted in Natalie screaming, becoming irate, throwing things, and threatening divorce.

Doctors, teachers, professionals, and I all have explained to Natalie and her schizophrenic mother that the amount of television watched on a daily basis should be excessively limited (1-2 hours at most). Apparently they are all wrong and Natalie and her mother are right by limiting to 12 hours a day.

I fully believe that the children's signs of receptive learning and emotional-social behaviors stem from their mother utilizing the television to "babysit" them while she is on the phone with her girlfriends and family. I have recorded her computer and phone times and they correlate with the television time which substantiates these claims.

Natalie and I discussed the situation more and eventually came to a "happy" medium. She refused to take Aaron out to social situations for interaction with other children and I refused to have him watch television every moment of every day. Natalie said she will sign him up for day care. So we did. He was in full day care to get more interaction with other children.

With Aaron in day care, Natalie continued to refuse to work and utilized this time to improve upon her social responsibilities with her girlfriends. As Aaron grew up, you could see he acted very different with Natalie and me. With Natalie, he would be defiant and when she asked him to do something, he wanted something in return. He would bargain with her, as she conditioned him this way. When I asked, he did the task without question, as I conditioned him this way.

Eventually, as I was pulled more and more out of his life, his condition with Natalie became worse and they eventually diagnosed him with ADHD. I still have yet to see the behavior they marked in his file. Children are smart. They know what they can get away with and with whom.

Natalie and I began having fights over Aaron's teachers. Aaron's school has been subject to various unethical practices failing students for not being bilingual, overloading teachers beyond the student: instructor ratio, and classifying students with disabilities for additional funding.

Natalie is hell-bent on classifying the children with disabilities. She is stating all the children (including the baby) have psychological disabilities, because she has disabilities.

I believe Natalie is placing our children at risk by placing unnecessary labels on them to make herself feel better to cope with her own problems.

I have met with his teacher and as he spoke to me with only half of his teeth in his mouth (literally). It was apparent that he did not wish to actually teach, but to remain behind a desk and wait out his work day.

During school meetings, he explained how he is the only teacher in the class for 22 students and is overwhelmed. He explained how he would like to "push" some of the students into another classroom.

He exhibited signs of being uncomfortable when I requested specific examples of his "concerns" relating to Aaron. After several attempts with this nonprofessional to cite his specific concerns, he explained that Aaron was "unable to hold a pencil correctly." He was asked if there were any additional concerns; he replied that there were not.

This nonprofessional "acting educator" was supposed to be providing a daily written progress report of Aaron's behaviors, but has failed to provide such documentation.

Natalie apparently signed without my knowledge consent to allow the school board to review Aaron's case. She did not retain the documents as "paperwork" is not a concern of hers.

When my middle guy, Eric was born; he was the same way as Aaron. Always smiling, giggling, responsive, and loved to repeat what he heard. This included saying "oh, shoot" after banging your foot on something. At eighteen months though, things changed for the worst for him. His pediatrician injected him with about six shots, two of them containing multiple shots in one. He became extremely sick after the shots and had extremely high fevers for days and we were forced to bring him to the hospital many nights. Once he got better within a week or so, his interactions, repeating words, and responsiveness were gone. He became a mute almost overnight.

I would keep an updated log with skills he used to have which he would lose as his condition worsened. He lost many skills and traits to include:

1. He used to respond to his name. You would call his name and he would look at you along with saying "ooo" or "ahh." After the shots, when you called his name, he stared blankly at the wall. Nothing would get his attention.

2. He no longer responded to "no," "sit down," or "come here."

3. We had a game where I would say "how big is Eric?" and he would respond: "So big!" He lost this as well.

4. He no longer pointed at objects he wanted. He did not want anything, ever!

5. Words he used to know and say, he no longer knows what they are; even words like "mommy/mama" or "daddy/dada" or "thanks" or "ring."

6. He rapidly lost his social skills. He used to go up to people and say hi and play with other children. Now, with his condition, he rather play alone.

7. He loved watching Dora the Explorer on television. He used to answer her questions on the show, but not anymore.

8. He began bowing his head to the right side and when he was excited, started flapping his hands in the air.

9. He stopped repeating words, stopped smiling, and was content with sitting wherever he was and staring blankly into space.

Many mornings I would go into his room and found him sitting in his crib just starting. I would go up and talk to him without any response whatsoever. It was heart-breaking. He began drooling excessively during this time. They call it "low toned."

The whole situation was extremely hard physically, emotionally, and mentally. I could write another book about this subject and what Eric was going through. One book at a time though.

I spoke to friends who had children with similar issues and received great information on doctors, services, and support networks. Eric's condition qualified him for a program called

Early Intervention. This is when state employed social workers come to the house every day to work with Eric and help him develop.

These workers gave Natalie and I exercises to do with Eric on a daily basis. Natalie refused. Once again, it's not her job. I did the exercises and also did other things. At the mall, there was a sporting goods store. They had hunting decoys and other plastic animals there, in particular; owls and ducks. Aaron and I would show him the owl or duck, let him hold it and told him what they said. "The owl says whoo whoo, the duck says quack quack." Eventually after two years of doing this, he finally was able to repeat it. That was a good day!

Natalie was pissed that these people were at the home every day. It would interrupt her social responsibilities with her girlfriends. As such, like any teenage girl would, she would talk on the phone in the same room as Eric which would interrupt his session. Other times, her mother would stop by and interrupt the session to carry on a conversation with the social worker and discuss her personal matters for the entire session.

Eric had speech therapy at a local hospital one day a week for an hour. While I was at work, it was up to Natalie to take him. After a few short months, Natalie cancelled his speech therapy at the hospital since driving ten minutes for her son and waiting an hour for his session to end was a "burden" for her. She much rather spend that time with her friends and family. This is your flesh and blood and his issues are a "burden?"

The social workers provided daily reports on Eric's progress in the form of an Early Intervention pink slip. These pink slips explained what their observations were, what he needs work on, and his overall mental health.

These important records were thrown around all over the apartment. Crumpled up, torn, thrown out, behind furniture, you name it. Most of them were destroyed in whatever vortex she placed them in. She had dozens of vortexes of paperwork. Natalie was a slob, and it was apparent what she thought of the slips and the services. I would collect all of the slips and place them in a folder. When I was removed from the apartment at the beginning of the divorce, I was able to get these pink slips, along with the children's important paperwork to keep them save for the children when they need them. As of today, Natalie has yet to realize that I have them and did not notice yet.

When Eric was old enough for day care, Natalie placed him into the same school as Aaron and told the state social workers to provide their services to him there.

Now both the children were out of the house during the day which left the home empty. During this time, Natalie had more time to concentrate on her social obligations. At times when the costs to excessively high for only one parent working and paying for two full-time day care students, I discussed with Natalie about having the children back at home until more money could be generated to send them back. My response was that we could not have the children at home too long; as it was not Natalie's responsibility to take care of them while I was at work. Natalie was a stay at home mother; just without the children.

For Eric's low toned drooling, the pediatrician gave me some tips how to stop it. One major milestone was to have him drink from sippy and regular cups to strengthen his bottom mouth muscles. So I began giving Eric them. Unfortunately, with these types of cups, you need to give your children a little teaching and regular cups you have to watch them a bit. This was too much for Natalie. Natalie continued giving Eric baby bottles of milk past his fourth birthday. She did the same with Aaron.

She told the pediatrician this and yes, she screamed at Natalie. The pediatrician and I had a conversation and she agreed that

Natalie needed to start listening to me as my ideals with Eric's development matched hers.

My ideas of parenting were quite different from Natalie's. My mother was always strict with me. She was on me like white on rice. She fostered ideals, imagination, controlled behavior, and independence. She wanted me to be both happy and strong. As a child, she was big with me playing outside without any type of electronic entertainment; no TV, video games, etc. Natalie on the other hand was different. Since her mother was mentally ill and father who was not around, she often explained that she was raised by television and how it was "fine."

My ideas of a parent were instilled in me from my mother. I want to raise them like their father was raised. I think we are all like that to a degree. We raise our children as we were raised, but give them more. We always want to give our children a better life than we had (well, some of us at least).

I want my children to be happy, big, and strong. I want them to have great imaginations and have a strong independence about them. I want them to thrive in any environment they choose, and not be afraid of anything.

Each day, I would prepare their meals, get their vitamins, plan the day's activities, and get them ready along with getting myself ready. During rainy days, we would do indoor activities. We would go to the mall, or the Lego theme park (in New York), or would play inside the house.

We would all sit at the dinner table and color, play with Play dough, or have a "Lego Night" where we would purchase a Lego set and all four of us would build it- including the baby (though I did have to re-due the baby's piece). After we built our Lego set, I would hang it on their ceiling, as the children would normally want a spaceship or airplane kit. We created an air battle on their ceiling.

During non-rainy days; we would go outdoors, followed by more outdoors, and even more outdoors. I would do activities like riding bikes, having picnics, BBQs, parks, running, going on trails, playing ball, etc. All this time, it was just the boys and I.

Natalie would negotiate with the children. If they were good, she would get them a toy. When she called over to Eric to get his attention, he normally would not answer. She would then yell out "cookie" and he would come over thinking there was a treat for him. Like a dog. I did not believe in this. I am strict with them. I do not negotiate, I do not repeat myself, and I am firm with them. Even to this day. I firmly believe children crave structure, and that's what I provide.

One instance I remember well; when Eric was learning how to walk, he would cruise around the apartment. One day he was by the computer desk and smacked his head on the corner of the desk. He fell and began crying. I was in the kitchen doing my normal duties. Natalie was on the phone with one of her girlfriends and was closer to him. Instead of checking and consoling him, she stepped over him to continue walking into the bedroom and shut the door. She didn't want her conversation to be interrupted by a screaming toddler. I continued over to him and checked him out. I consoled him and brought him into the kitchen with me to help cook his dinner.

Natalie did her food shop during the day. Already prepared meals, frozen meals, cookies, ice cream, pastry cakes; normally processed foods. At the wholesale market, she would purchase: hot dogs, pizzas, corn dogs, and these premade peanut butter jelly sandwiches in a box. When she decided to feed the children lunch it would always be the usual premade peanut butter jelly sandwich or a Lunchables.

I would always object to all this stuff that she bought. At some points, I began just throwing out the Lunchables kits. They are extremely unhealthy and bad for the kids. Natalie asked me to give her a list of stuff that I wanted the kids to eat. I provided a list of veggies (carrots, squash, broccoli), fruits like apples (which Eric used to LOVE), along with items to make various dinners and lunches. She would ignore the list or forget to bring it with her. She finally opened up and said that since I cook the meals, I must do my own food shop.

So when I would get home from work and finish up Aaron's homework, the boys and I would go to the market to pick up our items. For times when the boys were too busy during the day, I would have to go to the 24 hour Walmart and pick up the food late at night after the kids were all in bed.

Since Natalie and her mother do not know (and refuse) to cook; Natalie fed the children and herself the deliciously addictive McDonalds, Burger King, Taco bell, and premade sandwiches. She often visited these establishments for breakfast, lunch, and dinner. Even if I premade meals and placed them into the refrigerator, it was too much to heat them in the microwave and the children love their happy meals better than home cooked.

Even today, this is still the case as I get bank statements from the old checking account and see all the purchases she makes.

During my visitation, Aaron explains how Subway is very healthy, Eric begs for McDonalds and gets excited when we pass one on the road, and the children have not touched a fruit or vegetable since they last saw me.

According to the children's pediatrician, Eric has been diagnosed with obesity and he is only four years old and Aaron has a weekly severe case of constipation and requires Miralax due to his diet. Natalie continually blames Aaron's problems and Eric's obesity on me. I am still not sure how this is possible as I only see them a few weeks a year.

I have aggressively communicated with both Natalie and her mother about the children's diet. I purchased fruit, vegetables, eggs, and yogurt for the children to consume, however, it is left to rot in the kitchen because the female "parental" drones either do not cook or understand how to prepare basic snacks or meals. I have actually been in fights with Natalie because she refuses to cut up fruit since "it takes too long."

During the last few months of my marriage, I came to the apartment to see the normal unkempt conditions and found Eric eating old food on the floor covered in dirt and both children staring lifelessly into their true parental caregiver- the television. Natalie was sitting on the coach with her tablet performing social activities without a care for the children. My two year old son grabbed my hand and wanted to go outside. I took him twice and my other son another time.

This was the only times the children were outside (besides school for the four year old). We came back in and I begged Natalie to cook dinner for them, while I got changed. In her fashion she cooked a five minute microwaved meal, as this is "as far as she will go" and argued that she didn't have any more time to cook anything else since I wasn't there. Mind you I was already at the apartment for one and a half hours while she lay on the coach with her tablet while I was tending to the children.

During the children's dinner, I was engaging both children as she continued to bad mouth them, for example, explaining how the two year old does not respond, will never respond, and explained his lacking's in front of him and our other son.

The children explained they wanted to go for another walk. I was being forced to leave as I am not welcome there, so I begged Natalie to take them out. She refused (as normal) and was screaming at me about it.

I have never seen anyone, let alone a parent not want to take their own children out for a simple five minute walk. I asked if they could go to the park the next day.

Once again, I received a screaming ex-wife. I explained to not have her loose her temper in front of the children. This just made matters worse. So in summary, she parented them at evening like she does every night. No walks, no parks, no family time, no reading. Four to six sippy cups of milk in a sitting with the television on all day, and during bedtime, the same with the television turned on in the bedroom so they can fall asleep while watching.

All this so she can talk with her mother who already showed up three times that day and she spoke with on the phone for a total of three hours with the last call being less than an hour from the last.

She is constantly looking up the terms mental retardation and Asperger's because Aaron's nonprofessional "educator" and her mother explain that's what Eric has. Though I do not believe a schizophrenic or nonprofessionals could know such things. But apparently, I am overruled again and again.

Natalie's mother watches the baby during the day, me at night after work. Sheila is constantly smoking in front of the children, blowing smoke in their faces including the baby. I do not know if she realizes it or not. I have brought it to her attention, but I am just being "stupid."

I do the children's homework with them, prep their meals, and stay up with the baby at night. I support Natalie, even when she gets tired from her social activities. When I have a social activity, it's automatically denied by her. It is "not allowed."

Chapter 8: Final Straws

During all this time, I was going to school online (as Natalie was using my stipend benefits), working midnight shifts, teaching on my days off, and watching children during the day. On the nights which I did not work, I was already accustomed to staying up all night, so if the babies woke up, I was able to stay up with them.

Eventually, I joined the federal government and my midnight shifts and teaching jobs ended. But this put more pressure on Natalie to watch children during the day. This was not acceptable to her.

During my marriage, I missed multiple red flags. I stayed all these years because I thought her behavior was normal for someone, I didn't know any different. This is what all relationships are like. I always heard how relationships are difficult and you must sacrifice a lot. But it was becoming worse and worse.

One day, Natalie, the children, and I went to her College Reunion which was a family day. It was at her college campus in New Jersey and had lots of activities for the kids. Magicians, clowns, games, etc. When we got there, I prepared both Eric and Aaron for the day, got them fed, and started to bring them to the various activities going on. Natalie was able to see all her friends and catch up. Natalie began talking to a man that she went on dates with and dated in college. They were talking for a while and they left the party for a short time. I had no idea where they went. Natalie finally appeared and told me that I had to take the children and leave. I was curious why.

The boys were having fun and we were enjoying the family day activities. She did not care and just told me to leave. Natalie said she would call me when she was ready for us to pick her up.

She proceeded to leave with her ex-boyfriend back to the party. So I packed up the now upset little ones and found an indoor amusement park nearby to let the kids have fun, as they really did not want to leave the party. Natalie called me and we picked her up. During the whole ride home she was telling me about things she said to her ex-boyfriend and inquiring if what she said would come off badly since she really wanted to make a good impression. My response to each question was "who cares" or "why do you care so much about your ex?"

That night, she left to go to an after-party reunion to see her girlfriends and her ex-boyfriend. She did not come home until late at night.

Eventually over the next few months, Natalie would continue to go to parties with him and her girlfriends. When she got home, she would be asking the same questions she did above more and more until they became a daily routine. She would constantly give me hypotheticals in regards to new relationship problems and if she overstepped her bounds or make "him" angry.

Other times, while I was up all night with the baby, she would be up all night writing long love letters to him on Facebook and other internet messaging systems.

With all this going on and Natalie brining up her ex-boyfriend more and more, I became curious and started looking at her phone (as she does to me). I found her making more phone calls to him along with Facebook messages I found on her account. She made statements to him how her marriage to me is a slap in the face to them and their relationship.

I continued to ignore this behavior and just ask myself, why it mattered and why is this guy so important to her? I missed a HUGE red flag. I think with all of this, I stayed with her and in the relationship to abide with my vow of never placing my children into a broken home or a divorce situation. Essentially: staying for the children.

I was always very passive in the marriage. For most of the marriage, I always agreed with Natalie with any idea she had. I also supported her decisions whether I thought they were great or terrible. Near the end of the marriage, after I was taken advantage of, I began speaking up and voicing my opinion. I disagreed with many of Natalie's ideas. If I did, and Natalie did not get her way; she would have a severe temper tantrum, throw items, hit herself, and threaten to kill herself if she did not get her way. Almost like a teenage girl. If she did not do that, she would call her mother to come upstairs and she, her mother, and step father would just belittle me into submission how they were right and I was wrong (3 against 1).

My marriage is on the brink of destruction. Natalie and I went to counsellors. We initially went to a marriage therapist. He heard both of our stories and allowed both of us to speak. Natalie did not allow me to speak (as she is perfect, and the issues are with me). He attempted to correct her. She did not like that and we never went back. Instead we went to her normal counselor who is self-promoted as "New Age Feminist" which she sees twice a week. We went together one day and it was an hour session of Natalie and her counselor telling me that I am an abuser because

This counsellor said it was abusive of me to ask Natalie to take care of the children since she is not working. I am supposed to provide more support: both emotionally and financially. In today's world, a woman does not need to work, I must provide. She explained to me that I need to work from home to watch the children, provide the financial stability, along with my normal duties of cooking, cleaning, and the children's homework. "A woman's role for parenting ends when the baby comes out." That's what was said. I wasn't "empowering" Natalie.

At this point, I felt like crap. But I started to laugh a bit. We ended the session with the feminist explaining that if Natalie sought out emotional bonds with someone else; I needed to support and "foster" it. LOL! Natalie was having tendencies of finding relations outside of the marriage.

Natalie became more and more self-centered. I had an issue with her blasting the car radio. She would set the radio extremely high with its volume, not even caring if the children are in the car. She is like a teenaged girl. She would leave it on excessively high and it got to a point where Eric and Aaron said it hurts their ears. This was doing damage to the children's ears; especially Eric who already has issues with hearing and processing information. So, every time I started the car and the radio blasted me out of the seat; I asked myself why does she keep doing this to her own children?

Natalie and I have discussed this issue a dozen times. I normally would go inside the house and ask her nicely to keep the car radio at a reasonable volume, her response was no different from what she normally says; "I will do whatever I want, f**k you. When I brought up the children's hearing, I received the same answer. Aaron has told me that he requests her to lower the volume as well. But he says "mommy says she does not care."

In December, 2014, the children, Natalie, and I were travelling to New York to go to the Palisades Mall in Nyack, NY. While on the Garden State Parkway, Natalie began having a temper tantrum about being out with the family rather than her girlfriends.

I finally asked about her friend, the ex-boyfriend and her relationship with him. Why is she so concerned about him? She began screaming and finally said these words "She could have been with him instead of settling for me."

She then parked the car at a rest stop (in between the north and southbound lanes) and told me to get out of the car. She dropped me off and sped away. She drove all the way back to our house (20 miles away). I was told to walk home. I walked/ran about ten miles and ran across 3 highway lanes until a friend picked me up and drove me back home. She was not apologetic. Apparently this was a ruse so that she can pick up and enjoy the company of her boyfriend.

Her control continued during my divorce, and still does to this day. She attempts to control what I do, where I am, and who I am with. She has pressed me and the court to inform her of every time I am working from home, every time I am at training, and whoever I am with. Even though it is none of her business, she must know what I am doing to follow it up with a court order not allowing me to do it or attempting to get more money from it.

For instance, as you will read, I am not allowed to have a girlfriend be alone with the children, but she is allowed to have a boyfriend alone with them. I am also required to tell her when I am at training, where and for how long. This is for her to calculate my "per diem costs."

Chapter 9: Wife's Court Career

Natalie has a degree in Sociology. After the marriage, she went back to school to take classes in education along with teaching exams. After she completed the program and accrued thousands of dollars of student loan debt (which she claims I am responsible for), she explained that she does not want to teach. During that time, I stupidly asked what the purpose of it was and just received a screaming irate woman without any answer.

Natalie's limited work history involved working as a camp counselor here and there or working at liberal non-profits as an aide. She attempted working in retail, but did not last one day.

Out of nowhere she applied and became a Motions Clerk and Court Services Officer at the local Brendon County Court House. She worked in both the Family and Civil Divisions. There, she supported multiple civil judges by filing current motions and maintaining the court calendar, assisted in preparing judicial orders, logged transcripts, and court tapes, assisted with hundreds of divorce cases, developed a keen understanding of court rules and practices, and was entrusted to perform a variety of critical case management tasks.

She performed all these tasks with the various Family Law Judge's within their chambers for five years. She developed personal relationships with the other officers, probation case workers, child services investigators, Judges, and division heads. She consistently used the joking threat during those years "you don't want to divorce me; I know all the players and the game." She eventually quit her job prior to having our first child. She has not worked since.

This is the same court house you will read about in this book, as this was the court which had jurisdiction over my case and her personal relationships with the key individuals would play a roll into my demise. During the beginning of my divorce, my attorney stated that we could move the case to another system, but it would make it longer, costs would double, and we more than likely get the same result. We had no idea what was going to happen though. In retrospect, we should have done it. As my case developed, you will see her friends getting involved and making matters for me worse.

Chapter 10: Work

After many years of being an aircraft mechanic, avionics technician, and professor; I began a career with the federal government. I entered government service in 2012. I became an airworthiness inspector for mechanics and avionics shops. For me, this was ascension and the pivotal point of my career. I was extremely lucky to get this position, especially at my age. I was the youngest airworthiness inspector in the office.

Getting this job is being on the top of the food chain for me. No more midnight shift, paid holidays, pension, no more extra responsibilities after hours, and being paid very well. I was also able to buy back my time in the military to put towards my retirement.

When I started, I immediately made friends in the office. Not only did I meet Michaela there, but also other great individuals which have been great support both prior to the divorce, during, and after. I developed friendship there which will last a lifetime. During the divorce, I received a ton of advice, attorney contacts, and help from all my coworkers. They also supported me when they saw everything getting to me emotionally all joked how I acquired AIDS: Aviation Induced Divorce Syndrome.

Before my divorce, I heard about a prestigious program that my organization hosts. It is called the Program for Emerging Leaders. It is a highly competitive program which trains individuals for leadership roles. Out of the entire agency, 50 individuals are selected out of thousands. The program is designed to train for the next level of leaders within the agency. To apply, there are a dozen or so essay questions which you need to write in. Most of the questions involved how you are leadership material and how your experience makes you a fit for the program.

I knew it was a longshot to get in, but I applied. I figured; I won't know if I can make it in unless I try. Natalie was against me applying, I'm still not too sure why. Nonetheless, I knew what it could do for us and my career, so I wrote the essays and applied for the program.

Shortly after my divorce began and I was getting bombarded with paperwork to fill out; I received a letter saying I was selected and entered into the program. This program required some travel, along with management development within different offices. This development involved performing various assignments, management shadowing, and being in a management role while being employed within a different area of the organization. I was tasked to work in the Boston area.

The program was kicked off in Washington D.C. Both my manager and I attended. During this time, I received more bombardments of paperwork, but was able to vent. You will read about all this in the diary. I reported to my assigned work details in January 2016. However, I was eventually transferred to the Boston office a few months prior to that.

While you are reading the diary, you will see I do not mention work. Mr. Keville and Natalie bombarded me so much during this last year; it was extremely difficult to work on anything else except for them. All of my coworkers and managers heard and knew about my case because I had to constantly leave work for court cases and trials.

I had to record and transcribe every phone call, voicemail, Skype session, wrote in my daily journal of the day's events, wrote letters, printed emails, compiled hundreds of documents and statements, filled out dozens of forms, and the list goes on. Other times, I would have to gather information and respond to fraudulent accusations during work times. All of this; breaking me down to the brink of exhausting to defend myself.

To keep my head above water in the divorce, each day I went to the office a few hours early and left a few hours late to work on my divorce paperwork. I also worked on the stuff during slow times during the work day and on my lunch breaks. I wrote and compiled all this information during these times along with maintaining my normal workload and juggling my various work assignments and tasks.

Two questions arise with me. First, how do other people do it? I spoke to other coworkers who were recently divorced, and they could not believe the amount of court paperwork which was covering my desk. So in these aggressive divorces, how does anyone have the time for this stuff? I am working on this 12 hours a day.

Second, why didn't my ex-wife have to do all this? Someone who could barely spell her name did not have to do any of this. She did not spend hours upon hours compiling hundreds of statements, account information, writing letters, or filling out forms.

I have an entire attorney firm working for me and I am working 10-12 hours a day on all this. This was just crazy! Now I can see why Mr. Keville was requesting so much money from me, he is exclusive to my case. I am paying people to spend hours of the day to make my life a living hell. Just Peachy!

With all my dealings with this divorce and the daily onslaught of legal paperwork and threats, I was still able to accomplish my regular workload. Since I am normally a task oriented guy, I was able to finish my work. I tend to be anal with that sort of stuff; I even have a daily to-do list.

To save of costs, to pay all the court ordered expenses, I was skipping meals, even went days without eating. When I did eat, it was normally a cup of Ramen noodles.

After Natalie had me removed from the apartment, I was now homeless. During the next few weeks, I began moving clothes and personal hygiene items into the office to live there (unofficially, of course). There were days when I was living at the office and showering in office gym. I was able to store personal items gym locker room along with suitcases and duffle bags in my cubicle. All this was against the rules of the building, my employer, and the state- but what is the alternative? I refuse to go to work release and prison.

I began selling off all of my personal items, electronics, and other things in the office to raise money. It was an office yard sale. I needed to raise money to pay all the court ordered debts, for an apartment, and pay my attorney. My coworkers purchased many of these items to help me out. I sold a lot of other items on Craigslist. Every day I had a dozen or so people purchasing items from me. All these monies went right to my lawyer and the court ordered debts.

Natalie and her attorney knew that I had yearly training. They began their threats and harassment demanding that I hand over my training schedule to them along with any per diems I receive for food, incidentals, and lodging. Multiple times Natalie stated how she performed the calculations of my "per diem" monies and said they were hers to spend.

In government and military, "per diem" is a term used for money given to you during travel for food and small expenses. As I would be in a hotel room for one, two, or even three weeks without a kitchen, the per diem money would pay for food. It changes on the area, length of travel time, and other factors; but it is usually $50 a day which usually covered three meals and a snack.

Due to this harassment and the onslaught of constant scheduled court cases, both my management and I had to cancel my training courses until things settled down.

During July & August 2015, I was called into court multiple times. I was court ordered to pay amounts which I could not even remotely afford. My office management team and coworkers were extremely supportive during this time.

After each court case, the Judge ordered me to pay thousands of dollars which I had no ability to even pay. I researched what would happen if I failed to pay all these demands or if I paid them late. The county will arrest me with a bench warrant. I learned about civil bench warrants, and how New Jersey arrests people who cannot afford civil lawsuits. Since there is no such thing as a "debtor's prison," New Jersey arrests people for failing to abide by a court order, also known as contempt of court. Pretty convenient!

After each one of my court cases and trials, I had to go back to work. As I did not have enough vacation time to take an entire day off for these continued court games. Coworkers asked me how it went, I began crying. My managers called me into their offices each time. I provided them copies of the court orders and the list of items I must pay for.

My management team saw what was happening to me. I was in tears in their offices each time I had a new court order. They read through it all and were dumbfounded. Both they and I did not know how I was able to afford the demands the court placed onto me. They did not know how I could pay for everything, how I could survive. I told them that I had to vacate my apartment which I just moved into. They asked where I would live; I did not have an answer.

I told them about the continued onslaught of legal paperwork, the fraudulent claims, the constant harassment, weekly calls from the probation office, and the daily calls & emails from Natalie and her attorney with more demands.

I showed them the research I did if I failed to make any of the court ordered payments to Natalie and her attorney. They agreed that their office cannot have an inspector living in a homeless shelter or a prison-sponsored work release program.

Eventually, we all had enough. Not only did all these court hearings take time away from my job, but the demands and court ordered debts were so much it was stupid. My management team asked where my family and support network was. I told him about my family in Massachusetts and Michaela in New Hampshire. My managers worked together with the national union, local union representatives and the other offices on a solution. It was clear; I needed to transfer to another office.

They all worked tirelessly and received an initial approval to transfer me out of New Jersey as quickly as they could. I was to be transferred to the New England area. The moment we received word, my boss released me from duty the same day. I immediately moved to New England. I still reported to my office in New Jersey, but stationed in the Boston office. Eventually, my official transfer was completed and I reported to my new boss in Massachusetts.

I moved to New Hampshire and now had a two hour commute (one way). So four hours a day provides for a long commute. Luckily, my management team allows me to work from home which helps immensely!

After I officially moved to New Hampshire and started reporting to my new office, I met my new coworkers and management team. They are all wonderful people. One of my managers reignited my passion for becoming a Freemason. They quickly learned what I was going through as the court cases continued down in New Jersey and I had to continually take off from work.

There are other coworkers up here that have gone through divorces themselves and cannot believe what I am going through. From the games, courts, and the new garnishments which have been placed on me, even though I have been paying my support.

During my various work assignments and details shifting from office to office, it was severely difficult to perform my normal work functions as well as keeping my head above water producing letters and gather information for the divorce. There are never enough hours in a day.

The building I am in is quite large and houses multiple different divisions of the government. I was able to work with a lot of these divisions with my assigned details with the program for emerging leaders.

I worked with several divisions and while the divorce was going full steam, I had to keep them informed of what was going on. I gave them the reader's digest version, and they could not believe it. I got their full support as I continued to be summoned to court cases throughout the year. One of the managers went through a nasty divorce years ago and could relate.

As I went to court and eventually exhausted my vacation and sick times; my bosses in both of my offices worked with me to modify my schedule to help me attend to my personal matters and this divorce. On many occasions, I had required training rescheduled last minute because I had a conflicting court case which my attorney and I found out about with only a few days' notice.

My coworkers and managers in both in New Jersey and Massachusetts could not believe what I was going through. All in all, their support has been wonderful and amazing. I could not ask for a better support network. I don't think I would ever last in another job with this stuff going on. I cannot thank everyone enough. My management teams, coworkers, union, and union representatives. They all pulled together for me. I have never heard or seen a job do this for anyone. I am eternally grateful.

Chapter 11: Friends & Family

Background

During high school, I had dozens of friends. I hosted a lot of party's and was friendly with all of the various groups: nerd, jocks, cheerleaders, squares, etc. I was able to relate and hang out with all of them. At my house, I hosted various parties and everyone was there. It did not matter what group you were in. I also went to a lot of other parties. I was the extravert, the party animal. I was one of those people who could maintain a high GPA and party hard the day before.

But after high school, I moved to Florida and eventually I only remained in contact with one of my friends. This man now lives in Arizona, but still remains a close friend even today. We have a special bond as he was there when my mother died and she considered us brothers. She loved him too. He will always remain my brother and friend.

Divorce and hard times really show you who your real family and friends are. Yes, it is true that you will lose friends, especially mutual friends in a divorce and there are other friends who do not come to your aid in your moment of need. But for the others, I would not be here today, telling you my story if it wasn't for those people who are my select friends and family.

Simple words cannot express the deeply sincere gratitude I have for my family and friends. Without them, I would be lost. From the advice they give, to the phone calls checking up on me, to taking me in while I was homeless, to helping me move a dozen or so times.

My friends would drop everything on a dime and proved it when they helped me on my moving day when Natalie and her attorney gave me only a few hours' notice to get my personal belongings out of her apartment.

As you will read later, I was forced to move dozens of times with little to no advance notice. I was forced to call friends minutes before I was allowed to gain access to personal items. Without hesitation, they dropped everything they were doing to come and help me.

As you will read, during this divorce, I was being brought to court monthly. Each time, more and more demands of money from me to a point where it was above what I made was being forced on me. I had to continually move around from friend's homes, family homes, and eventually my own little apartment to being homeless. Eventually I moved out of state.

During the divorce process I moved a total of five times. Each time I had to buy new furniture, supplies, getting donations of furniture, renting a moving truck and scrambling friends to help me move each time.

Before the move commenced, I could not return the stuff without boxes or receipts, so I had to either sell, donate, or give away stuff. Such a waste of money and time! But they all went to good homes. I donated dozens of bags of clothing to Good Will, gave Harry all my baby stuff for his newest addition to his family, as he had a little baby girl, and gave the godfather of my little one my prized propellers for him to make a table from them.

Each time I moved, I had to downsize. When I moved to the new apartment in NJ, I purchased brand new low budget couch from Ikea. I picked up the couch and a futon there. A great friend who I met in Airplane Mechanic School helped me pick them up along with a donated bed at another friend's house.

Luckily I saved the receipt for the couch. Eventually, I had to move out of state since I could not afford an apartment anymore. So, before my move out of New Jersey, I had to get rid of them. A good friend from fencing and his two strong sons came with their truck to help me haul it back to Ikea. Luckily, they took back the couch and futon for a full refund!

Today, most of my friends I remain in contact with are from fencing and my previous jobs.

Unfortunately, as I do live so far away, I rarely get to see many of them nowadays, but I do get to see my family in Massachusetts, some of the fencers at tournaments in New York, and friends that come up to visit me in New Hampshire. I was never able to say goodbye to many of my friends, especially at the fencing club, but I just want to let them know that they are missed and I want to see them all again. I want to thank each and every one of them for being so great to me!

Fencing

As you will read, I was a member of a non-profit fencing club called "Fencer's Edge." I was a member ever since I was a child. I fenced with them, instructed, and eventually led the organization. I developed many personal friendships with the students and fellow instructors. The fencers were all present even when I got married. They performed the Arch of Sabers!

After fencing lessons were complete for the night, we made it a point to go out afterwards to a local dive bar and have some chicken wings and drinks. We made it a weekly tradition. I did this since I was legally allowed to drink until Natalie did not allow me to do it anymore or she gave me a severe guilt trip for doing it. One night a week for two hours was way too much on her to watch the children.

I had multiple friends at fencing. There was Tom, who was an older gentleman who was a machinist and fellow instructor. He was there at my stag party when I was married. He eventually had a baby with another fencer from the club. There was Joey, who was once my coach when he was with another club.

There was Colin, who made maps and worked in governmental cartography. He is a close personal friend, who before the divorce asked if I would be in his wedding party. He was the life of the party and was always quick with a comeback or joke.

There was Victoria, a beautiful Russian woman who had a son born the same time as my oldest son. We hung out a lot and let the boys play together. We celebrated both of their birthdays and had them fence each other. When we met up on Saturday's at the club, we would take turns watching children at fencing. Having boys play at fencing and at the school. When she moved to her new home, I was able to help her out, and she helped me move. During my move to get my personal stuff out of Natalie's apartment, I was severely stressed. She gave me a great big hug which instantly calmed me. It was funny, she was able to lift and carry more stuff than the guys. When I moved into my apartment after I was removed from the marital home, she and her family donated a bunch of supplies for me to use. She has been an amazing friend!

And of course, there was Garrett. He was the one who helped me move the couch and futon back to Ikea. Garrett joined the club about twelve years ago, when he first moved to New Jersey. We hit it off right away. He has been my strongest supporter at the club.

We would talk weekly about our lives, personal affairs, work, and club events. If one day went by without talking, there was something wrong. We found every opportunity after fencing to get together for food and drinks. We grew close over the years.

Before I had children, we used to have board meetings at my old apartment, where we discussed club matters and had significant amounts of alcohol. We would get together after classes and discussed club matters. After each of my children was born, I would always get a care package or baby toy in the mail addressed from the club. I knew who ordered it!

He was there at my wedding. The man who wed Natalie and I was also a fencer (and Pastor); during the ceremony, he forgot to say those words of "you may kiss the bride," Garrett noticed this and closed the Arch of Sabers until we did it.

Due to work obligations, he retired from the club the same time I did. He visits with other fencers in the club along with checking in on the other instructors from time to time. Recently, we met up at a tournament in New York and had dinner. It was great seeing him again! We will talk regularly, but not as much as we once did.

Miguel Air
During my career, I worked at a company called Miguel Air. This was my last job before I entered government service. Never before have had I maintained a close personal relationship with such a great bunch of guys. I am proud to be in our group.

Our team was small. There were about five employees all working the same midnight shift. Being in such a small area with a small group, we developed a comradery and became instant friends overnight. To this day, I maintain a strong friendship with them and we are always texting, calling, or visiting each other.

During my time here, we would share the workload and hangout while working. It did not feel like work. It felt like a social club. While other stations which were set up just like us had their employees work on their own; we would take the same car and do our work together; as a team.

We all helped each other. There were times when each of us had to do work outside of our jobs or even putting our personal affairs in order. Many of us were applying for jobs, so whoever needed to do their work; we would take their tasks for the night and let them work on their personal matters. For me, I was able to do my homework for my Master's degree. Many nights, after the workload was all complete, I would write my papers and do my homework. Everyone came by to help me out. I remember one instance, I was taking a calculus course and was having significant issues with certain problems I had in my homework. We wrote the problems on the white board in the office and tried to solve it. It was difficult for each of us.

Later on in the evening, we left to perform our normal duties. A coworker of ours, Aaron saw the problem on the board and in a typical "Good Will Hunting" fashion he figured out the problem on the board and never told anyone that he did it. He always said that he was terrible at math but was able to solve problems which none of us could. Aaron is of Asian descent with an Irish name. We grew close over the years and eventually we became the Godfather of my youngest son.

Also in our group, was a man named Tony. He graduated from the same school as the rest of us. He was a larger gentleman of Italian descent from New Jersey (so you understand the type of person we are discussing). He is a great guy, but does require smoke signals to gain his attention as his cell phone skills are to be desired. We would always go to his house for New Years; we didn't need an invitation. Eventually, he met a young divorced woman with two children. We went to his wedding and quickly incorporated her into our close-knit group.

Another close friend is Sean. Eventually Sean moved to South Carolina with his girlfriend. When he married her, another friend- Harry and I went to his wedding down there. Not only was it a road trip, but also an adventure. Sean along with his new wife remains good friends with me even today, though we don't speak too often.

Our group had another member. He didn't work with us in the aviation field, but I worked with him for years in retail.

He was in the computer repair business. He came out with us when we went on road trips to play paintball and go to breweries. He has helped me so much over the years and helped me on every move in my life. He also helped me move on short notice when I was able to get my personal items out of Natalie's and helped me build my furniture.

Unfortunately, he lives in one of the buildings owned by Natalie's father. We set him up in the apartment years ago, so that he could get a good deal. I haven't spoken to him since that day and lost contact with him. I do not know Natalie or her father has said to him. Hopefully one day we will talk again.

Harry

I have many friends, but I hold one dearly; a best friend. Everyone has a best friend, one whom they thoroughly rely on. Harry is mine. You will see his name mentioned in this diary often. He has been one of my strongest supporters throughout this entire adventure.

I remembered seeing Harry at the Aircraft Mechanic School I attended, but not really talking to him or developing a strong friendship. The same went with Tony. We first met and spoke when he first joined Miguel Air.

I also remember the first day I spoke to him. He was still working at another air carrier and came over to introduce himself to the crew. I was with a newly hired technician and was observing the trainee while he was looking for a tiny tool I gave him and he lost. He dropped it off the top of an aircraft as we were changing an antenna and he was looking for it on the ground. Harry came over to introduce himself and we spoke for a few minutes about losing tools.

Harry started with our company a few weeks after. On his first day on the job, the first words out of his mouth were the typical greasy mechanic sexual and derogatory jokes. He instantly fit into the group!

Harry lived close to me and decided to commute together, as we worked the same days and shift. We car pooled together for years. This was a great opportunity for us to bond, share stories, and develop a lifelong relationship. Harry and I had lots of time together. We hung out at work, went on various adventures like going to South Carolina, went out for drinks, dinners, and went on road trips for work.

Harry is from India and came over in High School. His parent's came here for more opportunities for him and his sister. He is younger man, but his wise beyond his years. He was there beforehand, seeing Natalie's behavior and telling me the God's honest truth. "You need to leave her, she is toxic." Harry explained that he know a lot of people who have been divorced and they all say, the woman you married, the woman you once knew is gone. In retrospect, he was completely right.

He was always the Mayor when we were out; whether going out to eat at Olive Garden, being at work, or going on an adventure somewhere; he was the always the traditional extravert. He is an EMT and paramedic on his off time. He is always helping others. He tends to do that a lot. He can never sit still. Eventually he left the company shortly before I did for a better opportunity with another airline. But in his normal fashion of helping out others, he reached out to his new contacts and scheduled job interviews for the whole group for various jobs with this new airline, to help us out with better opportunities. He did things like that, that's how wonderful a man he is.

He now has a beautiful baby girl and a beautiful wife. He met his wife through his parents. It was an arranged marriage of sorts. In his religion and culture, this is still a common practice but with a twist. They did date for a time to make sure they were compatible with each other. It was difficult for him to see her as she was in India. After they married, he brought his wife here and they started their family.

Before I was able to leave the state, I was able to give him some much needed supplies for his newest addition. I gave him all my baby stuff; high stairs, exo-saucers, swings, you name it, and lots of advice when it comes to children.

He and his wife were always coming by taking my children out to the park. Before I left for New Hampshire, he always invited the children and me over for food with his family. They would cook us a huge meal. Even if we stopped by unannounced, they would cook for us.

In January 2015, I was in the hospital for surgery. After the surgery, I woke up to him and his wife sitting there with flowers to check on me. He was my only visitor; no one else showed, not even my wife. Shows how much she cared!

I am an honorary member of his family and proud to be! His wife, daughter, mother, father, and sister are all amazing people! I enjoy our conversations and spending time with them. I love playing with his little girl too! I remember meeting her for the first time prior to one of my court cases. I drove down from New Hampshire to meet her.

Throughout this whole process, he was there for me each step of the way. He was there giving me advice before the incidents of the diary occurred, during, and after. He was there getting my important paperwork and packing my bags when I was first thrown out of my apartment, to renting u-hauls each time I had to move, to removing and storing my tools at his house, and storing, attempted to bring back Natalie's car twice, taking pictures of it, and dealing with police and Natalie's father threatening and screaming in his face when he tried to do the right thing. Later in this diary you will read about each constant battle and how he was there supporting me.

Harry has been my strongest supporter down there in New Jersey since the beginning. He has done so much for me and was there during every move, harassment, and court case. He has been there for each of my children and me. Words cannot express my sincere gratitude to have him as a friend and brother.

Masons

It was always a goal of mine to join the Freemasons. I remember seeing family members and their friends wearing rings with a square and compass on them. I always asked what it was and was fascinated by it. I was always told that I would learn about them when I was older. After I got older, life got in the way and with working and taking care of the children, I did not have any time to seriously look into joining or even have time to devote to joining.

Since my move to New Hampshire and as my divorce slowly came to an end, I had some extra time, and I wanted to meet new people in my area, so I did some research on it and discussed joining with my boss. He is a Freemason as well. So without the children with me full time, I now have time to dedicate myself to the fraternity and meet my new friends at the local Masonic Lodge. I have found my place with them and have the role of playing the bagpipes for them. Another thing I haven't done in recent years.

I have been going through the degrees and met my sponsor and teacher. He is an amazing man. He is all about family, honor, and friends. He is a retired police officer and has an amazing wife, family, and home. I see him weekly and it is always a joy hanging out with him. He and his wife recently treated Michaela, my children, and I on a trip to a local nature science center. We all had an amazing time and I was glad that he was able to finally meet my little ones. I continue to learn and use the teachings and principles of masonry from him and enjoy developing lifelong friendships with all of the members in my lodge.

Lost friends

I did hear that during divorces, mutual friends take sides and one side always ends up with the short end of the stick. I did not believe it at first, but unfortunately I did lose friends with my divorce too.

I do understand how mutual friends do not like to get involved. Mutual friends do not want to take sides, but eventually do; especially if their children still play with my children. Of course, I never want to affect that. The children play well and have a great time together. I never want that bond to be broken. So I take the high road.

I also understand that since I no longer live in the state, it is very difficult to defend myself. But why should I defend myself? If they are truly friends, they would know what type of person I am, what I am capable of (or not capable of) and my true nature. So if they choose to think I am a money hungry, deadbeat who beats his wife and abuses his children, then they never knew me at all.

Luckily, I only lost a few mutual friends out of this. It hurts, don't get me wrong. But what can I do? I state my case and they make their decision. The friends I lost were former fencing students of mine which I eventually worked with the husband as he is in the same field as me.

We hung out as couples and eventually when we had children; our children started playing with each other. As you read in the diary, after one of my children's birthday parties, they spoke to me and failed to understand what was going on. I got my standard "Why would she lie about that" routine and apparently learned that I was never removed from the home. I left Natalie voluntarily. Nonetheless, I eventually lost contact with them as they continued to spend time with Natalie and lost the friendship.

Family

As I grew up around my mother's family up in Massachusetts mainly, they were the ones who were there for me during my divorce. I have an aunt, uncle, and two cousins which I consider sisters and who are also the God Mothers of two of my children.

I have a strong bond with them which developed since my mother was alive. My mother was closest to her sister out of her entire family. She had brothers, but they were always concerned with money, squabbling, and creating family drama. My mother did not do well with drama, so her time was better spent up in Massachusetts with her sister. We visited my family regularly and at one point began looking into spending summers there at a local campground.

When my mother passed away, I was in basic training for the Army. My aunt and cousins were with her when she died. The death was sudden and unexpected. Her Lupus finally took her. Since then, my aunt became a maternal influence of sorts. As an only child, I did not have any siblings to embrace. My two cousins took that place and I consider them sisters even today.

My grandmother used to live with my mother and me. After my mother's death, she moved up to Massachusetts and my aunt now takes care of my ninety three year old grandmother. She is still kicking around and stays as active as she could, but it is tough on my aunt and uncle.

She was there for my family while I was married, they all were supportive of me when I out on my own and when I was married. My cousins were two of the bridesmaids at my wedding. Natalie did not like driving up to Massachusetts and seldom allowed me to. So during my marriage, my aunt and cousins came down to me in New Jersey instead. They came down to New Jersey for every baptism, important birthday, and other family functions.

My family is full a strong, independent, and hardworking people. They are the embodiment of what strength is. My uncle has a background in landscape design and works several days a week and 30 hours a day (in a 24 hour day). My aunt teaches in a grammar school, and my cousins; one is a special education teacher, the other a registered nurse. I am always calling them up for advice whether it is medical or child development related.

While you read my diary, I reference both my aunt and cousins alike. This is the aunt and cousins which I talk about often and has been with me since the beginning of this process. They would call to check up to me regularly, have the boys over when they came up for visitation, and they all would shower my children with gifts, especially during their birthdays.

I am able to visit with them when I am down there to pick up the children for visitation. Their home is very close to the halfway point between Natalie and me, along with the pickup area. During quick visitations while we were waiting for Natalie as she would be a few hours late for pickups, my aunt, uncle, and cousins would host quick birthday parties for each of the children.

My family in Massachusetts has been wonderful. I cannot thank them enough. They took me in when I was homeless and work transferred me to Boston. As she took me in when I first moved to New England, she still has an open door. I stay down with them here and there. It is still nice to catch up and spend time with the family.

As far as my father's family, I have a relationship with my father's side, but not as strong as my mothers. During most of my life, I grew up with my mother while my father lived in separate towns, as they were separated. He would come back into her life here and there, but nothing permanent. Thus, contact with his family was limited and the bond not as strong. However, over the past ten years or so, we began speaking more and spending more time with each other at family parties; especially my aunt's traditional Christmas party where the whole family attends.

One of my aunt's on my father's side has two daughters (now in College and graduated). But I still remember and appreciate what they did for me while I was stationed in Iraq. They worked with the girl scouts and were members of their local unit. They were my pen pals during this time and sent dozens of care packages and boxes to me and my unit. It was very sweet and I appreciate it even to this day.

My father did not come back into my life in any real way until my children were born. Since then, he spends time with them bringing them to parks and bringing them up to me, which I greatly appreciate. Natalie allows him to take the children up to New Hampshire any time he wants, as she does not have to drive herself.

After I moved to New Hampshire, my father never really called to ask about my situation, status, or what has been going on with the divorce. He did not have an understanding or idea of the events of the past year of the hell I was going through.

Recently he came up with the boys to see me. During his visit, he came across a letter from a creditor explaining that they will be suing me. He told me how I needed to curb my spending and be wiser with my money. He did not realize that the court took everything from me and that I still owed thousands of dollars a month for debts, Natalie's debts, her attorney, and even my own attorney. He also thought I was still married to Natalie. He either did not realize, did not care, or a little of both. So, in good fashion, I blew up on him as he had no idea about my divorce, my financial ruin, the threats, and harassment I went through.

However, my father's girlfriend has done so much for me. During the start of the divorce, before I found my own place, she took me in for a few months. She arranged with friends of hers to get donations of furniture for me. She got me a bed, sheets, microwave, cooking and kitchen stuff, and enough items to move in and be comfy in a small apartment. She also gave me some names and numbers of other attorneys who may be able to help me more than mine did. Unfortunately, the others were way too expensive. The $600 an hour rate of my current lawyer is just a drop in the bucket for other ones. But still, she did all this for me! I am blessed to have such great friends and family.

Unfortunately, to this day no one of my extended family has reached out to me. Not one phone call, email, or text message. I am constantly being told how the rest of the family sends their regards and would like to know how I am. This is nice, but as I always say; the family has my number, if they really want to know what's going on or send their regards, they can do it themselves.

Chapter 12: Enter the Angel

I first met Michaela at the government office in New Jersey. We both worked together and started working there only a few months apart. She was another inspector. We held the same position, but she was a pilot. We spoke on a daily basis as her desk was located next to the main office door. On many of occasions, we were able to sit in her cubicle and talk about both work and non-work related items. We were on dozens of different projects together, went to different operators and aircraft accidents. She is from New Hampshire and travels back home every weekend.

Eventually, after about two years, she left to fly for another company. I helped arrange a going away party for her, as she was a good friend. During the time of the going away party, I told my wife about the party and I would be home a little late after work. She became extremely irate and accused me of having an affair with my coworker, which could not have been farther from the truth.

About a year went by since she left and one day I was out and about with a close friend and coworker. We were talking about my separation, my divorce, and all of the games. We came across an aircraft which reminded us of Michaela.

We began talking about her and curious what she was up to. My coworker said I should call her directly and speak with her. I did miss talking with her. It's been a year since I have seen her. So, I figured I would call her after work that day.

We spoke for over an hour. We discussed her job, the office, and little bit about my divorce. We also discussed me coming up to see her. I was planning to go up to my aunt's house in Massachusetts during Memorial Day weekend in 2015 for some relaxation from all of my divorce headaches. My aunt is fairly close to where Michaela lives, so we set plans for that weekend to visit each other for the day.

Memorial Day came and went. We had a great time catching up. She showed me the lakes region in New Hampshire, and we visited the sites, went wine tasting, bowling, along with a nice Italian dinner. I was able to forget about all my issues down in New Jersey, and it was really nice. We had a great time! Neither of us knew this was the start of a lifelong journey together.

Since that day, we began talking more and more; spending hours on the phone with each other. There were often times that she spent the night in New Jersey with her job and we went on dates. Other times, I went up to her for an extended weekend.

During our courting sessions, while I brought the children to the local parks in New Jersey, we would Skype on the phone. She loved talking with the boys and me. Eventually, I opened up to her with what was going on with me and this divorce. She was astounded to say the least.

Michaela and I were first hesitant with starting a relationship with all the games within this diary, but slowly we became closer and closer, and eventually I became a full member of her family.

However, after a court case where the Judge court ordered me to pay excessive amounts of money, beyond my salary; I became homeless overnight and Michaela along with my aunt took me in full time.

After those court sessions which demanded I pay more than I bring in, I had to abandon my apartment and leave everything behind. Michaela was worried sick about me and hated the fact that I was living partly in the office and partly at other people's homes.

We discussed the situation, and since I had a temporary work assignment in Boston with the leadership program I was in, we decided it was time for me to move to New England and I would be shared between my aunt's house and Michaela's in New Hampshire. Eventually, I moved into Michaela's home permanently.

Michaela has a long history of overcoming all odds. She is the full embodiment of a strong, independent woman. Unlike others who use this set of words loosely without anything to back it up (like my former wife), Michaela overcame obstacles to include people telling her she would never be a pilot, and taking advantage of her. Each time she was told she could not do something, she used all her intuition, strength, and determination to prove them wrong.

Michaela has worked multiple jobs in her lifetime. She worked retail, school bus driver, aircraft fueler, and airport helper. Eventually, she achieved her dream of being a pilot and now she flies for a corporate airline, flying the rich and famous around the country. Along with her normal flight duties, when she is home, she teaches the next generation of pilots how to fly, runs a flight school, airport station, and helps around the airport.

I firmly believe she learned how to be so strong and determined from her parents. Her mother and father both owned their own businesses along with raising three children. In the past they have owned apartment buildings, businesses, salons, food trucks, construction businesses, the list goes on.

Her mother volunteers with foster children and teaches them how to contribute to the community and gives them self-confidence through work and experience. Her father, even at an elderly age, wakes up at 4:00AM every morning and continues to work in the construction business.

They built their own home and continually work to fix and improve it. Since I have moved to New England, I have learned more about home repair and building than I ever have!

Michaela is the middle child in her family; with an older sister and younger brother. However, her extended family is much larger. Her mother is one of twelve children; and her father, one of nine. I am still meeting cousins and family members each day. I recently hosted a yard sale at Michaela's parents' house and half the people who showed up asked me who I was as they were extended family. I had no idea who they were. I felt bad. Her family is huge and it is really nice that they all still live in the same area and keep in touch with each other.

Michaela and her family are all strong, independent, and show the full embodiment of loving, caring people. Michaela, her mother, sister, and niece are all strong independent women. Michaela's sister; Martha is an amazing woman. She does foster care within her home along with raising her own daughter, Emma. Martha; like her mother, provides a loving, fostering environment, while teaching life values to multiple foster children and maintaining a beautiful home. She has been a foster parent for years and has helps dozens of children. She does all this and also has her normal job at the Post Office. Martha's husband; Carlos is a joy. He is quick with his jokes, always has a beer in hand for you, and is always available to help. He can build or fix any home, car, tractor, you name it. He has since retired from working at auto body shops for years. Together, they have built a beautiful family & home.

Michaela's brother, Doug is extremely intelligent. He is a truck driver by trade but is capable of so much more. He is an amazing craftsman and mechanic. He fixes everything on his own truck, his cars, and the family cars. He knows how to troubleshoot all sorts of problems. He is an artisan when it comes to woodworking. Michaela showed me a chest he made in high school. It is perfect. Even today, as he is doing work around Michaela's home, her parent's, or his own, his woodworking and home building skills are on point. He just put together and installed an entire shower without any instructions or measurements. Doug and I have grown close over the past year. We found a love of target shooting and hunting together. So in between him showing me how to fix or build something around the house, we target shoot or go over to the local gun stores looking for the next firearm purchase.

But one thing is for certain, the family is extremely tight-knit and supportive of each other. They are always available to help family and friends. Never before have I seen a family unit help each other on a daily basis. Whether it is: doing an errand, cutting the grass, or fixing a house. They all help each other; including me. It is extremely honorable of each of them.

One example I remember was when I first moved to New Hampshire, Michaela and decided to move my personal items out of a temporary storage unit to the crawl space at Michaela's home. I was only expecting Michaela and myself that day to move all of my stuff, but the next thing I knew, the whole family was there to help. I was not used to seeing this, especially being from a city environment.

As I am a "flat lander" and do not have much experience with building homes or fixing them, we found a use for me. I try to help and learn as much as I can, but I am still learning how to repair things around the house. My main duties include fixing the electronics: Either fixing a computer glitch, reformatting something, or just fixing a phone which may have been thrown or dropped a few times.

The family is also great with the kids too. They treat the kids as part of the family. Each time they come up, Michaela's family has them over for dinner, treats them to new and exciting foods, swimming in Martha's pool and the whole family joins in. Every time the kids come up, it's a party.

Eric has developed a strong relationship with Carlos. Eric kept calling him his "friend." They started a game in the pool where Carlos would throw footballs into the pool and Eric would retrieve them and place them in a specific arrangement in the pool bar. Eric begs to play the "ball game" each time he comes up. When we would go to the pool, Eric would automatically begin playing the game with Carlos.

Emma, Michaela, and the whole family swim with the baby. Carlos gives the hose to Eric to spray his older brother, and Martha has snacks and food for them. Afterwards, the baby runs around the yard with his new found legs, and his two older brothers try fishing in the brook in Martha's backyard.

Michaela's family has been nothing but exceptional. Her family has been so supportive throughout this whole process. They have offered their help with everything. They took me in, supported me, fed me, clothed me, helped me get back on my feet, and have offered their help with all of the issues my ex-wife would bring into my lap. They have been strong supporters of me and have been my support network. I am so glad I have met them and cannot thank them enough for all the help and support. I am happy to be part of this family.

I remember during this past year, on my birthday, I attempted to talk with the children. Of course, their mother would not have it. I was severely depressed and upset. Michaela was out in California working. Knowing it was my birthday, Michaela's older sister invited me over for dinner. It was great. It was a great night where I was able to forget about the divorce issues, even for a night.

I have heard through other divorced men how finding a woman is hard after a divorce. Many women do not want a divorced man with children as "baggage" let alone an ex-wife who is constantly harassing them inside or outside the courtroom.

Even Natalie stated at certain points, "how would any woman take you in? You have nothing, you have nothing to offer, no money." That just shows you what she is looking for in a man.

But I have found my match. It takes time for someone to find the right person for them, some people never find theirs. Luckily I have found mine! Michaela is my Yankee bell. She has been my strongest supporter throughout this whole process. In my darkest hour, she was there holding the light.

We are constantly having adventures like kayaking, flying, or simply going to a craft show. I cannot thank her enough for everything she and her family have done for me and the children. She is an amazing woman and I thank my lucky stars each day that we found each other. She is still by my side, even with my ex-wife's constant harassment and games. That shows you what type of woman she is!

Michaela is great with my children. She treats my children like they are her own flesh and blood. The first time the children came up to visit me, Aaron and Eric asked her to read a bedtime story for them. So while I was getting the baby prepared for bed, all you can see is Michaela snuggling up next to the boys reading them a Christmas Story.

She is always figuring out and planning events for them before they come up and visit. She scheduled train rides, amusement parks, swimming, hiking, and other adventures. She makes s'mores with them, has fires, brings them swimming, takes them to the beach at the lake, and we are planning a camping trip with them. The children are always asking for her whether they are up here or through Skype. Eric wants to go flying with her.

She sees their living conditions and how they are treated while I am on Skype and is astounded. I have shown her pictures of the children's living conditions while I was living in New Jersey and she cannot even comprehend what she was looking at. When the children come up to visit, she doesn't want them to leave. She teaches them how to take care of themselves, cloth themselves, brush their teeth, and bathe. She feels terrible about how they are treated in New Jersey and wants them to live with us. I thank her all the time. But she says that someone has to care about these kids and be maternal to them.

Chapter 13: After the Divorce

Health:
During my divorce, money became tighter and tighter. One dollar a day for food was a luxury. This whole divorce process got me physically sick. I suffered massive weight loss and my overall health condition plummeted. I did not eat for days due to anxiety and I eventually landed in the hospital with severe chest pains.

I began breaking out in pimples and hives, especially around my neck. Natalie told the mediators and court about my appearance and claimed they were "hickies."

At one point, I was hospitalized for severe chest pains and had to remain overnight in the hospital.

All of this due to the stress of Natalie's false claims, harassment, Keville's lies, legal bombardments, and a corrupt system which enabled it.

Harassment:
Over the past year and a half, I had to endure so much. I had to endure Natalie's constant harassment on Skype, phone, and email about more money, more demands, and her temper tantrums just to speak with my children. At a point, this was going to be too much on me.

How can a woman who says she loves you do this to someone? How can a woman who stood at the altar saying "I do" end up being so vindictive, evil, and controlling? Harry said it best; during a divorce, the woman you once knew is gone. In retrospect, he is completely right. He is young, but his wisdom is beyond his years.

My attorney, other attorneys, friends, and family all saw the constant and aggressive bombardment of legal issues I was going through and everyone was in agreement: This was planned for a very long time. That became apparent to me at the beginning when all the bank accounts were emptied. I cannot believe what she did, how she can live with herself with doing all of this? Did she ever love me? How can someone go from "I do" to filing false abuse claims, lie to the courts, and put someone through a legal mess such as this.

During the divorce and after it; Natalie's Bi-Polar lows had her telling me that she wanted me in prison, so she can visit me and show me how wonderful a life she is having. She promised me that she would keep me in court, bankrupt, and "ensure my demise."

Natalie and Mr. Keville fired off bombardments of legal letters, paperwork, issues when I had my children with me or while I was away at work. I am done with her, her threats, harassment, and crying wolf about the children to get me to answer her calls. Every time she called me with an emergency, there was none, just another way for her to harass me.

Over the past few months, I endured even more harassment, threats, and games. Natalie is still utilizing my medical benefits under my name, playing games with visitation and using the children as the tools for more money and control. It's a constant harassment through emails and dozens of calls a day.

Every Skype session with the children is interrupted with Natalie and her demands for money. I also get phone calls and emails from her as well. She cannot provide any proof of the bills, but just gives me an exorbitant number which I must pay, or she'll "have me in jail." Every day I receive threats from Natalie, Mr. Keville, Judges, and creditors.

Unfortunately, I am now numb to it all as I am used to them by now.

During each visitation drop off, pick up, and Skype session, Natalie asks me where I am living and demands that I provide her copies of my rent checks and other bills. She asks the children in front of me "where is daddy living" and "what house were they staying at" when they came up to visit me.

She has performed research on Michaela's homes, mortgages, and personal affairs and brings them up constantly. She demands that I provide her all of my and Michaela's personal information. She also demands that I provide her a copy of my vacation schedule, places I plan to visit, along with my training schedule for work. If I do not comply with her demands, she threatens court intervention. I do not understand why she just cannot leave me alone.

During one of my last Skype sessions with the children, and Natalie began her constant harassment about wanting more money, less time with the children, and threatening me, I asked her why she was doing all of this? Why was she putting me through such hell the past year, and continuing it? I heard those hallowed words she told me sixteen years ago, "I am entitled to be happy, and this makes me happy."

Courts & Fear of Retaliation:

Since Natalie has still refused to remove me from her bank accounts, I still have access to them. Michaela and I got a paper statement in the mail and saw how just this month alone she received thousands of dollars in deposits and withdrew a total of $10,000. $5k of it went to her upcoming cruise. So with child support, alimony, welfare, and daddy, along with no bills; things are good. But we are now thinking, while she is getting all this money, and I am left with almost enough for just gas for the week, how will Michaela and I survive?

So now total, I have two divorce decrees which total 53 pages of demands I must meet over the next 23 years. Attorney's I have spoken to recently have lost track after seeing my finalized divorce decree that I must abide by. They lost track going through 53 pages of demands.

On the final decree, Natalie apparently can request the court to extend the alimony after the initial six years. New Jersey does not have lifetime alimony out of the gate, but they grant it on a renewal schedule. Natalie can keep going to the court and having it extended. Now, who pays for her lawyer every time she goes for an extension? Me of course! Can't wait, what FUN!

I was never in court, never on the stand, never in trouble with the law. I served my country and followed the rules. Almost overnight and automatically, I became a criminal with a criminal history because Natalie's attorney said so in his documents and the court ate it all up.

The moment the Judges and Courts entering in Mr. Keville's fraudulent claims into record and enter it in as fact without question, or evidence, they became legal evidence. When I inquired about what orders I violated and how did I abuse my ex-wife and children; no one can answer me or they just refuse to answer me.

Throughout this process, I have paid my attorney's office to respond to dozens of letters back and forth to the court and Mr. Keville. Most of which were answering false allegations.

I have responded to dozens of letters from Mr. Keville explaining how terrible of a person I am, how I am an "undocumented" abuser, how I am constantly ignoring court orders, and falsifying information.

I have given the court and my attorney evidence including letters and emails from Natalie and Mr. Keville with their own signatures on the documents.

Mr. Keville would lie to the court claiming he never wrote the letters and the emails from Natalie never existed. The courts, without even looking at the evidence would concur with him and tell me how those letters I provided do not exist and Mr. Keville never sent them, because he says so.

Mr. Keville cannot even keep track of his own lies. At first, I was removed from my residence because I assaulted and abused the children and Natalie; but then I vacated voluntarily leaving her barefoot to fend for three children. How can the judges not see these lies?

While I was evicted from my apartment at the start of the divorce, Natalie wrote a letter and signed it explaining that she was throwing me out.

Apparently the letter Natalie signed explaining she is throwing me out did not exist. During court sessions, my attorney showed the letter, but Mr. Keville explained that it doesn't exist. What did the court do with two conflicting stories? Without looking at the letter, they believed Mr. Keville and concurred with him. The letter does not exist!

Mr. Keville tells the Judge at first how I didn't provide any interrogatories for discovery, but then I failed to answer two questions which had nothing to do with my case: How am I a good parent and my thoughts about Natalie moving to Ohio? So first I didn't provide them, now it's answering bogus questions? How can the Judge not see this? He is lying right to her face.

Mr. Keville provided nothing for discovery and the Judge defended him and Natalie. The Judge told me that they "provided what they could." Are you kidding me?

I still cannot enter the State of New Jersey. I cannot ever go back to my hometown. Even my friends, family, and legal help concur. The fear of retaliation from Natalie, Mr. Keville, and the various civil bench warrants for my arrest, and Natalie's abuse allegations.

With all this, I still have the same probation case worker who knows my ex-wife overseeing my account even with all my letters to the courts, my issues with her, my complaints, and my requests for someone else.

I am living in fear seeing how the County Court is arresting people who are behind on their alimony, wrapping it under the umbrella of "child support." I hate reading the articles how they no longer have ability to pay hearings and keeping fathers in jail forcing them to pay support three times their salary. I hate reading how the Courts go after the father's family's social security to pay their ex-wives' alimony. These practices must stop!

Children:

I hate how Natalie requests multiple times to the court, mediators, and others that she does not want any other person watching or influencing the children to include Michaela. She wants to "approve" anyone who will be in contact with them. It is another form of her control. When it does go to court, I simply ask if the same could go for her. The mediators said yes; the Court Judges said no.

Since their birth, the children have heard their mother screaming, yelling, and having temper tantrums regularly. They have been accustomed to seeing this. It is no different now, while their mother and I are now divorced. The same temper tantrums and screaming fits are still displayed for the children to see. They often ask why she does this. I still cannot find a suitable answer to their question.

During each visitation, when the boys came up to see me in New Hampshire; Natalie would not pack them any clothing or if she did, they would be the wrong size. Multiple times, she would pack inappropriate clothes. During the winter months- packing shorts, flip-flops, T-Shirts; during the summer months- winter clothes. Michaela and I spent hundreds of dollars in clothes each time and brought the children to the local Walmart. Even Michaela's mother picked up tons of clothes at the local Community center Thrift Shop for the children. But each time the children came up to visit, they gained a significant amount of weight in between the visits and the clothes we purchased now did not fit.

I have noticed a complete breakdown of the children's eating habits and manners since I was removed from their lives. The only way I can get them to eat veggies is to tell them "that's what McDonald's French fries and hamburgers are made of. The children do not sit at a dinner table nor do they even know how to use utensils. Aaron and Eric are consistently using their fingers to pick up food and hold silverware wrong. I have to correct it every time they sit down to eat. I asked them why they do this, and I get the answer that I have learned to just accept- "kid's meals don't have them."

My visitation with the children is very limited being only a combined four week amount. Each time I am able to see them, I get word from my attorney about his office being bombarded with legal paperwork from Natalie and Mr. Keville. Other times, I get the same bombardment through email and paper letters. **This has happened during each visitation, without fail.**

These bombardments are preplanned attacks and I have been told by legal counsellors that it is done to increase my stress level while I have the children, so that I do not give them my full attention and love.

More importantly, it is gone so that I cannot complete the legal documents and defense properly or in a timely manner. Nonetheless, everyone has told me it is an unethical practice.

During a recent visitation with my children; my six year old, Aaron told me on the car ride home from picking them up that "mommy's lawyer has a gift for you." He thought it was a present and wanted to know if I got it and what it was. He had no idea that a lawyer's gift is a bad thing.

Initially, I was furious with their mother. I thought about it and I could not believe a mother would begin wrapping a six year old into her legal games and nonesense. The children should not be brought into these dealings. They should be completely left out and just enjoy their time with their mother and father.

So, I passed off his statement and left it alone. I do not want him to be concerned with a lawyer's present for me. I changed the subject and discussed the fun things we would do that weekend together. A few days later, I received "mommy's lawyer's gift." Pages upon pages of more false claims to the court and threats to me.

To this day, Natalie continues to draw the children into the legal games and unethical conduct. When I see them, both Aaron and Eric say things like:

"Daddy stole from mommy" & "Mommy says daddy hurts me"

She has no business drawing a four and six year old into these games. The children should be concentrating on school, having fun, and spending quality time with both of us.

Natalie's games with the children are putting undue stress on them. Because of it, both Eric and Aaron have issues pooping and peeing in their pants. I have multiple talks with them each time they do it.

After long conversations with them to see what was wrong, ask them about their feelings, and why they do it; they begin to cry. They say that they don't think I care and do not understand why I am asking them about their feelings. I tell them that I ask because I love them.

When I tell them how much I love them, they cry even more. They are either not told enough or at all when they are at their mother's. They do not have structure, they do not feel loved, and they are developing problems because they need love, affection, and attention. Unfortunately, they are not getting enough in New Jersey and I only see them on a rare occasion which is not enough for what they need.

I am trying to correct this and give the children the attention they deserve. I give them love, affection, structure, and fun. Each visit, Michaela and I plan a bunch of events for us to do and we enjoy many activities together. Every day, I tell them I love them and remind them during our talks and each night when I tuck them into bed. During the day and right before bed, we always give hugs and kisses.

I love my children, but I have been pulled out of their lives, I will never see any of their milestones, or be there for their games, accomplishments, good times, or bad. I tried so hard to be with them, to have them, but in the end the system awarded everything to their mother and treated me as a criminal. I must pay, that is all they allow me to do. That is what the best interest is for the children. I will only be a visitor in my children's lives. I will not be there for birthdays, or school events, or even seeing their smiles, their emotions, their proms, and first girlfriends.

I hate that I can only see my children on my ex-wife's schedule. Only when she says I can see them, when it is convenient for her, like when she is on a cruise. When I want to see them, I have to deal with her harassment and give her more money. This is extortion! They are my children, not your weapons!

If the children have any problems; whether it is health issues, weight gain, problems in school, or social issues; Natalie tells me how it is entirely my fault. I am to blame for the children. Their limited time with me is enough for me to cause all of their issues. Natalie is not responsible or has any share of the fault (if fault is even required). She often tells me how she had to seek counseling for the children because I moved to New Hampshire.

Eric (and all three children) crave attention. When we cuddle, go out, or even when I fix a toy, I love hearing Aaron and Eric say "daddy you are my best friend." It warms my heart! I love these guys so much!

I am losing my mind. I love to see my children, and I change around my schedule each week so that I can make the weekly Skype sessions with them, but with Natalie consistently cancelling the sessions last minute, not showing up at all, or harassing me during them; I don't even know why I bother anymore.

Since Natalie has not spent much time taking care of three children and giving them structure during the marriage; she is losing control with the children being alone with them.

During each Skype session, I see Eric and Aaron openly defy her, jump and climb all over the furniture, and run around either filthy, naked, or both.

Friends of mine in New Jersey see her and the children in local stores. Recently, a friend saw them in BestBuy. He explained that Natalie had no control over the kids and saw all three run in different directions in the store. Natalie did not last five minutes before having to leave. I have heard the same story multiple times from lots of people I know.

I miss my children, I love my children, I will always love my children; but I am losing them, and I am losing the battle. I haven't seen them, and she is using them as bait, as tools, as weapons. I am so depressed. Natalie is going to make sure the children hate me. She is already telling them that I hate them; I don't love them because I moved, etc. I have the Skype video tapes.

I hate watching those Skype sessions and tapes of her telling my children that I hate them, that I abandoned them, that I do not love them anymore. They get upset with her. Eric even hits her! I hate that Natalie cancels our Skype sessions (last minute or not). I hate the Court's word "Visitation." I am their father, not a visitor!

As far as my visitation is concerned; this finalized divorce decree is a joke. Natalie was hell-bent on the children being in the car for too long, but places inside the decree how I can only see the children for a few hours on holidays to include father's day. All in all if you calculate it, I only get to see my children four weeks a year. This is a catastrophe! This is so sad. I cried when I got this news. I tried to fight it, but to no avail. More time with the children would adversely affect Natalie's support payments, which was not allowed.

As far as seeing my children more, since I am financilly ruined and the garnishments are so much; I cannot even afford an attorney to fight for more custody or visitation!

Suicide:

At the start of my divorce, I felt that I failed in life. My goal ever since I was a child was to raise a strong family of my own and give my children everything that I did not have growing up. I felt like a failure. I failed as a husband and as a father.

During the beginning of my divorce, Natalie contacted my family to create more unrest. She contacted my family to tell them I still owe her money and that I was planning to commit suicide. I was, but she did not know it. That was a guess on her behalf. You would think she would ease up on the onslaught of lies and harassment if she thought I was. Nope, she just wanted to create more heartache for me.

Every day I sat in my car doing research on my phone looking up different ways to die. I would sit in store parking lots and research the subject for hours on end. I was looking up the peaceful bill handbook and other websites. A gun would have worked best, but New Jersey's rules with owning a firearm made it damn near impossible to own one.

I found two good ways to die. The first called Charcoal-burning suicide. This is when you light up a charcoal grill inside a confined space (like a car) but a lot of preparations had to be done so the car didn't burn. In addition, I would need to park in a secluded area so no one would try to open the door or break in a window to save me. I went to Walmart and purchased two portable charcoal grills, charcoal, and a fire-mat.

Afterwards, I began thinking about things. If I did this inside the car, the police would eventually find the car and trace it back to Natalie. I was ready to leave this world, as I have failed as a husband and a father, but I didn't want my body found or identified, I did not want to give Natalie the satisfaction!

I found an article about people jumping off the George Washington Bridge and how the bodies are difficult to identify. Perfect! I began looking into jumping off the George Washington Bridge. I researched and researched. I found videos of past jumpers and articles. All it involved was a short fence climb. The bridge had two walkways; one on either side. One side was closed due to the government installing an anti-suicide fence, but the other side of the bridge was open for pedestrians. I signed up for the Port Authority Walkway status report emails. I was ready to do it until my angel appeared. My Yankee Bell came into my life and made me promise her that I would never leave her.

My Final Thoughts:
I think this novel and diary shows how one person can be defeated by Courts, Judges, Lawyers, and the entitlements of money. Where accusations are proof, and evidence is thrown out if it proves you are innocent. You are no longer a father, but a pay check. The same courts who claim that the children are their #1 priority are the first ones to pull you from your

children and leave their "child support" as a fighting coin until the end.

During this whole divorce, Natalie would either make a simple phone call to the insurance company, police, the courts, a judge, or an attorney and it meant a weeks' worth of paperwork, heartache, and headache for me. Not even including all the legal costs! Other times where she was required to either just mail a simple form out, sign a piece of paper, or make a call to fix something she did; she refused and it once again creates more writing, letters, emails, legal fees, and work on my behalf. When she refuses to mail a required document or makes a simple phone call means hours of aggravation and stress; just because she can.

She is right, divorce decrees and court orders do not apply to her. She has violated so many I have lost count. When it was brought up to court, it ended up being either okay or my fault. She is above the law and Attorney Bar Rules and laws do not apply to her attorney. They both have been empowered and supported with these thoughts because the system allows it.

As far as my ex-wife, her family, her attorney, and her boss that presided over my case; there is a special place for people like you in the afterlife, no matter what your religion is. You will be judged for your actions one day.

There is so much more that has happened and so much more to come, but I hope you find this story enlightening. This novel may be concluded at the end of the diary, but my story is still going and will be continued.

Chapter 14: Support & Advice

As I stated earlier, this book is for fathers going through similar cases. I decided to write this book to let those other fathers know there is hope, there is light, and they are not alone. As you can see in this book, I have been down that path, the heartbreak, the suicidal thoughts, and the pain. All I can tell you is to keep going. There is light, I promise, but it is a long road. I hope you found this book enlightening and can help you find your path.

I am not a lawyer, or a professional in this field, but I can tell you things that have helped me and my case. First off, before your divorce, be prepared! It's the Boy Scout motto! Keep your eyes open to red flags. Once you start seeing them, and seeing them line up, it would be prudent to start the process yourself. You may tell yourself that you want to stay for your children, or your parent's stuck by each other, or you have seen how nasty divorces can be. But remember, you are not them! You are your own person and it may not be in your hands. It is in your wife's hands as well.

Whether you file for divorce or if your wife does, it doesn't matter. Once they file the paperwork, your wife is no longer your friend, she is your adversary. Be careful with what you say to her, or show her. She will use anything she can against you- good or bad. I have heard cases of wives explaining how their husband's military service and roles of police officers made them into horrible abusers with "undocumented" mental conditions.

Once you get the paperwork, you may think and feel that you failed as a father, husband, or both. Do not think this way. Lots of people get divorced and it is just a part of life. It does not make it your fault. As long as you fight to see your children and do what is right, you have not failed! But you will the moment you give up.

Begin removing yourself from accounts, divide up what you can, and get your personal items out! Possession is 9/10ths of the law. If you don't want her to have something of yours, get rid of it. Give it to friend, a coworker, or family. If you have weapons (even knives) get rid of them. Your wife can call the police and say you are threatening her with those weapons. They don't need proof during those cases and you will be arrested! Get important paperwork out. Taxes, pay stubs, social security cards, birth certificates, etc. You will have to produce these documents during the discovery part of your case.

If your wife has the documents and does not give them to you, guess what? You are the one who has failed to produce discovery and the court order. You will be found guilty and may be arrested. Just another game they play. Get those documents out. Bring them to work if you must!

Tell your job immediately. I don't care what people say when they can "split their time" with work and personal life, your divorce will consume you and it will show up at work. If your adversary wants to slip something through, she will do it while you are at work knowing you are not there to fight against it. If your employer knows what's going on, they will work with you.
Lots of men have been in your situation, they will have compassion. I have seen bosses at other places be complete pricks to employees, but when they heard about someone going through a divorce, it reminded them of theirs, and they gave those employees undying support.

Your friends and coworkers will all give you advice. Some of it could be good, some bad. You need to use your head and pick and choose. One thing they will recommend is their own lawyer. Everyone knows an attorney. Do not just jump on the first one. Shop around. Look at reviews. AVVO.com is a good website to look at. They have online reviews of attorneys.

The best advice I received from friends who went through this before was about keeping a detailed diary. I don't care what you call it; journal, diary, memoir's, book, etc. This diary has to have very specific information: including times on certain dates, things that were said, names, phone numbers, etc. Save this and give it to your attorney. Not only is it a legal, written document, but it is also a recording of what you are going though. They can use it in court. In addition, you can give it to your children one day if they come by and ask you what happened years ago when you were torn away from them.

Be careful on who you tell your case information to. If you have mutual friends, they may relay your plans or situation to your wife and it will come to haunt you. Even badmouthing your wife to mutual friends can have catastrophic effects in court as you are "smearing her imagine." For God's sake, do not post anything on social media (yes that includes Facebook). My recommendation is to temporarily close your account until things are settled. Even after things are settled, it would be wise to drop your ex-wife and any mutual friends which could relay information to her, as she will use this against you in court.

Keep a small notepad in your car to jot down notes for your main diary. You can't believe what you can forget in a matter of minutes, especially if you are angry.

Record EVERYTHING. Record your Skype sessions, Apple Facetime, text messages, and phone calls. If you don't know how to record it- google it! Everything is able to be recorded.

Legally speaking, you must inform the person you are recording that you are recording them to use that evidence in court. In my experience, you can inform the other party, sure; but you know what their answer will be!

How many times, have you seen somebody in court with a surveillance video being shown? No one got their permission with those. Better to have it and not need it, then need it and not have it. It may not be used in court for the purpose of getting back at someone, but it can be used to DEFEND YOU. Cameras have been used to overturn cases to show innocence in various cases. In addition, one day, your children may want to see them, to see what really happened between mom and dad.

Start learning your state's laws both during and after your divorce. Also learn your federal laws. State and County Courts have traditionally imputed demands on fathers which go against Federal Law. The garnishment laws by the US Dept. of Labor are an example. 60%, that's it!

Pick and choose your battles. If you have a limited budget, attorneys are expensive; you are going to need to save your money to fight for the big things. If your divorce is financially driven, like mine; remember alimony is tax deductible and temporary. Child Support, especially for little ones is going to be longer. As far as visitation and custody, it is an extremely long battle.

Any time you have to speak with your ex-wife, try to do it via email and safe it. Create correspondence folders. You can organize them by the month/year. If you mail anything, send it certified mail with signature. You will not believe how many times people claim to never receive something. I have seen cases where a husband would mail a bank check thinking once his ex-wife cashed it, that would be the proof, only to have her sit on it, claimed he never sent it, and after the court case finds him guilty, she cashed it. It's just another game to them.

Save all of these items to your computer. Scan in all court documents and anything you receive from attorneys. Keep all these files, organize them, and back them up on the computer.

You will eventually have to send all this to your attorney, the courts, and other attorneys if you change venues or attorneys.

Keep these documents on a "cloud" or flash drive so you can access them wherever you are. Lawyers like to bombard you with legal nonsense when they know you are in a situation where it would be difficult. So when you don't do it, it looks bad for you.

Keep a box of all the kids' items. Personally, I have three boxes. I have one for each child and it contains all their important paperwork, Baptism certificates, memoirs, baby books, birthday cards, etc. One day your children will thank you for saving all this stuff.

Be adaptable. Remember, a simple phone call from your wife to the police, the courts, a judge, or an attorney means weeks' worth of paperwork and headache for you. Having all the necessary files and paperwork with you is key to survive these tactics. The same goes for when your wife does not feel like abiding by a court order. Because she decided to not do something means you must write letters, certify mail them, and take a proactive approach to the situation.

Never give up. Find ways to fight and ways to make additional money. Perhaps write a book upon your experiences to pass along the information while making money.

If this book will help you with anything, it is to show you how to keep a strong diary if you are going through a nasty or aggressive divorce like this and to show you, that you are not alone. There is hope, there is help. It comes in a variety of shapes, sizes, and people. Help comes from friends and family. Support comes from others like you.

There are hundreds of books, resources, organizations, and community homes for divorced women. For men, there is work-release, full prison, or the street. There are only a handful of organizations for men which share our voice. One of which I fully recommend.

Michaela found it on Facebook one day and they have a ton of resources, guides, and help. But I am mainly interested in hearing the stories of other men going through the same thing I did and seeing that I am not alone. There are dozens of posts each day on their site with fathers going through turmoil and seeing the comments and support they get from fathers like you and me. They are called, "The Fathers' Rights Movement."

It is my hope that this diary makes it to the masses of good husbands, fathers, men who have always done the right thing, want the best for others, and love their families and children. I hope you will never have to go through this hell, but if you do just take it in stride and know you are not alone. It has happened before, it will happen again. The world is full of liars, cheats, and corrupt people in power.

Fathers' Rights Movement

Mission Statement:

As a collective movement, we are passionate about empowering fathers to stand up for their rights and to educate the public and family court system about the importance of fathers in society, as well as bring greater awareness to the imbalances and injustices that affect the rights of fathers.

Every day, fathers are losing their rights and contact with their children due to outdated biases that diminish the role and influence of a father. We are here in support of fellow fathers and families that suffer from this injustice, to share your stories, to connect you with the proper resources to overcome your blocks, and to inspire our society to address the issues in our family court system that are hindering child development and damaging the family unit.

We aim to collect valuable, helpful resources and tools that will further enable fathers to regain and retain their rights, as well as gather any available data and research that offers greater insight into the importance of fathers and the effect of father-absent homes. Our mission includes bringing the community of fathers together as a unified social force aimed at restoring society's ideals of the father and strengthening the connection each father has to his child(ren).

The Fathers' Rights Movement (TFRM) seeks to have a good relationship with all other organizations promoting and advocating for shared parenting and parental rights whose organizational standards, visions, and missions align with those of TFRM.

Despite the gender specific title of "Father" in the TFRM name, TFRM is a movement whose members, both men & women, are interested in seeing an equal custody presumption in child custody cases. Members shall be welcomed regardless of race, gender, sexual orientation, religion (or no religion) or other differentiating factors.

Contact Information:
http://www.Fathersrightsmovement.us

http://yourchildyourdivorce.com/wordpress/child-custody-rights-for-fathers/

Facebook.com/fathers4kids

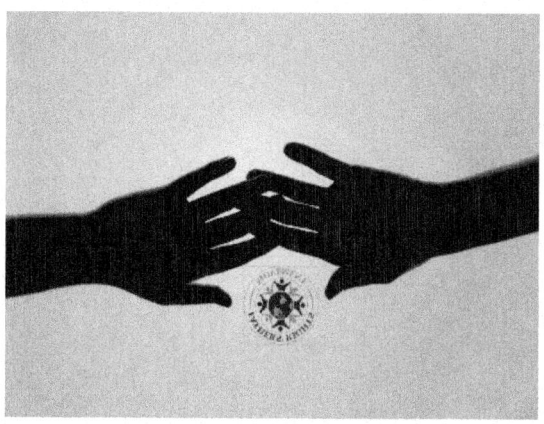

Part II

Entry #1: Pre-Divorce Diary (Quarter 1, 2015):

During the beginning of this quarter, on each of the weekends, Natalie would leave at 3:00PM on each Friday and would not come back home until Sunday evening. I asked her once if I can go out with some friends for an hour once; she told me to bring the children with me.

Saturday 3/14/2015--Sunday 3/15/2015: I got home from work at my normal time on Friday. Before I entered the front door, Natalie was leaving. She did not give an explanation or tell me where she was going. She left for weekend, did not answer her phone, and was missing in action. I took care of the children and planned some weekend activities. Natalie came back late Sunday night. I asked where she went; she refused to answer. I can only assume she was with her boyfriend.

Monday 3/16/2015: I came home after work. Natalie left immediately and did not come home until late at night (early morning). On occasion, I would ask where she would go. She would either say with friends or nothing at all. A lot of times, her friends would call the house looking for her while she was out. Hmm...I thought she was out with them.

I cooked dinner, fed the kids, and did Aaron's homework with him. Later that that evening, when Natalie got home, I asked if she would help with the baby at night, as like most babies, he was up every few hours to drink his bottle. She refused.

She quoted her counsellor saying that it is not a woman's role to stay up with the baby. As a stay at home mother, she does not have to perform those functions. I pressed a bit, explaining that I have to work the next day and all I was asking for is some help. She explained that I was being abusive and it helping with the children is not her responsibility. She is a "strong independent woman." Thus, I stayed up with the baby every night and went to work the following morning.

Tuesday 3/17/2015: I came home right after work. Natalie's mother was there watching the children. Apparently Natalie left at 3:00PM. Her mother explained to me that if I get out of work at 3:00PM, I must be home at that time. Commute time is not calculated, so Natalie will now start leaving the house at 3:00PM as her job to stay at home with the baby ends at that time. Natalie did not come home until 11:00PM.

I asked her where she went, she refused to tell me. But she was now tired, so she went to bed. I asked Natalie, as I normally do to get more help from her and to pitch in more. Once again, I received a screaming woman breaking down into a temper-tantrum, "it's not my job." I stayed up with baby all night. The baby had a rough night.

Friday 3/20/2015: Just as Natalie promised, she was gone at 3:00PM and didn't come home till late. When she got home, she was too tired to "handle" a baby. So, I stayed up with baby all night. I've stopped asking Natalie to help or pitch in more. I know I will get my answer of "it's not her job."

Saturday 3/21/2015: Natalie left today and did not come home until midnight. When she got home, she was tired and went straight to bed. I stayed up with the baby; he had a better night and slept for a few hours.

Thursday 3/26/2015: I came home at 3:45PM. Natalie left at that time till 12:00AM. I stayed up with baby all night. I've stopped asking Natalie to help or pitch in more. I know I will get my answer of it's not her job.

Friday 3/27/2015: Today, a few friends of mine were going out to Olive Garden for dinner and wanted me to come with.

I asked Natalie permission. She said "no" and decided to leave herself. She didn't come home until Sunday morning.

Sunday 3/29/2015: Natalie stopped over in the morning to grab some clothes and personal items. She then left from 9:00AM till 5:00PM. When she got home she was on the computer all night but could not help with the baby. She was on Facebook and writing. I stayed up with baby all night. I got ready for work the next morning. I am exhausted!

Monday 3/31/2015: I came home at 3:45PM from work. Natalie left at that time till 11:00PM. Where she went, no one but her knows.

Entry #2: Separation Diary (Quarter 2, 2015):

Wednesday 4/1/2015: I came home early at 12:30PM because I became really sick at work and vomited on myself. When I got home, that was the go-ahead for Natalie to leave to hang out with her friends until the late hours of the night. Once again when she got home, she was too tired to help with the baby at night. I stayed up with the little guy, who now is sick too. I am working on 72 hours without a once of sleep, sick, and having to work tomorrow.

Thursday 4/2/2015: I couldn't do it. I was too sick to go to work. Thus, I called out sick. The boys woke up, I got them ready and out the door for school and the day's activities. When Natalie woke up; surprise surprise, I was told "I decided to take a day off for myself, so I am too." She left and did not come home until the next day (4/3/2015). So when the boys came home after school, we did our normal routine and I stayed up with the now sick baby all night.

Friday 4/3/2015: Came home at 6:00PM. Natalie's mother was watching the children. Natalie left for weekend. Arrived at home on 4/5/2015 at 8:00PM. I stayed up with baby all night. I've stopped asking Natalie to help or pitch in more. I know I will get my answer of it's not her job.

Monday 4/6/2015: I came home at my normal time of 3:45PM. Before I could even get through the front door, Natalie was leaving. She didn't get home until around 9:00PM. No words, no update, just out the door with a big middle finger at me.

Friday 4/10/2015: I came home at 3:45PM. Natalie left at that time till 11:00PM. I stayed up with baby all night. I've stopped asking Natalie to help or pitch in more. I know I will get my answer of it's not her job.

Saturday 4/11/2015: I got some sleep with the baby. The two older ones woke up at 7:00AM. I got them ready for the day and breakfast. Natalie woke up and immediately left the house from about 11:00AM till 9:00PM. When she got home, she was way too tired to help with the baby; I stayed up with the little guy again. I am exhausted.

Sunday 4/12/2015: Today was a special day for the kids. Aaron and Eric LOVE cars, trucks, automobiles, etc. If it has wheels, they like them. My best friend, Harry along with his wife and sister were going to the Jacob Javits Center in New York City to the annual Auto Show, where they have all sorts of cars and trucks on display. I decided to take the children to it. Natalie liked the idea as well since it gave her a break from her break.

Because we had the three of them, me, and the kids; I decided to take my minivan to drive everyone into the city. Early in the morning, I started packing my kid's "Go-Kits" which are bags with all the children essentials (the name I coined myself) and started packing the car. The minivan was its normal disgusting self, so I started shoveling the old fast food wrappers, bags, candy, and soda bottles out. I made it cleaner, but not good enough it seemed. I started the car and the radio blasted me out of the seat; it was set extremely loud.

Natalie and I have been through this a dozen times. She will set the radio extremely high with its volume, not even caring if the children are in the car. She is like a teenaged girl. This is doing damage to the children's ears, especially Eric; who already has issues with hearing and processing information.

Why does she keep doing this? I went inside and asked her nicely to keep the car radio at a reasonable volume, her response was no different from what she normally says, and "I will do whatever I want, f**k you. When I bring up the children's hearing: I get the same answer.

The children and I left around 8:00AM and had a nice home cooked breakfast at Harry's. His family took really good care of them. Harry's mom and dad cooked a special breakfast for them. Eric loved the mangos. After breakfast, we all piled into the car. Harry's family could not even believe the shape the minivan was in. They noticed what a mess it was and it had a severe bad odor. I explained to them how I cleaned it for over an hour this morning. We drove with the windows down the whole way.

While we were driving, I was telling Harry about the issues with the car radio and Natalie keeping it so loud with the children in the car. I can care less what she does by herself, but when my children are in the car- now I have a problem. Aaron chimed in; knowing what we were talking about and he said that he "tells mommy it hurts his ears." I asked him what she says to that and he responded "she does not care." This is really sad.

Harry is wise beyond his years; he came up with the best solution. Car Radios have fuses, just pull the fuse. Brilliant! So, we pulled the fuse and that was the end of that.

We went to the Auto Show and had a great time. The kids enjoyed going into all the cars, meeting lots of people, playing games, and being in a new environment. After a long, busy, wonderful day with the family and friends the children wanted to quick go to the park at home. So we went to the park to unwind and release some more energy. We got home around 7:00PM.

We were greeted at the door by a screaming woman. Natalie began a temper-tantrum in front of the neighbors because we were supposed to be out longer and that I am not doing more for her. She left right after her tirade and did not come home until early morning the next day. So, I stayed up with the baby at night and went to work the next day. I was exhausted!!!

Monday 4/13/2015: After work, I came home and expected Natalie to be gone already or just about to leave. She was home for a few minutes. She started to scream again and kept asking me if there was anything I wanted to tell her. She explained that she went to the car dealership, as the radio was not working. She spent tons of money for the dealership to troubleshoot the issue and reinstall the fuse. She explained that she knew it was me who removed it and that she is going to call the police on me. I fought back somewhat and explained that first off, she cannot call the police on the maintenance that I do to my own car which is financed and registered in my name, in addition I brought up my concerns with the children's hearing and blasting a radio at a volume level beyond 40 is doing damage to their ears, especially the baby. She continued making the claims that she can do whatever she wants and she is going to call the police on me if I do it again. She stormed out at that point.

After Aaron and I did his homework, I brought the children to park to get some exercise, followed up by dinner and baths. Natalie did not show up until around 11:00PM and went right to bed. I stayed up with the baby all night. He had a rough night. He slept the better half of the day, so he was up for me at night. But I do enjoy the "ooosss" and "aahhs" throughout the night.

Wednesday 4/15/2015: After work, I did Aaron's homework with him and started getting the boys ready to go to the park. Natalie decided to come with the children and I, which I thought was good as this was a first for her. We went to the park, but Natalie did not leave the car. She sat in the car to talk with her friend (i.e. boyfriend) while I played with the children at the park.

After the park, we went a few towns over to get some dinner. After dinner, I began asking Natalie to help more with the children or pitch in more. I felt it was unfair that she considers everything to be "not her job." I also brought up the fact that I knew about her boyfriend. She became excessively violent and explained that she could have been with him instead of me, everything would have been better and that she did not want children with me.

Natalie opened the car door on the highway; she threatened to throw herself out. The children were witnessing this happening and began crying. This was not the first time she did this in front of the children.

When we got home, Natalie began to threaten to call police on me for domestic violence. This was extremely erratic, so I called the County Help Line for mental illness. I heard about this help line through a friend who was an EMT and paramedic. I believe her bi-polar depression is getting worse and after today, she has become a threat to herself and the kids.

They asked a magnitude of questions. Natalie began threatening me to get off the phone with them. She called her mother to come upstairs. I began answering the questions, but during the phone call, Natalie hung the phone up on me.

Once her mother arrived, she and Natalie began saying that I was abusing Natalie and was being violent. I told them that they know that is untrue. Her mother confirmed it but said she is holding to her story and she will to do whatever she can, include lying to protect her daughter from the doctors, or as she called them, "the dangerous men dressed in white."

From there, Natalie's mother left to go home and Natalie left to stay with "a friend" and didn't get home till late. I stayed up with the baby all night until it was time for me to go to work the following morning.

Thursday 4/16/2015: I went to work and immediately started to tell my closest coworkers what happened. They told me that I need to start calling banks, counselors, and attorneys. Legally speaking today would be my separation date.

I contacted my employee assistance program and crisis help lines. I informed them of my own suicidal thoughts and severe stress. They explained that someone will be calling me back and hung up. No one called back. No one cares. They referred me to a financial counsellor.

Eventually I cancelled this service as they were no help, charged me exorbitant service fees, and called me at inconvenient times to just check up on my "financial health." When I would tell them all the money demands, they did not have any answers.

Due to some work obligations, I was late coming home. I came home at 4:30PM. Natalie was not home. Her mother was there with the children. She left the moment I came home. Natalie did not arrive until 7:00PM. I stayed up with baby all night to take care of him. I love the way he looks at me while I am feeding him. I have always loved that look, with each of my little guys.

Before Natalie came home, and seeing the writing on the wall with what was about to happen; I took pictures of all the medications Natalie was on, pictures of the apartment mess, bottles behind beds, stacks of papers all over, clothes all over mixed with food, along with all of the other messes.

I also had multiple pictures on my phone from the apartment disaster after I was away for a week in Oklahoma City for training. The mess was left for me to clean when I got home. Same type of pictures of the apartment mess, paperwork, old rotten food, pictures of her medications, dozens of prescriptions for depression, Bi-Polar, and sedatives.

Throughout the divorce, I showed these pictures to my attorney and court, but they are not admissible. Pictures of mediations do not prove someone is on them, and the mess is apparently normal. I have shown family and friends these pictures and they cannot believe it. It is simply abhorrent.

Friday 4/17/2015: The day that changed my life forever:

Like every other day, I came home at around 3:45PM after work. When I got home, Natalie was preparing to leave for the day to go out with her friends as she normally does. Like normal, she didn't say a thing; not where she was going, or anything. Natalie left at 5:00PM. I started my routine with the boys. I fed the baby, checked up on Eric, and began Aaron's homework with him while I began cooking dinner. Usually after homework is done is when I get to change out of my work clothes.

An hour later, Natalie arrived with her mother. Aaron and I were almost done with his homework. Natalie came into the kitchen with a BIG smile on her face. Natalie demanded that I leave for good. This came as a shock. I asked why, but she didn't give me an answer. I explained that I wasn't going to leave, I have done nothing wrong, and anyways; I was doing Aaron's homework with him.

She then did the unimaginable. With that same smile, the vindictive look, she called 911 and said, "Emergency, my husband is beating me and my children." Knowing what was about to come I rushed. I called two friends. One, Harry who is a paramedic and knows how these things work and the other: a co-worker whose family is all police and knows the police procedures.

Harry said he would be right over and started to head to my home. My co-worker was very calm and collective. He told me to do the same. He told me not to raise my voice, follow instructions, and prepared me as I was more than likely going to be arrested.

I had only a few minutes to prepare myself for what was about to come. I kissed the boys, but did not say anything. Aaron and Eric knew something was wrong. Children have a six sense about things. They sat with me on the couch, holding me. Natalie sat at her computer texting someone (probably her boyfriend), laughing and still smiling.

When the police arrived, four officers and two vehicles rushed into the street and knocked hardly on the door before barging in. Natalie began crying the moment they came, almost like an actor. I was forced outside with my hands behind my back standing on the front steps with all the neighbors watching while the police were consoling Natalie as she was crying.

I was inspected from head to toe. They looked at my hands, my face, my body, and began asking a plethora of questions in the form of accusations. Leading questions, really.

"How long have you abused your children?"

"How many times a week do you drink and come home to beat your wife?"

While I was under observation outside, the other police officers were inside with Natalie and my children. I asked what they were doing. They said they were "consoling her." They were asking her more heartfelt questions. But now her story began changing.

The police officers were inspecting Natalie as well, from head to toe. They told her that there were no signs of physical abuse. She now changed her story, "Did I say physical abuse?

I meant mental abuse." So the police started asking more detailed questions. After a back and forth questioning, they explained that they could not determine if there were any signs of mental abuse. From there Natalie changed her story again. "I'm sorry, I misspoke- its verbal abuse." The police informed her mental and verbal abuses are the same thing. Now she changed the story again, now it was "nonverbal abuse." I have no idea what that is, neither did the police.

From there, she changed her story one last time; she stated "I was creating a hostile environment." This was the magical word which the police used to eject me from the home.

The junior police officer took me to the side and explained the law. He stated that if they have to come back, even for a hangnail, I will be arrested for domestic violence. I asked him about her continually changing story, and unfortunately they cannot do anything about the false claims.

The head officer called me into the room with Natalie. He explained how awful of a person I am and belittled me in front of the children. Natalie was crying at that point and explained that she needs to take care of three little children and my abuse will not stop. Once again, she stated that I physically abused her, which the police saw was a false allegation. The head officer told me that due to Natalie having to watch the children and her feelings, I must leave the home immediately. I asked about my personal items, he stated that I could pick them up at any time.

The moment the police left, Natalie cries stop like a faucet turned off, and she began laughing and said, "There's the door."

I began packing some small items in the bathroom and kitchen. Natalie was watching me like a hawk. Each item I was packing: toothbrush, paste, etc. she yelled at me what I can take and what I couldn't.

At this point, my friend Harry arrived; he asked if he could assist me with packing some bags of clothes. So, while I was packing small items from the kitchen; Harry went into the bedroom, and began packing my clothes (or so I thought). Harry, who is extremely intelligent, knew where my important documents were: taxes, children's birth certificates, social security cards, Eric's early intervention reports, & items which I would need for the now impending divorce. He packed them all underneath my clothes. He showed them to me once we got to the car. Natalie did not realize those documents left the home, nor did I even think about taking them. I don't know what I would have done without Harry. To this day, Natalie does not know or request any of the children's documents which I was able to get that day.

At my request, Natalie wrote a signed letter stating that she ejected me from the home because of my hostile environment creation. This would be eventually useless, as the Judges decided not to introduce the letter as evidence, but rather stated I left voluntarily as Natalie's attorney stated.

Once the car was packed and Natalie was done screaming at me, she told me that despite what the police said, I am not allowed any other personal items (to include more clothing and my computer). She also said in a nice firm voice, "Take your children with you too." I took my son, Aaron with me as I went to the hotel. It was now 7:30PM.

During my time outside with the police and loading my clothes and Aaron into the car, I could see a vehicle driving around the block. It was the same vehicle with a gentleman inside who looked familiar and he kept driving around the block, for now it had to be an hour. I finally realized what was happening. I'm out of the house- the boyfriend is now in. How wonderful this is.

I thought this was funny that she openly lied to authorities, both of my abuse, and that she has to watch the children, and defies them with barring me from my personal items and there is nothing I could do.

My cat, Tucker died this day as well. Natalie just informed me of this. I cannot believe she did what she did on that day knowing this information. She knew how much he meant to me. For the past year, her mother has been watching him, especially with the baby around. I had him since he was a little kitten. Almost 11 years. We were through a lot together: several apartments, lots of cuddling, and purring. I don't even have time to grieve.

Saturday 4/18/2015: I was with my oldest son, Aaron till around 1:00PM. We woke up in the hotel room and had a quick breakfast. We went to fencing together where he fenced with his friends and grandfather. Afterwards, we went back to his mother's apartment and picked up his brothers. I now had all three children with me for the weekend. Now, I was homeless, no food, nothing and had the children with me.

I went to the bank to take out some cash for some small expenses for them. MY ACCOUNTS ARE EMPTY! Natalie emptied the savings, checking, and even the children's custodial accounts which had birthday and baptism money in it. Why? Why? I had to use my credit cards.

Natalie demanded that I take the kids back to her home, as she spoke to her attorney and if I do not, they will charge me with kidnapping. I complied with her demands and dropped them off at 7:00PM.

I went to visit my friend Harry. He was calling me a lot to check up on me. He told me that since I was evicted, there needs to be a police report. So the next day, Harry and I went to the police station to get a police report. At the front desk which is extremely high with a small little window, the clerk could not find one. He did see the officer in charge and decided to get him. He told me since they did not arrest me, there is no police report. I demanded one because of the false allegations, their threats to remove me, and their actions to evict me. He said that "he will not write up a police report- end of story."

Sunday 4/19/2015: In the morning, after Harry and I had to deal with the local police station and their refusal to write a police report; we both knew how nasty this is quickly becoming.

Harry, who at this point was the most rational and clear-headed, had a long term thought process at work. He told me that we need to move out my tool boxes, as I need them for my profession and they can easily disappear under Natalie's watch.

I had two tool boxes full of specialized aircraft tools. As an aircraft mechanic, these are required for me to have. Moving these boxes was a whole day affair. But luckily, Harry was with me the whole day. We search all day to find a U-Haul. On a weekend and short notice, they tend to be hard to find or available. We finally found one and we drove it over to the apartment. My father also stopped by to assist with the tool box removal and other items.

In addition to the tool boxes, I had fencing equipment and archery bows & arrows which had to be removed. During the past few days, close friends and coworkers were explaining to me how bad this divorce can go. They knew I was an avid fencer (swords) and archer. I had both archery and fencing equipment in the garage. These both are considered weapons in the town. If Natalie contacted police stating I had weapons along with her false allegations of domestic violence, I would be screwed. So while Harry and I were taking my tool boxes out of the garage, my father came by to assist with moving out my archery and fencing equipment to bring them to his girlfriend's house.

As we started to move the boxes out, Natalie began screaming outside the windows. She was yelling out obscenities and saying that all my tools are hers. She continued saying that she owns all of my personal items and that she must get them appraised. She called her lawyer and they began threatening me. Harry stood tall and told me to do the same. Harry told Natalie that he gave me some of his tools to borrow and he did not want his tools to be included or mixed up in a nasty divorce.

Natalie came downstairs with a receipt of the tools explaining that I took "HER Tools" and they are appraised by her at $100,000.

Monday 4/20/2015: When I picked up the children to see them after work, I attempted to discuss having the children more, and perhaps even the majority of the custody. Natalie did not like this one bit. She began having a temper tantrum about wanting the child support (not mentioning the children- just the support). I reeled back and discussed a visitation schedule with her. She said Mondays, Thursdays, and every other weekend is acceptable.

End of April 2015--Through Mid-June 2015:
I have been sleeping over at my father's girlfriend's house every night. I cannot thank her enough for everything she has done. Not only does she have to deal with him, but deal with me too! My normal routine has been sleeping there, going to work early, working on divorce paperwork or hanging out with the children, spending hours in the car googling stuff and being severely upset and depressed, going back over to my father's girlfriends and sleeping.

When I have the boys, I cannot really have the children over. Her house is like a museum with expensive art work, glass, and breakables. It's not a good house for three little boys. I have a small bag of clothes and phone charger over there so I don't take up too much room. I have all my personal clothing, files, and bathroom sundries at work at my desk. I take showers at the gym and spend my days at the office, even after hours to keep up with the legal bombardment.

I live out of a bag, I have been forgetting to eat, and I am slowly loosing myself in depression. When I am out with the kids, the boys ask why they can't go to "daddy's house" especially on rainy days. The mall does get a bit old. But, how do you tell a toddler that daddy is homeless?

I still can't afford my own place yet, so overnight visits are very difficult and not having a kitchen to cook in even more difficult. I have to go out to eat with the boys and keep receipts because of Natalie's claims that I do not feed them. I have to save the receipts to give to her and keep in case she brings me to court. I called attorneys and apparently, food shop receipts at a grocery store are not considered for feeding children. It does not prove I fed them at a certain time and place. This is sad.

Natalie began going through my accounts on the computer. She logged into Skype, Facebook, and other websites to keep track of me and use whatever information (good or bad) against me in court. I am not able to get my computer, thus I was forced to hack remotely into my machine and infect it with as many computer viruses I could, effectively shutting it down. I also had to start changing my passwords, as she knew all of them. Each day was a battle as she would access an account which I would forget to change the password. Thing about it, how many passwords do you have?

Tuesday 4/21/2015: Since I began receiving threats from Natalie and her attorney, I really needed to protect myself. I now had to retain an attorney. At work, I google searched divorce attorneys in NJ and received over a thousand. How do I know who is good and who is bad? A good friend and coworker I know recently went through his second divorce. He explained that his attorney was amazing and really good. His lawyer also offers a discount through our employer. So I called him up, met with him, and retained him all in one day. Unfortunately, I am under so much pressure right now.

I told my attorney about my ex-wife working at the courthouse and if we should do a change of venue. He stated that we could move the case to another system, but it would make it longer, costs would double, and we more than likely get the same result.

I went back to work and spoke to other coworkers. After Natalie emptied the bank accounts and since I was still homeless, living at my father's girlfriend's house temporarily; we discussed my situation and they told me to open a new bank account and start my direct deposit there. Begin separating myself. So I did. I could not get an account from the bank which holds my old marital joint account. I called that bank and they explained to me that if I open a new account, they will automatically place her on that account. Peachy!

The old joint account was now empty, thanks to Natalie, so I went down to another bank close to work and opened up a new checking and savings account. I went back to work again and filled out the dozens of paperwork to get my direct deposit changed. I was at work till late, but who cares, where do I have to be?

It took a while for it to merge over; of course I had one more check go into my old "marital" account which was emptied out again by Natalie the moment it hit. I asked her If I could use some of the monies for myself to live on, the response I got "I hope you enjoy being homeless."

Wednesday 4/22/2015: I did some research on the subjects of divorce, child support, alimony, etc. Almost every single case I found indicates that Brendon County Judges are not looking at guy's (yes, men only) pay checks and setting child support and alimony which exceed their salaries…oh boy, what am I in for?

Today my lawyer gave me a HUGE list of documents I needed to complete and compile: over 50 pages of writing and hours upon hours of collecting bills, statements, benefits, insurance, etc. He will not move forward with my case unless he has all of this and needs it immediately. So in between work items and after work, I did my "divorce homework & assignments."

Thursday 4/23/2015: My lawyer is extremely expensive ($600 per hour) and I needed money. I began looking up options. Coworkers informed me of taking loan out against my TSP 401(k). I did the research on it, and it looks good. You take a loan against your own 401(k) and repay yourself back. But only one stipulation, and it even states in the instructions, I require my spouse's signature and approval, in black lettering it stated that even if I am separated, I must still have the spousal signature. Just wonderful! My divorced coworker told me she will not sign it.

After work, I picked up the children at 4:00PM. I asked Natalie about the 401(k) loan. She contacted her lawyer right there and said she would get back to me.

The children and I did our normal outdoor activities and had lunch at Subway. I still can't afford my own place yet, so not having a kitchen to cook in is a bit difficult. I dropped off the children at 8:45PM. Natalie requested to see the receipts to prove that I fed the children.

Natalie brought up her ideas about splitting "her" bank account once I deposit all of "her" baptism checks. I'm not too sure what she is planning here. Why would she bring this up especially around 9:00PM? She also explained that she does not want me to have visitation rights as she wants the full amount of child support and she "knows" that I did the "calculations."

She also gave me an answer to the 401(k) TSP loan. She refused to sign it along with the words "enjoy being homeless and good luck finding an attorney!" I guess her attorney informed her that she shouldn't sign it and they know I do not have enough funds to pay for an attorney. Just lovely!

Friday 4/24/2015: During work, once again, Natalie bombarded me again with legal nonsense, so I informed my attorney. I asked him frankly why this is going so fast and it is so much. Apparently this divorce was preplanned and Natalie along with her attorney had everything printed, signed, and ready to go.

Today was also Eric's big day; his birthday party. The party was scheduled for a 7:00PM start time at a local indoor bounce house. Natalie and the children showed at 7:15PM in her late fashion. I put my anger of what she did to me in the morning aside for the children's sake, and I assisted with bringing the children into the bounce house.

I took care of all three kids. The party was filled with all of Natalie's friends. While she was having her social hour, I took care of the baby and kept an eye on the two others. After the party, I followed Natalie and the children home to assist with his gifts, food, and putting the children to bed. Eric did not leave my side. He said he "misses daddy." I eventually left at 10:00PM.

Saturday 4/25/2015: Came to Natalie's apartment at 9:00AM. I left at 11:30AM. I watched Eric open his birthday gifts. Natalie stated to come later on that day for cake. I called her at 2:00PM, as she requested and she became severely aggressive. So, I did not come over due to the elevation of Natalie's temper.

Sunday 4/26/2015: Today was a big day for the little man (baby). Today was his baptism. He was baptized at the local Catholic Church down the road from Natalie's apartment. I got ready at my father's girlfriends and picked up children at 8:30AM. We all went over to the baptism and acted like nothing happened. We left at 3:30PM. I had some of my mother's old stuff in the apartment in a tote. My family wanted it out so it does not become an issue down the road. We went back to the apartment. Natalie did not allow family into the apartment. Only I was allowed in. Going inside, the apartment was worse than usual. I couldn't even walk. There was junk all over the place. I got the tote and gave it to my family. They were not pleased that Natalie did not allow them in.

Monday 4/27/2015: I picked up the children at 3:45PM and went to the mall and parks. I tried dropping them off at 8:30PM, but Natalie was not home. We waited and waited for her. The boys were restless and tired. She eventually arrived at 9:15PM (45 min. late). Natalie stated that she does not want me to have visitation during the week and needs additional monies. Then she changed her mind stating that I must drop off/pick up children at her house each time because "she has a life to live." I inquired why I have to provide her curb side service. She said it was too much for her. I guess that means too much to get off the couch?

Tuesday 4/28/2015: At work, I received my first paycheck since Natalie emptied the bank accounts; I needed to use it for food, expenses, and start saving for an apartment.

Natalie knew when I got paid, and so sooner than I did, she called and wanted the WHOLE thing as "child support." I asked my attorney if she could do that. He informed me to pay her what I can. I asked if $500 a week is enough, he explained that ½ of that would do. So I made it $250. Apparently in New Jersey, Child Support is fought over. It is not a set number. I always thought that the number is generated by the State, but nope, here it can be modified, changed, or anything by court battles.

Also on the phone call, Natalie informed me that she filed for divorce and I will be served. She also admitted to accessing my USAA account being unauthorized by me, since I received an email saying that it was being accessed by an unauthorized computer.

Before she hung up, I asked her I could use the Sienna minivan since I am financing it. She refused then hung up.

My attorney emailed me a list of documents they will need for the "CIS process." CIS stands for Case Information Statement. It is about 10 pages of financial information you need to fill out. How much are you paid, taxes, deductions, earnings by week, month, year, expenses, food, gas, tobacco, etc.? Names and addresses of all employers, insurance companies you use, and then you have to attach W-2's, pay stubs, taxes, affidavits of insurances, etc. It took me weeks to complete it all. Every day, before, during, and after work, I had to compile all this information, fill out, and file dozens of forms. Afterwards, I printed them and provided a CD to my attorney. I weighed all the documents: 35lbs of paper. Nuts! Who has time for this?

Wednesday 4/29/2015: I noticed that Natalie began making exorbitant expensive purchases on the credit cards. I asked her about it and she blamed them on me. She explained that I cannot prove that she made the purchases. Thus, I began calling the credit card companies and removing myself as an authorized user. In retrospect, this did not even matter since I have to pay all of her debts anyway.

Thursday 4/30/2015: I picked up children after work. We went to various parks and had dinner at the mall. I came back to Natalie's apartment at the designated time of 8:30PM to drop off the children. She wasn't there. The children were bored and were getting antsy to go inside for bed. She didn't show until 45 minutes later. The children were WAY past their bedtimes. I provided the receipts to her to show that I fed the children and accepted that her lateness was apparently my fault.

Friday 5/1/2015: My father's girlfriend was served with the divorce complaint from Natalie. It was dated on April 29 and was filed due to my years of abusing her and the children. It contained about twenty pages of false allegations of that abuse and demanded large sums of money. It was written by Natalie and her new attorney.

Natalie apparently retained a lawyer named, Mr. Harold Keville. I know this attorney as my mother used him years ago when she was being sued. Unfortunately, she died halfway through the case. My family attempted to get her expensive retainer back from him, but from my understanding, Mr. Keville considered it a "gift" and refused to hand it back over. He is renowned to be a shark in court utilizing his personal relationships, lying to authorities, playing the court games, and unethical behavior.

This was the lawyer whom Natalie always boasted about as he represented her mother and was a "very good, unethical, vindictive lawyer" who has the longest divorce cases in New Jersey history.

Saturday 5/2/2015: I picked up the two older children: Aaron & Eric at 9:00AM. We went to the fencing class and met up with Victoria and her son. The three of them ran around and played for hours. I dropped the kids off at 6:00PM. Natalie began questioning what apartment research I have done. She began telling me where I had to live. If I did not pick a town she approved, she would keep the children from me. When I got back to my father's girlfriends, I received a forwarded email from my aunt. Natalie contacted her about the divorce. I called Natalie and requested she stop contacting my family.

Monday 5/4/2015: Like normal, I picked up the children after work. Eric was extremely sick. I asked Natalie if she took him to the doctor's. Of course, she didn't. As it was too much for her to do, I decided to take Eric to the pediatrician. The doctor checked him and was released. Afterwards, the boys wanted to have a picnic in one of the local parks. So we went to the store, picked up some food and picnic items and had our picnic. The kids loved it. After the picnic, parks, playing outside, and some dinner, I dropped them back off at 7:45PM at their mothers' request.

Thursday 5/7/2015: After work, I got to Natalie's apartment within minutes. I gave Natalie the weekly check of $250 for child support. I took the children to various parks around the area. The baby really enjoys the swings and being a little ham. It started to get rainy. I still don't have a place to live to take the children, so we decided to go to the mall and walk around. I dropped off the children back to Natalie at 8:30PM. The moment I dropped them off, I received a forwarded email from my aunt. While the children and I were out, Natalie contacted her AGAIN about the divorce and how I am avoiding the children (even though I was with them at that moment). I called Natalie to request she stop contacting my family.

Saturday 5/9/2015: In the morning, my good friend from fencing, Victoria texted me around 9:00AM. Her and her son wanted to go out to the movies and asked if they could take Aaron and Eric with them as well. I called Natalie to see if the boys wanted to go. She said no, she did not want the burden of getting them ready to go to the movies today. I told her I would take them, but the answer was still the same.

Monday 5/11/2015: I provided Natalie with the $250 Child Support Payment and picked up the children at 3:45PM. Since I am still homeless, we decided to go to the parks and eat at the mall. I dropped the kids off at 8:30PM. Despite what Natalie said when she had me evicted with not allowing me to have my personal items, I begged Natalie for some personal items. So during the drop off Natalie and I discussed the distribution of my personal affects. We agreed on a distribution of personal items and furniture. Natalie offered the "marital" bed in her room as she did not want it anymore.

Wednesday 5/13/2015: I received an email containing a letter from Mr. Keville.

As you are aware, I represent your spouse, Natalie Arlotta, in connection with the above referenced matter. An urgent situation has arisen which must be resolved without delay in order to avoid a request for immediate Court intervention.

More specifically, I am advised that my client and the subject children are without sufficient funds with which to meet their ongoing economic needs. I am advised that, despite the fact that you are currently the only income-earner in the home, even though you appear to earn in the area of $100,000.00 or more annually, and even though my client and the children are completely dependent upon you for their financial survival, you have to date only provided a total of $500.00 towards support over the course of the last month.

I am further advised that you have taken the position that you do not intend to do more in terms of financial support until you "hear from (Natalie's) lawyer".

Finally, I am advised that you have been pressuring my client, e.g., to take over her own cell phone expenses, to sign papers to enable you to withdraw funds from your deferred compensation, and to accept that you have changed the location where your pay check is deposited. All of these things are a departure from your marital status quo, and all of these things will lead to unnecessary litigation if this situation cannot be resolved without delay.

We must have an immediate agreement that my client will receive adequate funds from you, effective immediately and on an ongoing basis, to enable her to meet her needs and the needs of your children for food, clothing, shelter, and other necessaries. The May rent on the marital residence has not been paid, and needs to be paid. We must be sure that the other roof expenses and the families other needs will be met. There can be no other efforts to alter the status quo, whether by unilateral changes in account status, (such as with the cell phones), by removal of money from accounts, or by any other means.

All of these issues are capable of resolution, but all of these issues, if not immediately resolved, will lead to an immediate request for Court intervention without further notice to you. If this becomes necessary, we will ask the Court to compel you to pay the legal fees and costs incurred by your wife in having to bring an application which should not have been necessary.

I urge you to make immediate arrangements to provide funds to my client sufficient to address this situation. The best way to deal with the immediate situation is two-fold: First, you should make sure that the May rent and utilities are paid, and you should immediately provide my client with the sum of $5,000.00 towards the family's immediate needs. This amount would be credited towards whatever your support obligation is ultimately determined to be. Second, you should fax or e-mail to me your 2014 form W-2 and your three (3) most recent pay stubs without delay so that I can calculate reasonable temporary alimony and child support.

I cannot stress enough that this situation cannot remain unresolved any longer. I am compelled to take action, one way or the other, to bring about a resolution to this situation for my client and for the subject children.

So, not only do I not have $5000, but he determines my alimony and child support? Rent is due? She lives in her father's apartment complex? $1,000 a month along with the thousands she emptied out of the bank accounts is not enough? I am homeless without a thing, waiting to get paid. I also have cashed checks for more than $500 he says I have paid. He is blatantly lying about that.

So with all this, I had to forward this letter and questions I had to my attorney. I explained to him that since my wife and I separated on 4/16/2015 and later thrown out of my apartment on 4/17/2015 (when police were called), I have only received two pay checks. Each check I provided her child support. I explained that I have noticed more checks being deposited into her account including a check from her father (also her landlord) and mother. I told him that I needed to start saving for an apartment.

I also inquired how rent is due to her father, but her father is giving her thousands of dollars (like this deposit)?

Thursday 5/14/2015: I picked up children at 3:45PM. We went to more parks and played outside. I eventually dropped them off at 8:00PM. Natalie was not there. We waited outside for her to eventually show up at 8:30PM. She blamed her lateness on me. She called afterwards to accuse me of not feeding children. I am now forced to take the children out to eat and save the receipts to provide proof that they have been fed. If I do not do this, she will bring it to court and have me arrested.

Saturday 5/16/2015: Picked up children at 10:00AM. Before the pickup, Natalie asked if I received email from her lawyer. I explained that if I get any email from a lawyer, I will forward to mine. She became aggressive and stated she will not allow me to visit the children if the money is not there. Shortly thereafter, she contacted me back stating I can visit the children. She explained for me benefit, I could use my car (excuse me, her car) since it has more room for the kids. I fell for it. She drove away with the car and when I started the minivan, the fuel light was on. She wanted me to fill it. Nice!

I brought the children to various parks, the mall, and we went to a family party at my aunt's house (father's side). I dropped the kids off at 8:00PM. During the drop off; Natalie's stepfather and mother were there and they started to harass me saying that I did not feed children.

They said to the children "poor boys, your father didn't feed you again?" Then proceeded to inform both Aaron & Eric that their father is a liar and bum. I could not say a thing, if I did, I would be in prison.

Sunday 5/17/2015: I picked up the children at their apartment at 10:00AM. We did our normal outdoor activities going on hikes, runs, and visiting various outdoor parks. We had lunch at the local mall. It was a fun day. We went back to their residence at the agreed time of 4:15PM.

While dropping the children off, I received a text message from Natalie to push back drop off time at 4:30PM. I am getting tired of Natalie constantly being late, but 15 minutes is fine. The children and I waited in front of their house. We waited and waited. 15 minutes went by, and still no Natalie. She finally showed up 45 minutes late at 5:15PM.

I told her that the children were restless and bored waiting in front of her apartment. I also informed her that her telling me that she will be late last minute every time is not appropriate especially since I am not allowed to enter the property. It was hot and muggy outside and it is unfair for the children to wait for that long. Her excuse, "it's your fault- you are a terrible father. That's why I am late." I'm still trying to process that response.

Monday 5/18/2015: I picked up children after work at 3:45PM. When I arrived outside the apartment, the children were already outside without any supervision. Apparently the thought process of when I leave work I do not have a commute time is still in effect. It was raining out, so the children and I went over to the local malls for some indoor activities. When it came time to drop the children off, Natalie in her normal fashion was a half an hour late (8:00PM scheduled time). She showed up to bring the children inside at 8:30PM. At least the kids were sleeping in the car while we waited for her to show.

Thursday 5/21/2015: Almost a carbon copy day from Monday. I picked up children after work, when I arrived; they were outside in the rain. Though, they were sitting on the apartment steps which had an overhang though, so they didn't get wet.

We went to the local malls for indoor fun. I went to drop them off at 8:30PM. Natalie was not home at the time of the drop off. But eventually her mother showed up to take the kids. These late nights waiting for Natalie are really interfering with the kids' bedtimes.

Monday 5/25/2015: Today is Memorial Day. I had off from work. I am still staying at my father's girlfriend's house. She has been extremely supportive. After taking a shower, I headed over to Natalie's to pick up the children at 9:30AM.

Today was a fun filled day. We went to three new parks around the area and our town had a Street fair with carnival. We went on all the rides, watched the vendors, entertainers, and clowns do their thing, and had a carnival style lunch.

Afterwards, we had plans to meet my father at the Palisades Mall (which is quite large by the way). We had more fun there going to various kids' amusement centers, gaming stores, etc.

During all this fun and excitement, Natalie called requesting that children be dropped off at 6:00PM. I arrived at her house at the designated time and in typical fashion: No Natalie. I called, texted, and emailed her with no response. Eventually she showed up half an hour late.

Wednesday 5/27/2015: I contacted Natalie requesting to retrieve some personal items from the garage. She informed me that all my personal belongings are hers since I did not take them before being kicked out by her and other items need to be appraised. She informed me that I cannot access those items or enter the premises without her permission.

Thursday 5/28/2015: Emailed and spoke to Natalie about removing personal items/furniture from marital residence which we agreed on 5/11/2015. Informed her that move would be on 5/30/2015. She agreed verbally and asked if I wanted any children furniture as well. She offered the children's dresser. I have since learned how binding a verbal agreement is…slim to none.

I requested to pick up my mother's copper collection on Friday 5/29/2015. She agreed. For visitation, I picked up the children at 4:00PM and dropped them off at 8:30PM with her mother since Natalie was not home.

When I got back to my father's girlfriend's house, I received the following email from my attorney:

Please be advised that Robert Morten has retained this law office with regards to the above referenced matter. Please direct all correspondence pertaining to the above matter to our office directly.

Additionally, we are in receipt of your May 13, 2015 letter and have had the opportunity to review same with our client. The parties do not have the financial resources to maintain separate households, yet your client evicted Mr. Arlotta from their home. She cannot kick him out because she feels some tension and then expect him to continue to pay all of the household expenses in addition to the costs incurred as a result of having to maintain his own separate household.

Moreover, your client is demanding that Mr. Arlotta provide her with $1,150.00 per month in rent. This is concerning because the parties' rent is only $400.00 per month. The apartment is located in a building owned by your client's parents and, therefore, the parties have always enjoyed a steep discount in their rent. To demand that Mr. Arlotta pay nearly three times the rent he was paying after your client had him evicted is absurd.

Mr. Arlotta has been providing support to your client in the amount of $250.00 per week. This is all he can afford to pay at this time.

Friday 5/29/2015: Per the agreement Natalie and I made on 5/28/2015, I went to the marital residence to pick up my mother's copper collection (including her urn). Natalie inquired if I paid for the moving truck and made arrangements. After I verified that those items were completed, she stated "good, because I'm cancelling it" and began laughing. She denied me my items.

She sent me an email saying that the move is off as well. She denied me access to the copper collection and my mother's urn so she could determine their asset value. Really? My mother's ashes require an "asset value." Then to make matter's worse, within minutes, Natalie's lawyer emailed me explaining I have no rights to my personal belongings or my own mother's Urn.

Through email, Natalie forwarded me another letter from her attorney. I am not allowed to remove anything from the house. I am not allowed access to my clothing, personal items, or mother's urn. I am not permitted to enter the marital residence.

According to the letter, when I "moved out" I gave up all rights to my personal items and that there are legal consequences if I attempt to disregard Mr. Keville's letter and get my mother, clothes, or personal items. Unfortunately, I have to give up my rights to this stuff.

- What possible use do they have with my deceased mother's urn or my clothing?
- In addition, this is completely against what the police officers told me when they removed me.
- Another question, how did her lawyer write these letters so quickly?

This is unbelievable; they had to have these already made. No one writes several pages within minutes.

Saturday 5/30/2015: I picked up the children at 9:00AM, we ran around some hiking trails, went to various parks, and had lunch and dinner at the mall. I still can't afford my own place yet, so overnight visits are very difficult and not having a kitchen to cook in even more difficult. I attempted to drop the kids off at the scheduled time of 8:00PM. Natalie was ½ late as usual. She also requested receipts to prove that I fed the boys.

Sunday 5/31/2015: Same as yesterday. I picked up the children at 9:00AM, we ran around some hiking trails, went to various parks, and had lunch and dinner at the mall. I still can't afford my own place yet, so overnight visits are very difficult and not having a kitchen to cook in even more difficult. I attempted to drop the kids off at the scheduled time of 8:00PM. Natalie was ½ late as usual. She also requested receipts to prove that I fed the boys.

Monday 6/1/2015---Friday 6/12/2015: I drove down to Washington D.C. on work related training. This training is for a selected few. It is called Program for Emerging Leaders. Out of the entire agency, 50 individuals were selected out of thousands. We are to train for the next level of leaders within the agency. This was the kickoff week. The program will last almost a year. I met great friends here. These people whom I just met were amazing! Awesome people who were very supportive and allowed me to vent these two weeks!

I previously informed Natalie a month in advance of this trip to Washington to inform her that I cannot pick up the boys during those weeks. Not only did she demand that I provide her my "per diem" travel allotments as she is entitled to them, but she decided to plot with her attorney to use this trip and bombard me with an onslaught of legal letters, interrogatories, and harassment.

They had full knowledge that I was away, without a computer and could not possibly answer them while I was away. I had to scrounge around for a computer and use every resource I knew of to answer these demands. My attorney also gave me some extra time when I get back home to complete it all.

During my trip, I received hundreds of pages of documents, threatening letters, and a list of personal items:

Thursday 6/4/2015: I received close to 300 pages of questions with hundreds of documents and questions I had to provide. They are called interrogatories or discovery. Of which almost half of the questions required me to answer at length (couple of pages each) and provide proof that I am a good parent to my children.

Wednesday 6/10/2015: I received a letter from Mr. Keville. Apparently Natalie and he need an exact list and proof of ownership for each personal item I wish to take out of "Natalie's home." They will determine what I personal items I should receive.

Monday 6/15/2015: I picked up the children at 5:30PM (Late due to work schedule change) and dropped off at 8:00PM. Natalie did not show till 8:30PM. It was great to see them again. I missed them so much.

Thursday 6/18/2015: I picked up the children at 5:30PM (Late due to work schedule change) and dropped off at 8:00PM. Natalie did not show till 8:30PM.

Saturday 6/20/2015: I picked up children at 10:00AM. We went to some parks and went to the Lego Experience amusement park in New York. I dropped them off at 8:00PM. We waited outside for Natalie to show. ½ hour later, at 8:30PM her mother came around and said she wasn't going to be there for the pickup. I dropped the kids off with her.

Sunday 6/21/2015: Today is Father's day. Initially, Natalie fought me on letting me have the children today. Probably just because it is Father's day! I picked up children at 10:00AM and did our normal parks. I met up with my father and his girlfriend at the Palisades mall where we all ate at a restaurant. They paid for my meal, but I asked them if I could save the receipt to give it to Natalie to prove the children were fed. I dropped off the children and the receipt at 7:30PM.

Monday 6/22/2015: First court case. At 8:30AM, I attended the Case Management Conference. This was the first time I got to meet Judge Cynthia Myers. I waited outside of her chambers for about two hours until she was able to call the case in open court. Natalie and her attorney, Mr. Harold Keville showed shortly beforehand and he was allowed a private audience with the Judge to discuss the case.

During the open court case, Judge Cynthia Myers explained the divorce was due to my "undocumented abuse" I guess I am an abuser without any proof or history. Natalie and her attorney explained how I abused both her and the children and these allegations had me removed from the residence by the police. I could swear that the police did not see any evidence of abuse or have a police report. The Judge agreed with them without any of any evidence.

The Judge asked if there were any open arguments that needed attention. Mr. Keville, my ex-wife's attorney explained how I have not been supporting her or paid him (wait, I have to pay him? What about the child support checks, what about her emptying out the bank accounts?). The Judge explained that they will host a number of court cases to grant them payments.

My attorney stated that I have been barred from the residence by Natalie and her attorney and I need my clothes, my mother's urn, and personal items. The judge asked if I can provide receipts for these items. Guess I can't get my mother's urn as I do not have a receipt for it. So the court left it at anything I can prove is mine has to be requested to Natalie and her attorney and I can get it if they allow it. So pretty much, all my clothes, my mother's urn, and my personal items are all Natalie's.

I asked about the kitchen Hutch which my family wanted back as it was an heirloom. The Judge awarded it to Natalie, because she said it would "disrupt the family home." My family was not pleased by this.

After court, I had visitation with the children. Because of these allegations of abuse and due to statements made by her stating I threaten her and abuse children in private areas, I requested Natalie to meet in public area to drop/pick up children. Natalie began yelling and screaming stating it is unfair for her to meet in a centralized public location and that I must arrive at marital residence if I want to see the children. She does not want to leave the couch. Natalie dropped children off at my place of work at 4:30PM. The boys and I visited multiple parks. Natalie agreed to a 7:30PM pick up time. She showed up at 8:30PM, over an hour late.

When I got to my father's girlfriend's house, a package and email were waiting for me. It was another threatening letter from Mr. Keville and another motion with Natalie and him suing me for additional monies and false claims. This one is 38 pages of demands and statements of me abusing Natalie, the children, and apparently they need an additional $7,500 for expenses, and Keville needs $5,000 a month.

How did they have time for this while we were in court all day? My boss, attorney, and friends all explained this was all preplanned, premeditated and they were ready for months before filing all this.

Tuesday 6/24/2015: Today is my mother's 15 year death anniversary. I signed a lease on a new apartment today. It is nothing special, just a tiny one bedroom. I do not have many personal belongings or any furniture, so it is completely barren. Over the next few weeks, I would be making daily trips to Walmart and receive donated household items from all my friends and family. The children were able to help me pick out items at Walmart (sippy cups, plates, utensils, placemats, etc.). These along with new bathroom items, sundries, curtains, rods, bed sheets, and furniture; everything we needed to set up our new apartment together!

Thursday 6/25/2015: Because of these allegations of abuse and due to statements made by her stating I threaten her and abuse children in private areas, I requested Natalie to meet in public area to drop/pick up the children. I texted Natalie at 3:20PM about dropping off the children at the Holiday Inn by her apartment for a public/centered meeting area. Natalie called and began threating about suing me about an Air Conditioner and my personal items I left with in April.

Natalie showed up at my place of work (not Holiday Inn) to drop off children at 4:30PM. She became irate in the parking lot and went into a non-medicated frenzy. She began threatening me about child custody and my ability to see the children. A coworker outside smoking saw what was happening. He helped put the children in the car and started to talk with them to keep them unaware of Natalie's ranting and raving about more money.

We went to multiple parks and ate. Today was the first time the boys came over to the new apartment. It is fairly empty, but the boys already started their planning for this tiny little one bedroom apartment. Aaron and Eric want the bedroom and I can sleep in the living room. They are planning their "sleep overs" to include movie nights

We arrived at the Holiday Inn at 8:00PM (as agreed with Natalie). Natalie arrived at 8:15PM (late). I provided her with a child support check.

Friday 6/26/2015: I received a phone call and email from Natalie at 5:00PM informing me that I am authorized for entry tomorrow, 6/27/2015 at 10:00AM to gather personal belongings. This was sent in bad faith as all moving companies and my attorney's office were closed for that time.

This was extremely late notice. I love the fact that the courts and these attorney's allow for this short notice for me to pick up my personal items.

I received a letter dated today from Mr. Keville. Apparently I stole an air conditioner in the future (on the 27th) and must return it. Wow, I must be good stealing items in future periods of time.

Saturday 6/27/2015: I have to tell you, finding a moving van and help with only a few hours' notice is just PEACHY. My best friend and I went to a dozen moving van rental companies and they were all booked.

We finally found one which had a tiny little truck and charged us as it was their largest (because we didn't give a week's notice). We split up and I drove his car, he drove the van. We went straight to the police station to get an escort.

We arrived at the marital home at 10:15AM with a police escort. The police stayed until 1:00PM. I had a few friends (that could make it in such short notice) come to help.

Natalie released the escort and assisted with the collection and packing of my personal items. Natalie requested that air conditioner in downstairs storage room be left as is. I did not remove it from the household (this will be important later on). In addition, archery stand left in storage room was left to be picked up at a later day.

Natalie explained that all assets which include the motorcycle are hers per NJ divorce law and I cannot have access to the motorcycle. I cannot retrieve the registration information as it is located on the bike.

My friends from work and fencing helped me move into my new apartment which is about 20 minutes away from the children. The good news is it is a block away from another fencing club. I thanked all my friends and got them each pizzas. It was a long day; everyone was exhausted, hungry, and tired. It is done though. I left lots of items at Natalie's, but it is just stuff. It is replaceable.

Monday 6/29/2015: Both my attorney and I received a letter from Natalie's attorney stating that they are seeking court intervention, as I stole an air conditioner from the marital residence. My attorney responded to them.

After work, I picked up children at 4:00PM and did our normal parks. I dropped off at 8:00PM. I asked Natalie why she and her attorney are lying about that stupid air conditioner. She began laughing and explained that she can do this, she wants me to "enjoy my legal fees" to ensure that I cannot afford an attorney and she will ensure that I am "financially ruined." Her lies "do not have to be proved." As she explained, "who is the court going to believe?"

Entry #3: Divorce Diary (Quarter 3, 2015):

During this quarter, I was constantly changing all of my passwords, locking online accounts, setting preferences to notify me of unauthorized access. You wouldn't believe how many times I was alerted for Natalie attempting to access and change my accounts. Whether Facebook, LinkedIn, bank accounts, insurance, etc. She was attempting to get more information on me to use in court.

Thursday 7/2/2015: Picked up children at 4:00PM and dropped them off at 8:00PM. We did our normal parks and dinner routine.

Saturday 7/4/2015: I took the boys to the Lego Experience amusement park with my fencing friends, their child, and my father. Afterwards, we all ate at a restaurant together. I picked up the children at 10:00AM and dropped them off at 8:00PM. Natalie was late again and showed at 8:20PM.

Sunday 7/5/2015: I picked up the children at 10:00AM. We did bicycle riding and an amusement place called Bounce U. It's an indoor bounce house. Afterwards, the boys came back to my apartment for dinner. I was scheduled to drop off the children at 8:30PM. Unannounced, Natalie came by early to pick up the children at my residence at 7:30PM. She arrived insisted to come inside. She explained that she had to use the bathroom. Apparently, she took notes of what was inside my apartment.

I later received a letter to the court from her attorney stating that I have purchased a new TV and air conditioner (which I did, on credit) and that I have adequate resources to increase my alimony and child support payments. She came into my apartment to take notes and snoop around, not to use the bathroom!

Monday 7/6/2015: I was late picking up the children and showed at 5:00PM. I was late due to Natalie's car having mechanical trouble and had to take it in. We went to a few parks and had dinner. I dropped them off at 8:00PM, well really 8:20PM as Natalie showed late as usual.

Wednesday 7/8/2015: Natalie's car I was operating broke down again and I was at the Enterprise Rental Car. I was going to be late for the visitation pick up; so Natalie decided to come to make sure I was "telling the truth." She arrived at 4:30PM to drop the children off to me. I got my rental car and took the children to various parks and dropped them off at their mother's at 8:30PM.

Friday 7/10/2015: My attorney asked Mr. Keville and the courts about out of network medical bills and insurance reimbursement checks. Natalie is utilizing out of network doctors and having the bills sent to me. In addition, when the insurance does cover an expense, they send me a check to Natalie's address. Natalie deposited the checks and spent them. So without any money, I am still stuck with the bills.

We asked the court about the reimbursement checks so that they can be paid to the medical providers. The court will do nothing. That money is Natalie's. Eventually, I am going to have to forget about them and let them go to collection, I cannot possibly pay them all. My attorney sent this letter to Mr. Keville:

Please be advised that this office represents Defendant, Robert Arlotta. Mr. Arlotta has begun receiving medical bills, which are either out of network or contain services that are clearly not covered by his medical insurance. He has requested that your client stop going to doctors and incurring services not covered within the insurance. He has also requested that she cease utilizing the insurance reimbursement checks for personal purchases.

Unfortunately, like everything else in this case, Mrs. Arlotta continuously plays games and cashes the reimbursement checks without paying the invoices. Please be advised that Mr. Arlotta has changed his address and future checks will not be sent to your client.

Sunday 7/12/2015: I was on my way home in New York and called Natalie to explain to her that her car (the Corolla I was driving) broke down on Tappan Zee Bridge. Aaron explained over the phone that I am not his father and he has another father. When I inquired about this comment to Natalie she began laughing and hung up the phone.

Monday 7/13/2015: I picked up children at 4:45PM. Natalie gave Aaron & Eric ice cream right before the pickup and then took it away from them when I arrived so children became upset when they had to leave with me. Eric was covered with food/dirt on all his clothing.

I took them to my apartment and after games, puzzles, dinner, and a sleeping baby; the children did not want to leave. I requested Natalie pick them up at my residence. Natalie was reluctant to this request and showed at 8:45PM. She refused to allow me to say goodnight/hug Eric when he came up to embrace me.

Wednesday 7/15/2015: Today, at 9:30AM, I attended the first of many "Parenting Time" Visitation Mediations.

I arrived twenty minutes early and was waiting outside. Natalie arrived shortly afterwards and sat down in the same hallways as me. Before the meeting commenced, a woman in a dress-suit walked down the hallway and greeted Natalie warmly. Natalie was talking on a personal level to this woman, who was explaining she is now the Assistant Director for Family Division in the Court House. She explained to Natalie how they will "take care of her." After she departed, Natalie was boasting that she can override the judge.

During the mediation session, I had no rights. The mediator was taking Natalie's side for everything. In addition, the mediator jokingly explained how my wife looked familiar and discussed courthouse jargon during the meeting. The mediator and Natalie worked together and had a personal relationship.

Friday 7/17/2015: I received a reply certification package from Natalie and Mr. Keville. This is for temporary support. In it Natalie claims I am living a life of luxury with my millions of dollars in hotel rooms, the kitchen hutch which I requested the court give back to me as it is a family heirloom which has been in the family for generations was outrageous and rightfully hers, and the marital bed issue. During a previous phone call, Natalie offered the bed to me when I moved into a new apartment (as she did not want it). This was now turned around to reflect negatively on me. It was a trap.

There were 28 pages of nonsense in this document. None of which could be proven. What did the court do with it? They took it as fact verbatim. I could not even defend myself. As far as my issues with her: nothing was requested by the court. I could not even write a letter stating the issues I had and produce evidence.

Tuesday 7/21/2015: My attorney wrote a letter to Mr. Keville asking them to provide me more parenting time with the children. No response was given. It is not a priority to Natalie or her attorney.

Sunday 7/26/2015: I received a forwarded email from my aunt. Natalie contacted her about the divorce. She was explaining how I did not want to see the children and how I was not paying her attorney or support. I once again requested Natalie to stop contacting my family.

Friday 7/31/2015: Natalie began calling and emailing me saying that I had an impromptu court case this week that her attorney set up and I did not show. Apparently, Natalie and her attorney set this up with the Judge and did not inform me or my attorney. It was an "oversight" of the Judge's chambers.

It couldn't have any possibility that the person who is supposed to inform me is a close friend of hers from her court house days. I am finding issues like this a lot. But I guess it is just tons of coincidences.

I informed her that my attorney and I did not have any information about a court case and I was unable to attend anyway as I was attending a close family member's funeral. She began demanding that she get a copy of the death certificate and she (or the court) will not accept any obituaries. Where did this come from?

Monday 8/1/2015—8/9/2015: Natalie decided to go on a cruise and dropped off the children at my apartment for ten days. Before she went, she explained that I'll get the bill for the cruise.

I had to quickly plan some activities with the children since this was so prompt and impromptu. I pulled it off with carnivals, farm & horse shows, parks, outdoor activities, you name it. We all had a blast!

During this time with the children, Natalie and her attorney made a preplanned attack and onslaught of paperwork. I received more interrogatories from her attorney, Mr. Keville.

They preplanned giving me the interrogatories while I had the children, 150 additional questions and items I had to provide. A lot of these questions dealt with the fencing non-profit which I operate. Mr. Keville wants bank account information, salaries, accounts, and everything pertaining to both me and the non-profit. They are planning to take the non-profit's meager accounts and ownership of the fencing club.

Natalie and her attorney wanted all of the bank statements, invoices, and all financial information for the fencing non-profit. I called and asked her why she was going after the fencing club. She thinks it is a multi-million dollar entity, and she is entitled to their profits.

Eventually, I had to leave the non-profit and quickly gave up my access to the bank account to attempt to protect them from the Natalie/Keville onslaught of greed. This was really sad as I was part of this club since I was a child and as you read earlier, the fencing club and I have a long history and I hated leaving my friends behind and "giving up" on the club. But I had to protect them.

I received a bunch of interrogatory questions which were for someone else. They used another person's name, a different case number, and asked questions like why am I opposed to having Natalie relocate the children to Ohio and Virginia? But, I still had to answer these questions.

I had to provide statements and write pages upon pages of writing on how I am a good father and why the court should allow me "some visitation" with the children. The amount of writing I did far exceeded the pages in this book.

So during the day, the children and I played. At night, I had to fill out these interrogatories and questions which did not relate to me or my case, along with having to write short novels on why the children should be allowed to be with me for a weekend or visitation day. Sleeping during this week was not an option. I was exhausted!

These games of sending documents with short notice while I have the children are important to know, as it has happened every time without fail during the divorce. When I have the children for a weekend, it is guaranteed I will get something from Mr. Keville which if not answered within a few days; the court will take action against me.

When Natalie picked up the children, she began demanding more child support and I have to pay for the cruise she just went on, along with repaying her "losses" at the casino on the ship. I ignored her. She began yelling in front of the children that she will be brining me to court for these expenses.

She requested that I give her the receipts and provide proof that the children have been fed. As I already knew that I was forced to take the children out to eat and save the receipts, I had them in hand.

Thursday 8/13/2015: Another court case. This time it is for something called temporary support or pendente lite. I have been providing Natalie $250 a week for child support, but apparently her landlord (her father) increased her rent from zero to $2,000 a month overnight. So Natalie and her attorney are brought me to court to make sure that I pay this increase along with a whole bunch more. Their list of demands is 15 pages long and FAR exceeds my pay.

My attorney and I sat in court for two hours until the Judge arrived late. She came in and my ex-wife and her attorney were allowed a private audience with her before the court case. It was now 11:00AM. We were supposed to start court at 8:00AM.

Walking into the courtroom, I observed a case in front of me. This case was a prelude into what I was about to experience. It was another divorce. The man appeared to be in his late 60s and his wife (sitting on the plaintiff side, who files for the divorce) was in her mid-30s. A blind person could see what was happening here. The man was explaining that he cannot pay the alimony which the court is forcing on him. He is a retired Sheriff Officer and the alimony exceeds his retirement income. His attorney was trying to tell the Judge that the young girl needed to get a job and she can easily work. The Judge explained to him that his ex-wife should not be forced to get a job and it is his responsibility to pay for her lifestyle. She went on to explain to him that since he was a Sheriff's Officer, he can easily go back into the police force along with getting a night job as security to make payments to his ex-wife. The man broke down in tears in the middle of the court room. After that, it was my turn for judgment.

The Judge looked at the case documents and began the session yelling at me. Apparently after years of "undocumented abuse" I forced my ex into this divorce and since my ejection from the marital household, I have not provided a dime in child support. My attorney did provide her all the cashed checks I was giving, but the Judge did not consider them proof of payment. The Judge further went on explaining that since I am an abuser, I am barred from the property. If I step foot unto Natalie's premise I will be arrested. This does not make sense as I must pick up and drop off the children there.

The judge ordered me to pay $350 a week in alimony, plus all Natalie's bills, her rent (to her father), her entertainment costs, all medical expenses, child support, additional child care costs, day care, after care, children's entertainment, all vehicle payments, insurance, etc. It is eight pages of items I have to pay for.

The judge asked only Natalie's attorney, Mr. Keville how much money he is owed for his court appearance. He stated $5,000 for this appearance alone. She told me that I have thirty days to pay him that money. I began getting upset. I stood up and said that I cannot pay all Natalie's increased rent, all her bills, alimony on top, child support, and now try to find $5,000 on top of all that. All these expenses are beyond what I make. I further asked to see an invoice with his numbers.

The Judge explained, they do not need it and I must find the means to pay what they order me to. I asked if anyone even looked at my paycheck or my expenses (also known as a CIS). The Judge actually admitted that she did not look at my information! How can they court order me to pay more than I make?

Judge Cynthia Myers yelled at me to sit down, as I have an attorney and cannot speak on my own behalf. So my attorney stood up to try to defend me. She told him to sit down as "she has nothing to say to him." Absolutely NO DUE PROCESS.

I received a copy of this kangaroo court order. It is typed with marks and handwritten notes throughout it. I cannot even read the Judge's handwriting. It had the lists of demands by my ex-wife's attorney with each line saying "granted" and I had paperwork with my defense and in big letters, the Judge wrote "DENIED."

After my court case, I had to go back to work. I did not have enough vacation time to take an entire day off for these continued court games. Coworkers asked me how it went, I began crying. My boss and his boss called me into their office. I provided them copies of the court orders and the list of items I must pay for.

They read through it all and were dumbfounded. They did not know how I could pay for everything, how I could survive. I told them that I had to vacate my apartment which I just moved into. They asked where I would live, as I was already homeless for the past few months. I did not have an answer.

After work I picked up the children for visitation. During the pick-up and drop off times, Natalie made harassing statements and threats in regards to money. She wants more and told me they are going to bring me back to court again. I ignored the harassment and kept on track. I had to request that she provide usernames/passwords to her accounts, so that I can pay them.

I do not know how I can pay any of this; I can't believe I did not even get a chance to defend myself. I am being treated like a criminal and I did not do anything wrong. I am being punished for my ex-wife wanting to fool around. This makes no sense.

I was shaken up. I began crying at work and home. I am now homeless. I cannot afford food, shelter, anything; not even gas. I fell asleep on the floor. My co-workers say that severe stress can do that. I don't remember a thing when I got home. When I awoke, I saw that I had a dozen missed phone calls from Michaela. She is worried sick about me.

I told the court I cannot afford to pay all of their demands and live myself. I cannot afford an apartment or a roof over my head. As the Judge said; they do not care how it is paid. I must find the means. If I cannot; their answer is simple- work release. If you never heard of this program, it is designed for men (not women) as every piece of information states. Go ahead, look it up. It does not say "individual" or "person," it states "men."

This program was developed for men who are court ordered to pay support obligations and civil lawsuits above and beyond their current salaries.

Brendon County invested thousands of dollars into a new wing in their jail for this program, and this is their answer to fill the cells. I refuse to live there. I would be fired from work if I lived there. The government would never allow me to live there, what impression would it leave with the private industry organizations I have oversight of?

In the next few weeks, I moved clothes and personal hygiene items into the office to live there (unofficially, of course). I was able to use the showers at the gym on the premise, and use a locker in the same room. All this was against the rules of the building, my employer, and the state- but what is the alternative? I refuse to go to work release.

To pay my attorney his $5,000 biweekly bill, I had to open various lines of credit. Over the next few weeks, I opened multiple lines of credit including credit cards to pay for an entire attorney's office to fight the onslaught of lawsuits, motions, and false allegation paperwork. I was paying thousands of dollars in fees each week. The moment I was unable to pay, the attorney would drop my case in an instant. No working with you. He is paid, or nothing. Eventually, all these lines of credit would be exhausted and all credit cards maxed out.

Friday 8/14/2015: I went to work, as I normally do and my phone began ringing a dozen or so times. It was the NJ Child Support-Probation Office. I found out that my alimony case worker is Ms. Jennifer Mason. They began threatening me saying that I am severely delinquent on my child support and alimony obligations. I asked the harassers on the phone how this is possible since I just had court the day before.

Apparently, the Judge placed on the order that I must pay $350 a week since the start of the divorce and since it has been a few months since I was thrown out, now the probation division requires all the back payments immediately, or I will be placed into prison.

It took a few hours, but I was able to set up my online account, found out the details on when and how to make payments along with sending my first payment to them.

I began having suicidal thoughts. I contacted my employer's crisis help line. I informed them of the suicidal thoughts and severe stress. They explained that someone will be calling me back and hung up. No one called back. No one cares.

Of course, the moment I hang up the phone with the crisis line, I get the emails about the Cable TV getting upgraded to the Premium version, insurance being changed, and later in the next few months I began getting out of network medical bills. All of which I am supposed to pay.

After work, I picked up the children. Natalie made harassing statements and threats in regards to money. She inquired if I was to live in a homeless shelter as she began laughing. I did not respond. All I asked was that she provides me her usernames/passwords to the accounts I now have to pay.

Saturday 8/15/2015: Natalie contacted my cellphone requesting the names and information of the parties which were playing with the children. She informed me that she is in control of what I do with the children while I am with them.

Once again Natalie stated I did not feed the children. At least now I am taking the children out to eat and save the receipts to provide proof that they have been fed.

Natalie demanded for my work travel schedule, as she is entitled to my per diem rates for food and lodging. When I explained to her the process that I pay out of pocket and it is my reimbursement, she did not care. She wants "her per diem and salary."

Natalie also began demanding that I continue paying her alimony direct to her. I told her that I began making payments through the NJ probation system and my case worker handles my account. She began explaining to me that she knows this information, as my case worker, Jennifer

Mason is a friend of hers and that her friend is going to "handle me." It's funny; I never mentioned my case worker's name. Natalie knew it without me even saying anything.

Natalie began threatening me that if I do not pay her directly in addition to the NJ system, her girlfriend will make sure that my accounts show that I have not paid. Her threats are starting to get old.

Sunday 8/16/2015: Natalie arrived late to pick up children (7:45PM). Natalie made harassing statements and threats in regards to money. Requested she provide usernames/passwords to accounts so that I can be in compliance with the court order. She has yet to provide them, and still refuses.

I informed Natalie that I will be away on Friday 8/21/2015 to begin moving process to vacate my apartment as I no longer can afford it. She began laughing and told me to enjoy the homeless shelter.

Monday 8/17/2015: During my lunch period, I went to a few banks to secure a loan for the $5,000 I now have to pay to Mr. Keville. Finally, after three banks, I found one that would give me a loan. It's an unsecured loan, with an extremely high interest rate. However, the money is not going to come in until after the due date of paying him. Hopefully he will not make an issue out of it.

I received a voicemail from Ms. Jennifer Mason, case manager for child support & alimony. She informed me of a long, tedious process called a "direct payment credit" for the arrears. If I have any questions, I must contact the main call center and leave a message with them to speak with her (2 day waiting period). She said she would mail the paperwork.

After work, I went out to the car and saw it now has a flat tire. Wonderful! Life keeps throwing stones at my head. As it was visitation time, I had to contact Natalie. She became excessively aggressive and requested proof of flat tire. I provided pictures of the car to her. She demanded additional funding not covered in the court order.

I explained that the current order will require me to move out of state, she replied telling me about the homeless shelter availability and that she must approve where I move.

Eventually Aaron contacted me about his mother's temper and was scared. I was only able to spend one hour with children at the local park (6:30pm-7:30pm) because the car being in the shop again. When I dropped the kids off, I informed Natalie that I will be away on Friday 8/21/2015 to begin the moving process to vacate my apartment. She laughed and said "good."

Tuesday 8/18/2015: Informed Natalie via text message (at her request) that I will be traveling to MA on Thursday after work to begin moving process and will not be able to visit children. She confirmed receipt and requested the date I will return.

I began paying her bills and saw that she began upgrades to her cable (Platinum) and others. Since I have to pay them, she figures why not get the best of everything.

Thursday 8/20/2015: I received a message from Child Support Service about more money being due on 8/24. I contacted the hotline and spoke to a woman named "Dorothy." Last payment made for two weeks was received and no money is due. The phone message is a pre-recorded message and does not factor in two-week checks. She made contact with Case Worker about arrears payments as they continually want more than I make for back pay.

Thursday 8/20/2015: Due to the interrogatories requesting detailed information about the fencing non-profit, I brought up this information to the other Co-Directors and board. Unfortunately, to protect them and the students, I must resign immediately and give up all rights to the bank accounts. I removed myself from the club and the other Co-Directors and I visited the bank to remove me off all accounts.

In the mail, I received the direct payment paperwork for the alimony arrears from the NJ probation department. I filled it out and mailed it in. Over the next few weeks, I made copies of these packages and certified mailed them to my case manager four times. I left messages for her multiple times as well to inquire why she did not process it. I did not receive any response from her. I just received a continual silent refusal. Natalie's threat appears to be working for her.

Thursday 8/20/2015: Natalie texted me inquiring when I will be picking up children. Informed her that on 8/16/2015, 8/17/2015, and 8/18/2015 she was informed I will be in MA to begin moving process. She explained that she did not receive this information and began making opinionated justifications stating it is for my "work."

Later this day, I began seeing Facebook access requests and emails. I asked Natalie if she accessed my Facebook account without my permission. She confirmed that she did and inquired if I began dating. She blamed the Facebook hacking on Eric, saying he knew my password. How does a three year old know case-sensitive passwords?

Thursday 8/27/2015: I received Natalie's interrogatories (discovery) items. It contained a letter that had almost nothing in it. Natalie and her attorney are above the law and do not need to provide anything to us. However, I still must product everything they requested or I will be thrown into prison for failure to abide by court order.

In their letter though was a demand that I continue making direct payments to Natalie of child support and alimony on top of the checks I provide to probation. Mr. Keville also informed me in his letter that we must retain this letter as "his representation as an Officer of the Court."

I called the probation department and they said this is illegal. So now I am in a tight spot. Probation states it is illegal to give Natalie money directly, but Keville is now going forward with another lawsuit/motion because I will not do it. Damned if I do; damned if I don't!

Friday 8/28/2015: After work, I went over to the children's home to pick them up for my visitation weekend. After about a ½ hour waiting for Natalie, I called her. She told me to come up to her home to assist with the children. I informed her that I cannot do that as she knows I am barred from the residence. She began laughing "oh that's right."

She brought the children downstairs and began her temper tantrum and harassment in front of the children about her idea of me "cheating on her." Not sure where that came from and it is completely unfounded. She was screaming at me that I have begun dating other women because I am on the phone with them and I have female friends. She explained that I am still technically married to her, so if I do start dating, it is cheating and it will not go over well with the courts when she brings it up. To top off the conversation, Natalie began her threatening about getting more money and if I didn't comply, she'll bring me to court.

Saturday 8/29/2015: Natalie contacted me with harassment about her idea of me the "defendant" was "cheating on her" which is unfounded. Natalie was threatening about money and inquiring if I began dating.

Sunday 8/30/2015: After visitation, I dropped the children off at their mother's house. Natalie was not around. Her mother was present at the children's return. Natalie was out with her boyfriend. Her mother had her phone in hand and requested that I bring the baby up to front door (despite the court order barring me from going there). I love these set ups.

Monday 9/07/2015: I picked up the children after work. After some exercise, homework, and dinner, I attempted to drop them off at 8:00PM. I waited inside my car with the three children for ½ hour until Natalie arrived. I informed her that she is constantly tardy and these games must stop. She blamed her lateness on me and continued her threats about money and inquiring if I began dating anyone.

Natalie invited me to the front door after the visitation. She showed me her new furniture to include black leather sofas, love seats, a huge (table sized) ottoman, tables, and entertainment center. She boasted how she purchased it all at the upscale furniture store in town along with the words, "look what you bought," before slamming the door in my face.

Thursday 9/10/2015: I picked up the children after work. After some exercise, homework, and dinner, I attempted to drop them off at 8:00PM. Once again, I waited inside my car with the three children for ½ hour until Natalie arrived. I reminded her that she is constantly tardy and these games must stop. She blamed her lateness on me again and continued her threats about money and inquiring if I began dating anyone.

Friday 9/11/2015: I picked up the children at 4:30PM and dropped them off at 9:30PM. Natalie was an hour late again.

Saturday 9/12/2015: I picked up children at 8:30AM. During the pickup, Natalie was threatening me about money and if don't comply with her demands; I'll be thrown in prison. She was also inquiring if I began dating. I dropped the children off at 9:00PM. Natalie of course was not present. Her mother eventually showed up ½ hour late (9:30PM).

Sunday 9/13/2015: Picked up children at 8:30AM. I dropped the children off at 8:00PM. Natalie of course was not present. Her mother eventually showed up ½ hour late (8:30PM).

Monday 9/14/2015: At work, I sent off an email to Natalie informing her about my move to Massachusetts. The email was a follow up to our conversation on Thursday 9/10/2015. I told her that I will be moving to Massachusetts on Saturday, September 26th, 2015 and will be unavailable during that weekend.

She responded with:

Also officially where will you be moving to? Your girlfriends or your aunt's? What is the address where you will be residing? What office will you be working out of? And as of when? Or will you be telecommuting? Please answer these questions.

I informed her that I do not have any girlfriend, I will be moving in with my family as she already knows. My work schedule is none of her business. Her response:

Robert there really is no need to lie about the girlfriend... I am happy for you I just have a right to know where you will be. Why lie? I know you were up there in May. You certainly were not visiting a female co-worker over Memorial Day weekend for no reason in New Hampshire. I know you have been having sexual relations with her. I know since May you have regularly been on the phone with her between 1-2 hours a day. I know you applied for jobs that would take you in that area while we were married. I am sorry I wish I was stupid and play along with you but out of respect to me and our children and our marriage why lie? Oh I know why gods forbid anyone knows what a POS you are!!!

So what I got out of this email is she still has my passwords to my EZpass Toll account and my cell phone. Apparently she is still snooping into my accounts. I did see Michaela on Memorial Day and we have been talking.

But I have been applying for jobs in New Hampshire and Michaela's area? That is news to me. So while I was married to Natalie, I was having an extramarital affair with Michaela? I see what she is going to be presenting in court next. It doesn't matter about her extramarital engagements. She'll just lie and say I was having one to sway the court. So, I'll just add this accusation to the undocumented abuser file too!

After work, I picked up the children at 4:30PM. I dropped them off at 7:30PM. Natalie's mother was there for the drop off. The kids asked her where mommy was and she explained to them that Natalie was at school meeting. I inquired why I was not informed. She explained that I do not need to know about the children and began threatening me saying that they will never tell me about the children's activities (apparent that her schizophrenia was active).

Tuesday 9/15/2015: Natalie texted claiming there was an emergency with the children. I called her back right away as I was nervous. The conversation had nothing to do with children. She inquired about divorce case and began threatening me about money she informed me that she is not expected to follow court orders because of her friends at the courthouse.

Tuesday 9/15/2015: I was furious about Natalie going to school meetings about the children which I was not informed of. I have family that work for schools and they gave me some great advice. They told me to write letters to the schools, so I did.

I have not been receiving any information from the children's schools. I called the two schools and they continue to refuse to send me information at Natalie's request. I began writing and sending letters to the school Principals, administrators, and teachers demanding they keep me in the loop and involved. The letters were sent to both Aaron & Eric's schools:

During the past few months, I have been undergoing a fairly aggressive divorce proceeding in which I have been forced out of the state due to financial difficulties. However, I still have joint legal custody in regards to my son. Due to my former spouse intentionally withholding my son's educational information from me, I must request it from you directly.

This letter is to officially request all correspondence and meeting information in regards to your student. As per the attached NJ Superior Court Civil Action Consent Order Custodial Arrangement, I am requesting duplicate information which you normally provide to the parents:

Item 4. Each parent shall be entitled to complete detailed information from any teacher or school giving instruction to the children, or which the children may attend, and both parents shall be entitled to be furnished with all reports and notices.

Item 5. The parties agree that they shall provide each other with the notice of significant events at school, social activities, sporting activities, and in other matters of interest that the children may be involved in, agreeing and understanding that both parties shall be entitled to attend all such events and activities.

If you have any questions, feel free to contact me at the information listed above. Thank you.

Unfortunately this was to no avail. Eventually the schools told me I would have to file motions in the court for them to keep me involved each school year. My attorney and divorced coworkers told me this is normal and unfair, it is a losing battle. How much money is a grade school report card worth?

Thursday 9/17/2015: After work, I picked up children at 4:30PM, did our normal routing, and dropped them off at

8:00PM. Natalie, with her phone in hand recording, tried to get me to bring the children up the stairs to her. I knew what she was doing, trying to get me on video entering her residence. I told her that she knows I cannot go up to her and that she needs to come down for the curb side pickup. She refused as the court ordered curb side pick-up only pertains to me. Aaron and Eric ran upstairs to her and the baby was placed on the upper level grass yard (safe and sound). I did not go up to her.

Friday 9/18/2015: Today ½ day off and rented a Penske truck. I moved all of my personal items out of my recently moved in apartment and pulled an all-night trip to Massachusetts and New Hampshire. I finally made it to both states dividing up my stuff between Michaela's, my aunt's, and storage unit. I have tapped out my friends for helping me move again and again, so I did this one myself. I am exhausted and hungry. When I got up to New Hampshire, I was greeted with open arms by Michaela and her family.

Saturday 9/19/2015: Natalie called me a dozen times. She was claiming there was an emergency with the children. Frantic, I called her back to see what happened. The conversation had nothing to do with the children. She inquired about divorce case and began threatening me about money. When am I going to learn?

Sunday 9/20/2015: I returned the Penske truck and got a rental car to go back down to New Jersey. Natalie called claiming another emergency with children. Called her back, conversation had nothing to do with children. She inquired about divorce case and began threatening me about money and interviews in accordance with interrogatories.

Monday 9/21/2015: After work, I picked up the children at 4:30PM for visitation. I dropped them off at 7:30PM. Natalie in normal fashion was fifteen minutes late. I provided a check to her for her T-Mobile, Optimum, and PSEG bills.

Tuesday 9/22/2015: Another Court Case:
This time it was for an Early Settlement Panel (ESP). This is when the court brings in 2-3 attorneys to review the case issues and propose their views on the issues for potential settlement. The purpose is to receive impartial review of the issues. Apparently, it is good because attorneys experienced in matrimonial law get to give us a confidential review of the issues. It is bad because every attorney's view on a case can be different. At a minimum, it helps bridge the gap on some issues.

They explained that I should be paying $30,000 a year in alimony for nine years, $30,000 in child support, and a whole bunch of other numbers. I counted them all up and it was about $200,000 in support numbers for a salary which is half that. It was obvious they used Natalie's claims about my salary, not my actual pay check.

But one good thing, they said that they recognize that Natalie has no bills and receiving a significant amount of financial help from her father, with that in mind, she should pay for her own attorney.

Her attorney told her it was a homerun and my attorney stated the same to me (homerun for her). Later on in this case, I heard the same from the financial mediator. My attorney told me this is a baseline; we do not and will not agree to these terms.

Wednesday 9/23/2015: Natalie scheduled a birthday party for Aaron at a Chucky Cheese sort of place. I paid for the party, and was allowed to attend (I needed her permission). While at the party, it was made up of the three children and Natalie's friends. While Natalie used this birthday party as a social event for herself, I played with and took care of the three boys and celebrated Aaron's birthday with him.

After the party, mutual friends of ours wanted to speak with me afterwards. We decided to go to the local Dunkin Donuts. I informed them about the case, the removal of me out of the apartment, the lies about child/spousal abuse, and Natalie's demands for more and more money. Nonetheless, I got my standard "Why would she lie about that" routine and I am an asshole for being an abuser. I guess you can be an abuser with just an accusation. "The accusation is the proof."

I did hear that during divorces, mutual friends take sides and one side always ends up with the short end of the stick. I guess this is it; I too lost some friends with this divorce.

Thursday 9/24/2015: I picked up children after work and returned them back at 8:30PM. During my visitation with the kids, Aaron pooped in his pants. After cleaning him up; I asked what happened and if he was feeling okay. He began asking me questions out of the blue and inquired why "daddy is going to jail" and why "daddy is a bad person." I was shocked to say the least. I asked him who is telling him that stuff. Mommy & grandma of course! He hugged me and started to cry.

During the drop off of the children, Natalie was late as normal. When she did show, I requested for her father's address to send her "rent check" to him. She refused to provide it, explaining that she wants me in prison. She still does not understand. If I go to prison, she doesn't get any money. She still thinks that she will get paid and have me in prison at the same time.

Friday 9/25/2015: Picked up children at 4:30PM and returned them at 8:30PM. Informed Natalie about a trip I was making a trip to Massachusetts on Sunday morning and we agreed for a late pick up during the afternoon as Aaron had a soccer game anyway. Natalie told me to cancel my moving plans for tomorrow and pick up the children as she made last minute arrangements with her friends. I tried telling her that I already booked the rental van, but she began laughing and said "oh well."

Saturday 9/26/2015: Picked up children at 8:30AM and returned them at 8:30PM. Aaron pooped his pants again. He inquired why "daddy is going to jail" and why "daddy is a bad person." I love what she is feeding to these children.

I dropped the children off and Natalie was not there again. Her mother was at the doorstep demanding that I bring the children upstairs to her. They are fully aware I am barred from going onto the property. I do not understand why they keep going against court orders, well, I do know- as they have already explained to me, they do not have to abide with court orders. But I do.

Natalie texted messaged me at 2:00AM in the morning cancelling the agreements we made on Friday 9/25/2015: She cancelled the meeting time to the normal time. This was purposeful, as I am not awake at 2:00AM. This is her attempt at more control and disrupting my already made moving plans.

Sunday 9/27/2015: I picked up my children at 8:30AM and returned them at 6:30PM. After I dropped them off, I compiled more paperwork, pay stubs, and information to email to my attorney. Apparently, his office is receiving more court documents and letters from Natalie's attorney claiming that I haven't been paying alimony, how my pay just tripled in a matter of days, and I have been abusing the children and threatening Natalie. So much work just to defend myself over pure stupidity and lies. As they can just write whatever they want, the burden of proof is on me to defend.

Monday 9/28/2015: I reminded Natalie again via email as she is already fully aware, the email was to remind her that after today I will be fully relocated and will be living in Massachusetts. I explained that my residence and work position have been moved and I report tomorrow, Tuesday September 29, 2015. Moving forward, we must revisit the Visitation Order and have it changed.

In addition, I told her that I will be calling tomorrow after work to speak with Aaron for his birthday.

Keville Letter:
I received a letter from Mr. Keville to the Brendon County Court House Finance Division called a "Notice of Motion for Litigant's Rights." It stated that I was late with his $5,000 payment, and because of that he is requesting the following be immediately issued against me:

2. Directing that in the event that defendant is not in full compliance with the counsel fee Order dated August 13, 2014, on the return date of this application, defendant shall be sanctioned for his non-compliance, as follows:

a. Defendant's New Jersey driving privileges shall be immediately suspended by the New Jersey Motor Vehicle Commission as provided by the Rules Governing the Courts of the State Of New Jersey until such time as defendant is in full compliance with all Orders of the Court;

b. A Bench Warrant shall immediately be issued for the arrest and incarceration of defendant as provided by the Rules Governing The Courts Of The State Of New Jersey, with full compliance with the Orders of the Court being the condition of release; and

c. Such other and further sanctions the Court determines to be equitable under the circumstance **;(Means more money).**

In addition, he stated (well, lied) that I did not produce discovery and requested the following:

Dismissing defendant's pleadings with prejudice, barring defendant from introducing affirmative proofs at the time of final hearing, and limiting defendant to cross examination at the time of final hearing in the within matter, as a result of defendant's failure to provide discovery.

However, we have his signature when he signed for the discovery documents. Guess that does not matter.

County Court threats to Federal Government:
I received a dozen or so letters from Ms. Jennifer Mason about me not paying my court ordered alimony. I have been paying and I am up to date with all my payments. This is unbelievable! How can she just blatantly lie about this?

I received another letter in the mail today: this one from the Brendon County Probation Department and Court House. It is a notice to my employer. It was addressed to the CEO of the "federal government." Which is funny in a way as the CEO of the Federal Government is the President of the United States. Guess he didn't get the letter.

I was carbon copied into their letter. It was mailed to an office which was a completely different division in the government and it was also located on the opposite part of New Jersey. I had no idea where they found that address. It was sent to my employer for them failing to garnish my wages to their liking.

Apparently, the probation office requested that my CEO garnish my pay multiple times to pay Natalie's weekly alimony. The CEO of the federal government did not answer their letters; so the county court is now threatening the CEO for failing to garnish me on the timeframe they demand. The federal government will now have to pay fines and be subject to the initiation of court proceedings against them for non-compliance with their Court Order.

The letter stated the following:

NOTICE TO EMPLOYER OF NON-COMPLIANCE WITH INCOME EXECUTION ORDER

On 08/15/2015, an ORDER/NOTICE to withhold income for child/spousal support was sent to you directing the deduction of $350.00 WEEKLY from the income of ROBERT ARLOTTA. The deduction must be made payable to and forwarded to the New Jersey Family Support Payment Center.

According to our records, we have not received payments from "FEDERAL GOV" in accordance with the order of the court. Please immediately remit the required payments. If you fail to do so, you are liable for the accumulated amount and a fine.

Each payment must include the name of the employee, amount withheld, date of withholding, the child support probation case ID and the employee's social security number. This information must be included to ensure that payments will be properly identified to a case or employee. Otherwise, we will be unable to verify your compliance with the ORDER/NOTICE.

If there is any reason why payments have not been forwarded or if your records differ, please contact the Probation Division.

Please be advised that non-compliance with this ORDER/NOTICE will result in the initiation of court proceedings against FAA (N.J.S.A.2A.17-56.11). Therefore, your immediate attention is required.

Thank you for your cooperation and attention in this matter.

Please complete if employment has been terminated/ or employee laid off and return to Brendon County Probation Division, Care of Ms. Jennifer Mason.

My Reaction:
I contacted the child support hotline. The woman over the phone "knew for a fact" that I worked for a private company called "federal government" and their system is completely correct.

They reiterated their demands for my CEO to comply with their orders! I still find it funny how a pitiful little county court is threatening the United States Federal Government.

This is just pure stupidity at the highest level. They really don't understand and haven't realized yet that the CEO of the federal government is the President.

As the letter was addressed to a technical center which is located on the other end of the state, I asked them about the address and where they got it from. That is the only address they had on file for "federal gov" and since "I have to" work in New Jersey; that is my work address.

I still think it is weird how they got that address. If the court actually looked at one of my pay stubs, they would see the address of the office which actually handles my pay (as their address is on each pay check). But if the court did that, they would see how much I actually make and know that I cannot pay the demands they placed on me....

To defend against the letters saying I haven't been paying alimony, I collected all my cancelled checks that went to the NJ payment center. I forwarded them to my attorney so that he can now show the judge that I have been paying.

I also scanned in the letter to my employer and sent it to my attorney. He has never heard this before, let alone seen a letter like this. The letter was written by Natalie's friend; Jennifer Mason.

My attorney thinks that this is the unethical behavior of her friends to now harass my job, so that it creates more tension. He responded back to me that he will forward this information to the court, and this harassment of my employer must stop. He will also try to get me a different probation officer to handle my account.

I followed up with a letter to the probation office requesting a different probation officer and explained to them how Natalie and Ms. Mason are friends. I never heard back from the probation office and my attorney's request to the court fell on deaf ears. If probation wants to bring the President of the United States to court, they can. I never heard of such stupidity!

So in essence, I have Natalie's girlfriends in the courthouse being able to harass my job and lie about how I haven't paid child support; and the court will allow it. Just peachy!

After reading these letters, I packed up the last of my things into the car and I officially moved out of New Jersey. I headed up to my new home, my new life.

I was upset. Over the past few months I have purchased and gave away almost all of my possessions. I purchased items and received donated clothes, supplies, and just plain "stuff" to have a nice little apartment but now I have to abandon it all. Such a waste of money and time! I should have never signed a lease for an apartment or purchased any of the living supplies!

Tuesday 9/29/2015: Texted Natalie about Aaron's birthday. Today was his birthday. Natalie limited my phone call time to two minutes with Aaron. I requested additional time; however Natalie began harassment about additional money and her vehicle which I am utilizing. She requests her vehicle back, as she requires two vehicles and a motorcycle to survive.

Entry #4: More Divorce Games (Quarter 4, 2015):

Friday 10/02/2015: Natalie has begun scheduling school meetings for the children. Apparently she is classifying the children and performing IEP sessions and not including me on anything. I contacted the schools and informed them that we have joint custody and I am entitled to the same information they are giving her and allowed a say. They claimed that they received explicit instructions from Natalie not to contact me (as I am dangerous) and they do not want to get involved with our legal matters. They will continue to refuse my attempts to get information about my children. To gain access to their records, I must file a motion with the court and sue them for it.

My attorney sent a letter to Natalie's attorney about her conduct and that this behavior must stop.

We received back letters from Natalie and her attorney. They do not agree. What about the NJ Court? They don't agree either. Their reasoning: None. No proof is needed; Natalie's word is truth and gold while the burden of proof lies with me.

Sunday 10/04/2015: I requested from Natalie the pictures from Eric's Pumpkin coloring day (I received notification of this event from his school). She told me that she would only provide them once I pay her cable bill and On-Demand videos. I paid the bills, and then she provided a forwarded email from school. During this whole time I had to endure additional harassment from her in regards to vehicles and additional monies. Just for a picture!

Monday 10/5/20115: Provided my attorney more letters, documents, and items to defend myself. Natalie just keeps on going with this stuff. I inquired with him about the process and how the New Jersey Court can arrest me over her lies and why the court has not gone after her for lying to them?

Essentially, courts do not prosecute women who lie in family court. There are dozens like me that have ex-spouses lie and get them falsely imprisoned without any repercussions for the false claims when they are overturned.

Since I moved to New Hampshire, my medical insurance had to change. I began researching medical "national" plans. I had to provide this research to my attorney. Apparently Natalie and her attorney must approve my change in insurance.

In addition, my transfer resulted in a decrease in my pay. I provided my attorney the new information. Unfortunately though, he explained that New Jersey will keep the highest number. This is what they do, even if I lose my job. I am always held at the highest pay for alimony and child support. How is this fair again?

Tuesday 10/6/2015: I sent the attached letter to the following individuals to assist me with my case as I do not know what to do with all this corruption and games. With help from Michaela and my family, we edited the letter line by line. I wrote the same standard letter to them all with the exception of the addresses. I marked it as Urgent: Public State/Local Corruption. In the next couple of months I would be getting letters from each of these individuals explaining that they cannot help as it is a civil matter:

Letters were sent to:
Federal Bureau of Investigations
Governor Chris Christie
New Jersey Advisory Committee on Judicial Conduct
New Jersey State Ethics Commission
Office of Professional Responsibility

Local Representatives

My name is Robert Arlotta and until recently, I was a Brendon County, New Jersey resident and a veteran of the Iraq war. I have three beautiful children all who reside in New Jersey with their mother. The oldest is six years old and youngest is nine months old. I am a decorated war veteran. Through my military service and time being overseas in Iraq, I received the following awards:

- *Army Commendation Medal*
- *New Jersey Distinguished Service Medal*
- *Armed Forces Reserve Medal*
- *Army Reserve Components Achievement Medal*
- *Army Service Ribbon*
- *Global War on Terror Expeditionary Medal*
- *Global War on Terror Service Medal*
- *Iraq Campaign Medal*
- *National Defense Service Medal*
- *Overseas Service Ribbon*

I served with the US Army both active duty and reserve for eight years. I am currently a Federal employee. My position involves maintaining contact and working with police and government at the local, municipal, state levels.

I am reaching out to you and your office to inform you about a grave injustice and to request your help. During the past few months I have been undergoing an excessively aggressive divorce.

My ex-wife; Ms. Natalie Arlotta has a limited work history, but most notably, she worked at the local Brendon County Superior Court where my case is being handled. She worked as a Court Services Officer for the Family Division which deals with divorces. During her time with the court she befriended many clerks, officers, case managers, and judges to include those involved in my divorce case. These relationships are still active and the reason for this complaint. My ex-wife has bolstered that she is in contact with these individuals and how her relationships will ensure my demise. She has threatened that her "friends" can override court decisions.

There have been small occurrences which have happened such as the court initially losing all of my filing fees. However, there have been other more significant factors which have been affecting my divorce proceedings. For example, during the custody and child visitation mediation session; the Family Court Mediator recognized my ex-wife and began discussing court proceedings. This was a conflict of interest and she failed to excuse herself.

I have concerns with the children's welfare as my wife has primary custody. I have been threatened by my ex-wife that if I contact the NJ Department of Children and Families, she will contact her friend: a Family Service Specialist/Case Manager to get involved and discredit my claims.

For about a year, my ex-wife has engaged in an extramarital relationship with a former love. My ex-wife planned this divorce for many years and has made multiple false allegations to support her position to create a divorce which ruined me financially and continues to utilize her friends within the court to promote her case.

In early April I was removed from the marital residence due to allegations of domestic violence. This was disproven when police arrived. The police officers which arrived on scene did not create a police report which I contested with them. The night I was thrown out of my residence I was homeless and had my oldest child with me. Over the next few months, I continued to be homeless as my ex-wife emptied all bank accounts. Eventually I finally secured an apartment and signed a year lease.

My ex-wife and the court have played games with me and my livelihood. My ex-wife has made extravagant purchases and enjoyed vacations and cruises in which I am expected to pay. Even against court orders, she utilizes out of network doctors and requests out of network medical procedures. I am consistently being bombarded with medical bills for these out of network charges and cannot pay them.

She began the process of getting elective surgeries (i.e. Bariatric Weight Loss Surgery) to ensure my financial demise. When approached about these issues and why she continues to do this, I get the same answer- "Because I can, and the NJ courts support me." I cannot fathom why the NJ Family Courts allow this.

My ex-wife and her family have stated that they do not have to abide by court orders regarding this case. As such my ex-wife has been consistently ignoring and violating the court orders which have been issued. Some of the violations include:
1.   Harassing and verbally assaulting me in front of the children
2.   Claiming false emergencies regarding the children in order for me to respond
3.   Utilizing out of network doctors and services

During court proceedings and documentation, I am accused of "undocumented abuse" and treated by court officials as a criminal. I have never abused anyone in my life nor have any records of abuse.

The County Judge handling my case is: Honorable Cynthia Myers

Judge Cynthia Myers combined both child support and alimony into the child support payment. My attorney asked why they cannot be separated and the judge just replied that she didn't want me to be able to claim the deductions on my taxes. My attorney began to argue this as it did not make any sense and she simply replied that she did not care what we have to say.

Judge Cynthia Myers listened to both my ex-wife and her lawyer and did not allow me to state my defense or allow me to speak. My ex-wife made accusations claiming that I never provided child support and my attempt to show proof of payment during court was not allowed. My attorney attempted to defend, only to have Judge Cynthia Myers state she was not interested in what he had to say.

This is a one-direction court and to state that it is a "kangaroo court" would be an adequate statement. I am being punished for being a good husband and father.

In addition, my ex-wife made claims that I have not provided any child support. Judge Cynthia Myers determined that I have not paid my ex-wife any child support and owe it as arrears. However, I provided the court copies of the cashed check images from my bank which shows that I have been paying child support since April 2015; but the court refuses to listen and is continuously imposing arrears payments on me. I have sent multiple requests via certified mail to the Probation Office which I am told they have not received which contradicts the signed certified receipt.

My Child Support Case Manager, Ms. Jennifer Mason, has received arrears adjustment paperwork four times and refuses to process it. I became aware recently that she and my ex-wife have a relationship which began when my ex-wife worked with her at the Brendon County Court.

My ex-wife states that she cannot work because she feels depressed, but cannot provide substantial evidence of those claims. She is able to work, but the courts determined that she is unable. If she is unable, why does she not collect disability is she is in fact "disabled?"

My ex-wife lives in an apartment building owned by her father and has the children being watched by her mother as she continues her social lifestyle. We were living the high life, with a monthly rent of $400, free babysitting from her family, and her father providing her $2000 a month as spending cash.

Since I was thrown out, her father signed a sworn statement stating that the rent went up to $1150 a month (290% increase) and that he never provided his daughter $2000 a month. In addition to this, there are documents by her attorney stating that he stopped giving her the money months ago. However, I have check images which state otherwise. They forged a lease stating the increased rent and stated that I agreed to it and printed my name to it, however my signature is nowhere on the lease.

I bring home a little less than $4300 a month. Judge Cynthia Myers knows that I make this much, however has determined that I can pay all of the ex-wife's expenses in addition to paying my ex-wife's attorney $5000 in 45 days. Attached is a court order in which I am expected to pay. However, these numbers go beyond what I actually make. The question arises on how a court can make you pay more than you actually make?

Now with all these expenses going beyond what I make, I am being threatened by my ex-wife, her attorney, and the courts that my driver's license is going to be revoked and bench warrants for my arrest. How can this be done when the court wants me to pay more than I make? How will I pay anything if I am in jail? If I am in jail, I lose my Federal job and license to work.

I have been informed that my expenses are unnecessary. One dollar a day for food, gas to get to work, and having a warm bed at night are not required. However, my ex-wife's Optimum TV and HBO channels are necessary in order for her to live.

While she continues to live beyond her means, I am forced to pay these means while I am homeless living out of a car which will be taken away from me soon by her as she must have two cars to be "comfortable."

With the lies of her family and manipulation of the Probation Division and Courts, I am expected to pay more than I make and now forced out of my apartment and being forced out of state to live with my family in Massachusetts to pay these ridiculous charges.

I am constantly being harassed by my ex-wife. I consistently get phone calls under the premise of an emergency with the children, only to find out after calling her back that she begins verbally assaulting me about additional money. The issues always involve money. Children are the least of her worries.

I was accused of stealing items from the marital home which I had to write letters and pay my attorney to defend myself. How can she make a simple five minute phone call with lies which forces me to perform days of work defending myself? How is it that she can make a false accusation and not be punished; but if I make an accusation it is denied immediately?

There are hundreds of questions which arise out of this case so far. How can a court force me to pay more than I make? How does the court expect me to work when I cannot afford gas or a car to get to work? How do I work when food is considered an unnecessary expense for me? Why is this blatant misconduct allowed?

I have performed research on the New Jersey Veterans Legal Assistance program and as I am a Veteran and not currently serving, I do not qualify for legal or pro bono assistance.

I have attached copies of the documentation pertaining to the matter. I respectfully request assistance with my case. I am requesting assistance with the investigation of the individuals named above with the misconduct and conflict of interest, in addition to a referral for legal pro bono assistance.

Thank you very much for your time.

Wednesday 10/07/2015: Natalie contacted me about the dental insurance. She explained that Aaron needed to go to dentist and that I changed the dental insurance and took her medical card. I did not change any insurance nor took her card (as I currently live in MA and barred from her property). Natalie became irate and started harassing about additional monies and requesting her vehicle. If I do not return her "assets" she will contact police and her lawyer will file motions to have me in prison.

Friday 10/09/2015: Natalie emailed my aunt whom I lived with briefly. She requested that she bring the children up and I watch the children during this weekend. I again requested to Natalie to stop contacting my family.

Saturday 10/10/2015: Since money is getting tighter and tighter, Michaela and her family helped move all my personal stuff from the storage unit to the crawl space in Michaela's house which I have been living at.

Sunday 10/11/2015: Natalie contacted me about watching the children in New Jersey (and lied about emailing my aunt when asked). I informed her that I cannot afford the gas, tolls, or feed the children (as my $1 a day for food for me was claimed by her and her attorney as outrageous). She became irate and demanded more money, to watch the children, she still wants her "assets" i.e. the vehicle which she is entitled to all assets. She further explained that I make "high six figure income" and I am a big boy and can afford all of these items. She began threatening more court fees, judgments against me, and will ensure that her "friends in the system" handle me. She demanded her Corolla back or she will call it in stolen, as it is still in her name.

Monday 10/12/2015: Natalie demanded I take children the weekend of 10/23, but I must stay in the State of New Jersey (while they are pushing for a bench warrant). Once again, informed her that I cannot afford the gas, tolls, or feed the children (as my $1 a day for food for myself was claimed by her and her attorney as outrageous). She once again became irate and demanded more money, to watch the children, she still wants her "assets" i.e. the vehicle which she is entitled to all assets. She further explained that I make "high six figure income" and I am a big boy and can afford all of these items.

She began threatening more court fees, judgments against me, and will ensure that her "friends in the system" handle me. She demanded her Corolla back or she will call it in stolen, as it is still in her name.

Tuesday 10/13/2015: I attempted to deliver Natalie's car (Toyota Corolla) back to her at her request. My friend was doing me a great favor and attempted to return the vehicle.

He visited Natalie's local town Police Department. The Dispatcher advised him to draw up a receipt letter and they provided an officer for peace keeping during the return. He drew up a receipt letter for the vehicle.

I contacted Natalie about the vehicle and she became irate threatening that I will not take the minivan (which I never explained that I would). She explained that she spoke to her lawyer and that she would never ask for the vehicle and I am mentally ill. She further attacked my living arrangements in the New England region and "my girlfriend."

My friend along with the local police department went to her apartment shortly after the phone call. Natalie's father was present and began screaming at my friend and the police officer. The officer had to intervene and get between my friend and her father.

They threatened my friend about stealing the minivan which he explained he was not there to do, he was there to drop off Natalie's car. Natalie's father said it was his property and he will not allow the car to be parked in front of his property (even though the car is owned and registered in her name).

They refused delivery of her vehicle. The car was moved to my friend's residence until the court can determine its status. However, I still cannot drive it because there is court document allowing me to or evidence of ownership. I unfortunately have no claim and can't use it until the threats of me "stealing the car" end.

*Down the road this will be important, as Mr. Keville will once again request this vehicle and these events were deemed never to have taken place.

Wednesday 10/14/2015: My attorney sent a letter to Mr. Keville explaining that my friend attempted to drop off the second vehicle to Natalie (as she needs two cars to survive), but she refused it when he attempted to drop it off. He also stated that this is against status quo and asked why she needs two vehicles while I have none. He received no response from Mr. Keville.

Now, with no vehicle, I had to go out and buy a car. Michaela helped me out with that. But now, with a new car, Natalie and Mr. Keville could press the court stating that she needs three cars and a motorcycle to survive, and they would more than likely grant it. So with each visitation after this, I had to use Michaela's family's cars so Natalie did not find out I purchased a car or she could technically get it.

Friday 10/16/2015: I received multiple text messages from Natalie to pay her T-Mobile bills along with her new phone today. If I don't pay, I will get brought back to court and eventually arrested. Thus, I had to pay.

Monday 10/19/2015: The arrears payment paperwork is still not filed. My Case Worker is refusing to process it and Natalie is refusing to hand in her portion. I sent text messages to Natalie requesting why she has not filed the Child Support Arrears payment paperwork for the state. No response, she is not going to do it, she isn't required to. The proof that I have is meaningless unless she says it's true. I love how this system works.

Wednesday 10/21/2015: Received multiple text messages from Natalie Arlotta regarding children visitation and child support. Money, money, money…that's what she wants. Anyway child support is already being given by court order. She is demanding that I need to pay her more or she will keep the kids away. This is extortion!!! The kids are just weapons for her! I am so pissed!

Wednesday 10/21/2015: I received a forwarded email from my aunt. Natalie contacted her about the divorce and more harassment. Natalie explained to her how she needs money to survive and that I have not been paying her, supporting her, or speaking with the children. She also explained that I was an evil person. I again requested to Natalie to stop contacting my family.

I told my family how the email had lots of lies and it's too bad I still have bank access to see the checks from her father and brother and don't make all that money. I told them not to worry about this. I requested multiple times to her to keep them out of all this. She is getting desperate as her father and brother failed to show for their depositions and she is seeking additional money.

After I read the email, I requested to her again to stop making contact with my family. I asked her why she is trying to involve them. Simple- She wants them to throw me out. She and her attorney need me in New Jersey to pursue their bench warrants which are only enforced within the state. So she wrote up a whole bunch of lies. Fortunate for me, I keep all emails, text messages, this diary, and record EVERYTHING. So when she performs games like this, I have the burden of proof with me (as long as the Judge wants to even see it).

I forwarded this email to my attorney. Apparently these are games to get me thrown out and living on the street again. At least Natalie is keeping her word about wanting me homeless and in prison. I sent him all the emails which had more harassment and the email she sent to my family. She is putting a strain on family up here. I asked him what can be done to stop this.

My attorney said that they will notify her attorney of her actions and demand it cease and, since it is harassing, if it continues, I will have to seek a restraining order.

Natalie's email to my aunt demanding her entitlements and her continued attempts to draw my family into her games:

I am sorry to write you both but Robert I want your Aunt to know what's going on. Robert was not paying me enough support. He was giving me $1000 to pay for all household expenses and bills/ car payment/ rent etc. It was not enough. My dad was furious with the divorce and does not want to help us financially. (Nor is it his responsibility)

My attorney wrote Robert a letter requesting more support. Robert ignored it. Robert gets paid every other week and has that he is single and has no dependents. If he changed his w2 form to the correct amount of dependents or even just one dependent he should be making at least $5000 a month. Net. He was giving me 20% of his net income to support me and the three children. My attorney said if he did not give a proper amount of support he would have to file a motion to get the money. Robert did not comply so my attorney had to file a motion for support. The judge deemed the fact that I even had to file a motion to get the money to be crazy. So the judge decided to make Robert have to pay my attorney to even have to bring the motion before the court. In the order the judge gave a timeline for the money to be paid.

Robert did not comply with the order and pay my attorney. My attorney wrote Robert a letter reminding him it had not been paid. Without my knowledge my attorney filed a motion to get the money for failing to comply with the court order as well as to compel him to answer questions to interrogatories which have not been provided.

There were two questions that were not yet answered. (Which my attorney wrote a letter requesting before the motion was filed) Robert did not respond. As far as I know the money has been paid. I don't know if the two questions have been answered but as far as I know as long as there answered there should be no order issued as long as Robert complies with the court.

There is no "warrant for his arrest" this is just legal terminology they use in court. To threaten if he does not comply a warrant can be issued. Robert's arrears have been paid so currently he should only paying $1200 a month in child support $400 rent $535 car $250 for cable/phone/internet/electric.

That is less than half of his net earnings each month that 4 people live on compared to one. (My father is not helping) Yes he is an asshole. Again if he corrects his w2 and has the appropriate amount withheld. Last year tax time we had a $16000 refund at tax time for example. None of this is really important though.

There is no war here. There is no warrant! Nor will there be as long as he answers the two silly questions my attorney wants answers to. Which my attorney did without my knowledge he is just representing me to the best ability he knows how. Which is what I would want your attorney to do for you.

Let's please try to make the best of things. For our children sake. I don't know if he is in NJ or MA. I think he likes me not knowing. Could you imagine if I moved away with the children and did not tell him where I was going? My children have no idea where there father is nor do I. I don't know if he is living with you or not or if he is staying at his girlfriends and that is why he can't make the effort to see them. I have offered to drive them up there.

I resent the fact that he blames this on me for not seeing our children. If I don't make him pay an appropriate amount of support I would only be hurting our children. It's going to cost me $2000 just to put our children in child care to work I don't know if I would net that. We also have a 10 month old baby and two other children in special education. I am doing the best I can here. But don't for one minute blame me for not making the effort to see your children. If you want to be involved in their lives the door is always open. I have no hard feelings. I just resent the fact he is using our children as pawns in some sort of negotiation tactic.

Refusing to see them unless I don't make you pay for child support? What is wrong with you! I don't want to get you involved and I am not trying to create drama. The kids miss him and I don't know what to tell them.

But I will be damned if he blames not seeing the kids on me! It's been almost a month since he has seen them. He called on Aaron's birthday.

We called him once when Aaron wanted to tell him about his day. Other than that. Robert has made no effort or contact in regards to the children. I don't want this to become the status quo. Again if "money" is the issue as you claim. I will give you formula and pack lunches and dinners for you for the weekend since I am floating in money myself.

Thursday 10/22/2015: In the mail, I received another court order stating that my arrears suddenly went from zero (after I paid them) to now I owe an additional $2000 out of nowhere. I sent more direct payment credit paperwork packages to the New Jersey probation department. I am still assigned to Jennifer, even though I have requested multiple times to be assigned to someone else as Natalie knows her. Apparently, looking at my account, I am still in arrears. She continues to refuse to process my child support payments I made before the court order.

Sunday 10/25/2015: I received multiple harassing text messages from Natalie asking where I am living. I called her up and told her that she already knows where I am living: with my family in MA. I inquired why she called me about this. As my family took me in, Natalie made attempts to have me thrown out. Natalie assumed that they threw me out and she wanted my new address. She explained that "I hoped they did throw you out."

Monday 10/26/2015: I received another EZpass bill. Natalie apparently added herself to my account. I informed my attorney.

I asked Natalie to speak with the children on Skype. She allowed it. The session lasted 20 minutes and ended when Natalie began demanding more money and telling the children how I "stole money from mommy."

Natalie sent multiple text messages requesting more money for bills. Bills have been paid, however she wishes additional funds. I informed her that I found out about the EZpass.

She expressed no knowledge and after repeated attempts to provide Natalie the copies of the bills via email and text message, she consistently explained how she did not receive them (though she responded in line to the emails) and requested copies be provided during mediation.

I informed Natalie via email that I will be changing the medical insurance to nationwide plans and to ensure that she utilizes in network doctors and services. In addition, the premiums will be going up. Aetna nationwide: Plan stays the same, only premium goes up. Emblem will be changing to Blue Cross and Blue Shield Service Benefit Plan -Basic- Nationwide (Plan Code 112). It is the most comparable to what I currently have. Provided Blue Cross Benefit Plan Manual.

My attorney sent a letter to the NJ Court Probation Services for the games being played with my account. My case worker refusing to process check images that proved I have paid Natalie, her continual games claiming I have not paid into the system (though I have the check images), and the continual arrears adjustments going higher and higher.

He stated in the letter:

Please be advised that the undersigned represents Defendant-Obligor, Robert Arlotta, in the Above-referenced matter. An issue has come to our attention that we ask be addressed by the Probation Department immediately. Although Mr. Arlotta is sending his payments in timely, they keep getting processed late. We are also aware that the probation officer is an acquaintance of Plaintiff-Obligee, Mrs. Arlotta. We sincerely hope that this is just a coincidence. Either way, we ask that this issue be remedied as soon as possible because it gives the appearance to the judge presiding over the parties' divorce that Mr. Arlotta is non-compliant with his court-ordered obligations. We ask that you kindly address this issue as soon as possible

*Even after this divorce, I still have the same case worker handling my alimony, child support, and garnishments. Complete conflict of interest, but no one cares!

Tuesday 10/27/2015: My attorney sent a letter to Mr. Keville:

Please be advised that this office represents Defendant, Robert Arlotta in the above referenced matter. Please be advised that your client continues to harass our client, and it must stop immediately. On October 10, 2015, your client sent an email to our client's Aunt, whom he is living with at this time, advising that he is failing to support the children and that he is ignoring the children, in a bid to create unrest between our client and his Aunt.

This is simply abhorrent, and there was absolutely no reason for your client to involve our client's Aunt in the matter. This is harassment, and it must stop immediately. If your client continues this sort of harassing behavior, our client will be forced to seek a restraining order.

Tuesday 10/27/2015: Today I had court ordered "Financial Mediation" with a court ordered attorney and friend of Mr. Keville as the mediator. Natalie, her attorney, my attorney, and I were all present. I left my house in New Hampshire at 6:00AM and got to his office in New Jersey that afternoon.

Michaela and her family gave me a Thomas the Train Halloween pumpkin and outfit for Eric (since he loves Thomas) and I gave it to Natalie for him to wear for the holiday. I eventually looked on Facebook and saw him wear it. He loved it! But moving on…

To start off the session, Natalie made claims of all children being classified with disabilities (including the baby), me having an affair for several years, and apparently I am making an additional $100 a day in per diem monies on top of my "high six figure income." Natalie demanded that she is "entitled" to this per diem money which I have no idea where she came up with this. Here we go again with Natalie's "entitlements."

Natalie and Keville brought up the children next. Even though this was financial mediation, they wanted to sway the mediator more. They lied about me not wanting to see the children and making claims of abandonment. My attorney attempted to show all the requests we made to change the visitation order after my relocation. He provided letters and emails he provided to both Keville and Natalie. Apparently they did not receive them or did not read them.

My attorney mentioned Skyping with the children. Natalie and Keville agreed (surprisingly). I will Skype with the children after work at 5:30PM every Monday and Thursday. For visitation, Natalie agreed to once a month. Initially, Natalie and Mr. Keville said I had to pick up and drop off the children at her residence. My attorney fought this explaining how it was unfair. We pushed for a midway point. I looked it up on my phone and saw that Bayville, Massachusetts was the half way point. This would be great since my family is there and will be able to see the boys along with a bathroom break for them. Right off the highway is a Cracker Barrel restaurant. I mentioned this to Natalie and her attorney. They refused stating that she has to compete with New York traffic. I rebutted with me having to compete with Boston traffic. They eventually agreed.

After this, more money was being brought up and the mediator wished to sit in privately with Mr. Keville and Natalie to their discuss case. He put my attorney and me into a spare room, which looked like a storage room. Natalie and Keville got the conference room. After a ½ hour, the mediator came to me and explained that I must pay Natalie a sum of $30,000 plus additional other monies as he took her side. He believed her sob story about my infidelity, my thousands of dollars in per diem, and a high six figure salary.

I attempted to explain how much I make and show him a pay stub. He refused to see an actual pay stub and said he was listening to Mr. Keville and "why would they lie about how much you make?" I looked at my attorney, he attempted to give the mediator the items as well, but he refused. This is unbelievable!

We went back into a group session again. Natalie began pressing me in which my attorney had to intervene. I provided again the EZpass records to Natalie per her request which I previously provided on 10/26/2015. The car was brought up by Mr. Keville and they made claims about the cars having to be returned to the dealership. I explained that the Toyota Corolla was attempted to be dropped off due to Natalie's threat to contact the police and claim it is stolen. The mediator defended Natalie, asking to me why she would do that. I responded that it is a control tactic and there is no basis for it. He told me that I am able to operate the car. I asked if she forgets to take her medication one day and decides to call the police and call the vehicle in stolen and I get arrested; what is my legal basis?

Mr. Keville interjected saying I cannot speak "ill" about his client (however, she can against me- which still doesn't make any sense, how can she make all these accusations and I get yelled at if I make one?).

The mediator explained that she will not call the police, but when I pressed asking if she does, he repeated that she wouldn't. If she does, I do not have a legal stance and will be arrested for stealing a vehicle.

The mediator explained that his own daughter has a similar degree as Natalie and he can understand her. He explained I would have to pay for full time child care and Natalie's advanced degrees to better herself. Due to her depression, she cannot work either. Question- Why should I have to pay for degrees if she cannot medically work?

The mediator scheduled a second session in which I guess I have to pay for in which he will be asking Natalie again for a plan if she is going to work or not. She must provide a written plan when she will begin to work again; in addition, she must provide proof of this "marital debt" in the hundred-thousands of dollars she claims. The mediator said I can appear by telephone for this next session since I have a six hour drive.

The drive back was solemn. I was so upset. Michaela and I spoke on the phone practically the whole drive back home. I got home right before midnight.

Wednesday 10/28/2015: Received harassing text messages from Natalie explaining that I did not pay child support and she contacted probation about not receiving any child support. She made false claims about me not paying. When requested about EZpass bill, she began playing games with bills and money.

I also received a summary letter from the financial mediator via my attorney:

This shall confirm we proceeded with mediation on October 27, 2015. We have scheduled the next session for November 24, 2015, 10:00 a.m. at which time Mr. Arlotta may appear via telephone. One week prior to the session, Mr. Keville will circulate Mrs. Arlotta's rehabilitation plan with appropriate documentation. Please note, the parties have utilized the free two hours. Thus, any additional time associated with mediation will be billed at $300.00 per hour.

The parties also agreed to the following at mediation:

1. Skype sessions shall proceed on Mondays and Thursdays at 5:30 p.m.;

2. Mr. Arlotta will advise as to exercising parenting time one weekend per month with a midway pick-up and drop-off point;

3. Mrs. Arlotta will maintain the minivan. Mr. Arlotta will maintain the Corolla.

Thursday 10/29/2015: I wrote and mailed in the NJ Bar Association and NJ Courts Ethics Committee Ethics Complaint Form & Letter against Mr. Keville. It was a four page letter along with all the proof, emails, and documents. It was a large envelope with at least a full tree worth of paper.

Thursday 10/29/2015: Performed Skype session with children. Call lasted approximately 16 minutes. Natalie began inquiring where I was, where my home address is, and the requests for additional funds. Via email, requested Natalie to return her EZpass transponder as I have closed the account and to reimburse me for her tolls.

Thursday 10/29/2015: Informed Natalie via email that as of October 29, 2015 I have to change over the dental and medical insurance to a nationwide plan due to my relocation. The request with my job will be placed today. Once I receive the effective date I will notify her immediately.

The dental insurance is the same as the only thing changing is local coverage to national coverage with an increase in the monthly charge. The medical insurance is changing from Emblem Health (which is not accepted in New England) to Blue Cross/Blue Shield Nationwide Basic. I have included the information to the email and provided it to her last week as well.

The children's pediatrics group along with their main pediatrician is covered under this plan. There are slight differences within this plan, but it is the most comparable to the local plan that we have had in the past.

Saturday 10/31/2015: Contacted children via phone to wish them a Happy Halloween. I received a voicemail from Natalie about Halloween pictures I requested. She explained that she will only send one picture which she did of Eric & Aaron. I requested a picture of the baby, but she did not provide any.

Sunday 11/1/2015: Natalie sent an email to me explaining that instead of paying me directly, she will deduct what she owes me by paying a portion of her own bills. However, she will not pay the full amount of what is owed because she feels that the child support is not enough to pay for the meal/dinners for the children.

I informed her that the child support has nothing to do with this issue. The child support is calculated by the judge and I pay separately. As this was now becoming an issue, I will continue to pay the bills directly as per court order. In addition, she has been informed that the bills she wanted to pay have been paid by me (PSEG/Cable) and are on automatic pay. I requested that she provide me a check for the full amount.

I also reminded her that the EZpass account has been closed and USAA has been notified to deny any charges associated to it. She must return her transponder back to EZpass and open a new account. I no longer drive in NJ and the account has been closed.

Natalie provided a response email certifying that I paid her PSEG bill earlier this day (which is on automatic pay) and also reminded me that I am a "lying POS." I am still processing this; she emailed me saying that I am lying about paying her PSEG bill but does it on a forwarded email from them saying it was paid?

Monday 11/2/2015: During work, I received a new medical proof of insurance. I provided this to Natalie via email. She responded with multiple emails requesting where I am living and my household arrangements.

After work, I performed the normal Skype session with the children. The call lasted approximately 5 minutes. Natalie left explaining she had to leave and did not say who was watching children.

I heard her mother's smoking cough in the background. My aunt was next to me during this whole session, as I was at her house at the time. Natalie's mother ended the Skype session when the children were talking to me midsentence.

Tuesday 11/3/2015: Car Insurance Fiasco:

I received a phone call and voicemail from NJ Manufacturer's insurance. This company covers the marital vehicles. The car insurance investigator contacted me about the car not being in NJ.

I was informed that Natalie contacted them to inform them that the Toyota Corolla was lost/stolen out of state and they require the whereabouts of the vehicle. Due to my relocation, the company must break up the policies and I must cover two premiums instead of the one which is currently covered. A refund check will be issued to Natalie for the months of November and December. We went through this previously during the separation and Natalie is well aware of the process.

I received several text messages from Natalie explaining that she informed them that the vehicle is abandoned, and if she gets a new policy I will have to pay for it, and to "Pay her f**ing insurance and stop bitching." I explained that per court order, the insurance cannot be removed and if I am forced to purchase two separate insurance plans I would like the reimbursement check for the months I have currently paid for.

Natalie and I contacted the insurance investigator via conference call over the phone. Due to Natalie's phone call, the investigator had to remove me from the account (even though I still have to pay it) and insurance requires the Corolla to be parked at her residence. I informed them that the vehicle is in NJ and my friend's house in Brendonfield. Natalie informed the investigator that she agrees to take the Corolla and move it to her residence. She explained to the investigator that she will be picking up the vehicle today. She ended the phone conversation explaining that she will be calling me later today when she is going to pick it up so that I can inform Harry who is looking after it for me. I requested that she send me an email with that information. She never called nor sent an email in regards to this.

Later that evening, I inquired when she will be picking up Toyota Corolla at Harry's residence, as he requests a time so he can ensure he will be home and she informed the car insurance investigator that she will be relocating it to the marital residence. She did not respond to this question.

Tuesday 11/3/2015: Visitation:
Natalie inquired via email about the children visitation. She requests that I speak to my aunt in MA about this upcoming weekend.

Tuesday 11/3/2015: EZpass Emails:
As a stall tactic, Natalie emailed me to provide (once again) the amount of the EZpass bill. I was not at my computer and did not have the exact amount on me at that time. I reminded her that she has been provided the amount via email and in front of both attorneys and the mediator. In addition, she must return the EZpass transponder and get a new one as that account is closed and they are charging me a monthly fee until it is returned.

Tuesday 11/3/2015: Medical Bill Games:
I sent Natalie an email informing her that I received a dental bill for Aaron receiving a second set of x-rays on 10/07/2015. She knows (and confirms via email) that this is his second set and well aware that insurance does not pay it (non-reimbursable). She explained that the out of network bills are my responsibility (though against court order).

I received a letter from the health insurance dated 10/15/2015. This is in regards to the predetermination for bariatric surgery for Natalie. The plaintiff is attempting an elective bariatric (weight loss) surgery which will be out of network and means a lot more medical bills for me.

I informed her via email that as far as the unreimbursed health expenses, she and the doctor are required to give me advanced notice of the expenses so that I can see options, I cannot afford all these medical games she is playing. In addition, I cannot pay for her bariatric surgery as it is an elective surgery and she did not give me advanced notice before she started that process either.

I received more bills from an out of network dentist. I sent them the following letter explaining my position:

To Whom It May Concern:

I am in receipt of your invoice dated October 26, 2015 for services performed on 10/07/2015 for Aaron Arlotta. It appears that these services have been paid by the Dental Insurance.

Please be advised, I am the primary holder of the dental insurance, however per court order (attached to this letter) page two, item #5; I am not responsible for unreimbursed health expenses. For reasonable health expenses, I did not receive advanced notice of this expense.

You are not the only medical facility which has fallen for Natalie Arlotta's games. My ex-wife has been visiting out of network doctors and requesting out of network services to play games and drive me into financial ruin. These games have forced me out of state and currently, I am forced to pay more than I make. I am currently sitting on thousands of dollars in medical bills which I cannot possibly pay as I do not make this sort of money.

After careful consideration of the issues involved in this invoice and claim, and a review of the Dental settlements, there is no overdue balance nor any current balance due for the services mentioned above. This matter is closed and I respectfully request that you update your records accordingly. For future service, you must give me advanced notice of the expenses involved and the un-reimbursable charges which can occur before authorization. Thank you.

Wednesday 11/4/2015: Natalie contacted me via phone to request information on the dental insurance. She claims that her tooth cosmetic procedure is an emergency and needs the dental information. This information has been given to her previously. Inquired when she will be picking up Toyota Corolla at Harry's residence, as he requests a time so he can ensure he will be home. She did not provide a response. I informed her that I spoke to my aunt and due to availability; we are looking at Saturday 11/21 to Sunday 11/22 for a visitation with the children.

Thursday 11/05/2015: EZpass sent me an email to return all transponders back to them (as they haven't received Natalie's). I forwarded the email to Natalie and requested she return the transponder.

Thursday 11/05/2015: A New Jersey Manufacturer's car insurance investigator left me a voicemail explaining that they require my address in New Hampshire to send correspondence. This is also to remove me from the account, as they do not cover vehicles residing outside the state.

Thursday 11/05/2015: Natalie left me a voicemail 20 minutes before the scheduled Skype session cancelling the session with the children. She is not home with them.

Thursday 11/05/2015: Sent an email to Natalie to confirm our conversation earlier during the week. I spoke to my aunt and due to availability; we are looking at Saturday 11/21 to Sunday 11/22 for a visitation with the children. In addition, I requested that we discuss the two upcoming holidays. I would like to have the children Christmas Eve (Thursday 12/24) through the weekend pick up on (Sunday 12/27). I also asked about the Toyota Corolla status. Per our conversation with insurance on 11/03/2015, I requested a timeframe when she is planning to pick up the vehicle from Harry's? I need to inform him so he knows when to expect her. I did not receive an answer to any of the questions.

Monday 11/09/2015: Michaela and I met with an attorney up in New Hampshire. Unfortunately he cannot help. We discussed the case with him. He does not believe it. He explained that everything we are talking about is illegal in New Hampshire and other items just did not make sense to him, especially paying Natalie's attorney. He explained that he would be able to look at the case and work under a New Jersey attorney's license, but with everything I have to pay already, he doubts I can afford his $20k retainer.

From my attorney, I received a letter dated October 30, 2015 from the NJ Superior Court. This was in response to my letter to the Governor. The letter was sent to me, my attorney, Natalie's attorney, and Judge Cynthia Myers. It was written by another friend and former coworker of my ex-wife. She explained that the letter is not accurate as Natalie Arlotta did not work in the Family Division:

I am in receipt of your letter dated October 6, 2015, that you sent to the Governor's Office. Your letter was forwarded to my attention for review and response. Your letter indicates that your former wife, Natalie Arlotta was employed in our Family Division. Please note that your former wife did previously work in the Brendon Vicinage. Ms. Arlotta worked for a few years in our Civil Division and at no time did she ever work in our Family Division. Your letter also contains a number of allegations regarding your court matter and rulings that are clearly not accurate.

In the event that you are not satisfied with the decisions made by the trial judge, you may either file a Notice of Motion for Reconsideration with the trial judge or, file an appeal of the decision with the Appellate Division. You should consult with your attorney regarding your concerns.

Since your case is currently pending in our court, all communications with the court must be on notice to all parties. Therefore, I will be providing copies of your correspondence to your attorney, plaintiffs' attorney, and to Judge Cynthia Myers.

I love how she sent this to all parties involving an ethics case (when not required) and states I have a number of allegations that are not accurate when I provided the proof: including documents that my ex-wife did work in the Family Division. I have all the documents and proof. I provided the court orders I complained about along with proof of Natalie working for the family court division. How can they just say that it is untrue? This is unbelievable. I cannot believe all these people are putting their jobs on the line for their "friend."

What type of court system does nothing with a complaint, does not do any investigation, denies everything right off the bat, then proceeds to send that complaint to and inform the individuals you are grieving about so that their decisions can be swayed or those letters be used against you?

Monday 11/09/2015: Performed Skype session with children. Session lasted approximately 20 minutes. Prior to session, Natalie sent a text message requesting if the Skype session was going to happen and what time (even though I have never cancelled and the time was set during mediation).

Monday 11/09/2015: Natalie Texts & Phone Call:

Sent Natalie a text message at 6:00PM requesting she contact me to discuss open issues. She responded back to email her. Natalie later contacted me via phone at 8:15PM. Phone call lasted approximately 1.5 hours. Spoke to Natalie about the following items:

1. The current motion for me failing to answer interrogatories. I informed her that her attorney has been paid and all interrogatories have been answered. I inquired why her attorney is pressing forward with the motion; she explained that she does not know. I explained the hypocrisy of the situation and mentioned about how Keville used his other client's name in the interrogatories, the questions involving her relocating the children to Ohio and North Carolina which has nothing to do with our case, and her lack of responses to the interrogatories (as she failed to answer any questions). She informed me that her attorney made clerical mistakes when drawing up the interrogatories and he instructed her not to answer them. So with this answer from her, I asked why can she not answer questions and her attorney make mistakes, but when I answer one question in a way he does not like, why am I subject to legal discipline? She responded that her attorney is very aggressive and I must follow the law. She does not have to.

2. Natalie confirmed that her father is paying her attorney.

3. Marital Debt: Informed her that I am currently on the verge of financial ruin. I have no money. She requested that I place her debt into my name. I informed her that I do not have any available credit

to perform such a task. I explained that her attorney has no right to place into the divorce decree that I cannot seek additional avenues for financial help if I am financially unable to pay all her debts and mine. Who would put in such a thing? If I am broke, there is no money. If he is prepared to put that in, perhaps he could pay my bills if I cannot. I also explained to her that there is no way of getting around this, as I cannot afford two homes. She responded that I must maintain her standard of living even if I rot in jail.

4. Inquired when she will be picking up Toyota Corolla at Harry's residence, as he requests a time so he can ensure he will be home. Natalie responded that she will not pick up the vehicle from Harry's address. (This is against what she informed the insurance investigator).

5. She received the letter provided to the Superior Court of NJ. She observed that I provided the names of the people she is in contact with and her threats with using them. She further threatened me explaining that if they are disciplined for their misconduct, I will be "sorry."

6. Natalie agrees and is open to 5 year alimony with a step down method. ($25,000/2 years, $20,000/2 years, $15,000/1 year).

7. She agreed that child care expenses will be split between us.

8. She explained that her father has not been giving her money (though the deposits within the bank account claim otherwise). I requested why she keeps explaining to the court that the money he does provide her is an "inheritance" instead of the original deal which she consistently boasted about prior to the

divorce explaining that he pays her a living stipend if she does not go back to work. She informed me that she was instructed by her attorney to do this.

9. I inquired about the large cash deposits within the account which have been appearing. She has no knowledge of these deposits, but they do show in the bank account.

10. The check provided by Natalie's brother was a debt he owed her in regards to a cruise. I asked why I am held responsible for her cruise debt and he pays her back and the fact that she has disposable income to give him $2000 during a cruise when I cannot afford to feed myself. She provided no response.

11. I requested that the children come live with me. She refused as she explained that it will have drastic effects on her alimony and child support. I informed her that I will continue to pay her, but she refused to listen. "I want my money."

12. Throughout the conversation, Natalie was "unaware" of many of the letters/motions I have received from Mr. Keville (i.e. denying a payment plan for his money).

13. Natalie explains that I take home over $10,000 a month after taxes and I am able to pay her large sums of alimony. She also explained that I could have paid her attorney the sum of $5000 immediately out of my savings and pay stub (if only I would change my dependents). I informed her that I changed my dependents for taxes to pay her attorney, but it takes a month for changes in my tax dependents to take effect into my pay stub, hence the lateness of the pay. I also rebutted about the $10,000 a month net earnings, as I do not make this and reminded her that

she emptied the savings to her mother back in April before she had the police remove me.

14. As visitation must be changed, Natalie requested that I provide a proposal. I informed her that a visitation proposal was provided to her by my attorney. She explains that her lawyer never gave it to her.

15. I do not make $100 a day in per diem as she claims; this is only for travel and not $100 during those times.

16. She wants a $16,000 tax refund check when I get it from the US Treasury; I explained that I will not be getting a refund check in that amount. She does not care.

17. Natalie explained that her attorney has reached out to me on multiple occasions before sending motions to the court. I responded that I have not received any letters from him in regards to matters involving motions. All I receive are threats within motions.

18. Natalie agrees to keeping a fairness and split with claiming the children on taxes (1 each, and 2nd every other year).

Tuesday 11/10/2015: Waited for phone call from Natalie to discuss November 2015 visitation, Thanksgiving, and Christmas breaks. She never contacted me.

Wednesday 11/11/2015: Sent Natalie a text message to contact me to discuss visitation for this month and the Thanksgiving/Christmas holidays. She never contacted me.

Thursday 11/12/2015: Contacted NJ Manufacturer's Insurance Company to give them an updated address, informed them that all marital vehicles are in NJ (as they do not cover out of state), that Natalie continually refuses to move the Toyota Corolla to her address, and request documentation about her phone call to them on Tuesday 11/3/2015. They may be able to provide some documentation but only if I send a letter of request with pin pointed dates and information required. The request will have to be made to my case manager.

Thursday 11/12/2015: Performed Skype session with children. Session lasted approximately 20 minutes. Eric showed me his class photos. I requested that Natalie contact me prior to class pictures (as asked of her previously) so that I can order copies myself. Natalie became irate about this request.

I also attempted to inquire about seeing the children this month (perhaps Thanksgiving break). Natalie explained that she will call me as she does not want to discuss it through Skype. I waited for a phone call, she never called me to discuss.

Friday 11/13/2015: Natalie contacted me via phone (3 times).

1st Phone Call: Natalie contacted me to discuss children visitation for November and December. For December I requested either the weekend of Wyatt's birthday (12/12) or Christmas break. Natalie denied both claiming that I voluntarily moved out of my apartment and the state. For November, I requested to have the children with me in New Hampshire from Wednesday 11/25/2015—Sunday 11/29/2015. She explained that she will go to Connecticut as the centralized drop off as during mediation that is where I was living. I informed her that due to her harassment of my family, I since moved to New Hampshire. She explained that the children have a ½ day on Wednesday 11/25/2015 and the children will be home at 1:00PM. She will leave at that time and drop them off at the Cracker Barrel in Bayville, MA around 5:30PM. She also discussed taking the children on a train which arrives in Boston for that day. I requested that she provide me a firm time/location on what she wants to do with the children.

I inquired about the Toyota Corolla that is currently at Harry's house. Natalie explained that she requires her car there and Harry must drop it off to her. I told her that I will speak with him about that.

Natalie brought up the alimony payment and explained that she is entitled to $30,000 a year for six years. She went on to explain that her father is not giving her money and the large cash deposits going into the account are none of my business. I asked what happened to the agreement made on Monday 11/09/2015 and she did not have any reconciliation of that conversation. Natalie explained that she will be moving, but will not tell me where or when and do whatever she must (with her lawyer) to protect herself. She consistently told me we are still married and asking multiple times if I was in a relationship and having an affair.

2nd Phone Call: Informed Natalie that I just got off the phone with my friend Harry and he is able to drop off the vehicle at her residence. I inquired at what time she would prefer he do this. She now reverted back stating she does not want the vehicle there, despite what she told insurance. She wants to think about the car and will contact me later today. In addition, she changed the time for the drop off on Wednesday 11/25/2015 of the children. She explained that she will be pulling them out of school early and bring them up at around noon. She requests to drop them off at my aunt's house which was denied by me as she is not allowed to contact them due to her harassment.

3rd Phone Call: Natalie contacted me cancelling all plans with seeing the children for Thanksgiving break. She said it is too much travelling and does not want the children to spend thanksgiving with Michaela. She explained that if I am to have the children and celebrate the holidays, I must be down in New Jersey and she will not take the boys away from the area. She does not want the children to be in New Hampshire. I inquired on why she is denying my rights to see the children and denying the agreed centralized point to perform the drop-off/pick up which was determined during mediation. She did not have a response. I told her to think about what she is doing and the children want to see me.

She continued to harass me about my schedule. She informed me that I can have the children the weekend of 12/11-12/13, but this will most likely change. Natalie began demanding where I was going to be the first week in December. She claims that she must know and I am required to inform her of my work travel and constant whereabouts.

I inquired about the car relocation and she stated that she will need to contact her lawyer about picking up the car and informed me to leave it at Harry's house.

Friday 11/13/2015: Sent follow up text message to Natalie requesting finalized answer if I can see my children for Thanksgiving break and to request Eric's current weight and height as I need to purchase a new car seat for him.

Natalie texted me back multiple times just asking if I got rid of Eric's car seat and refused to provide his height and I must contact the pediatrician. In addition, she will not give me a firm answer whether she will allow me to see the children for the Thanksgiving break.

Monday 11/16/2015: Sent email to Natalie requesting final answer to seeing the children for Thanksgiving break. Due to traffic, I was unable to speak with the children via Skype.

Instead, I contacted them through the phone. Natalie asked what divorce proceedings were coming up. I informed her of the motion for their lie about not receiving the interrogatories. She began laughing and was well aware of the court date.

I requested to have the children for Thanksgiving. She informed me that she must consult her attorney before letting me see my children.

She came back to me refusing to let me see the children and she sent multiple emails with erroneous information and lies. She now claims that I did not bring car seats with me to New Hampshire (untrue), I am still living with my father in New Jersey, and claiming I lied in mediation about living in Massachusetts (untrue).

Tuesday 11/17/2015: More harassment from Natalie. I received text message from Natalie to pay her cell phone and electric bills.

Wednesday 11/18/2015: I informed Natalie that I checked online and her bills are not due for another two weeks. She claimed that they are due now. I requested the status of her payment to me in regards to her EZpass account tampering. Initially, she refused to answer. She then explained that she did not send my reimbursement because I would claim I never received it. I requested that she stop these games. She once again said she will send the reimbursement check. However, this has been claimed multiple times already.

Later this evening, Natalie left a voicemail stating that Aaron wished to speak to me and to contact her. I called her shortly afterwards and her reasons for calling had nothing to do with Aaron. She contacted me to threaten me explaining she will never bring the children to me and will ensure my "financial demise." She explained how things will not go in my favor tomorrow (court motion hearing).

Wednesday 11/18/2015: Attorney: Requested information for calling into court for motion hearing on Friday,

11/19/2015. Attorney lost my payment information and dates for the checks which were sent to Mr. Keville. Resent check images to him.

Thursday 11/19/2015: Received medical ID card from Blue Cross/Shield. Included hard copy for Natalie (placed in rental check envelope going to her father). Took picture of the ID card and text messaged it to her explaining hard copy is with rental check to her father.

Thursday 11/19/2015: Sent letter of request for information to New Jersey Manufacturer's insurance company.

Thursday 11/19/2015: Another Court Case:
I had trial at 1:30PM for counsel fees/interrogatories motions.

Judge Cynthia Myers contacted me via cell phone. Apparently, once again Natalie and her attorney, Mr. Harold Keville showed shortly beforehand and he was allowed a private audience with the Judge to discuss the case.

Judge Cynthia Myers began the session asking the plaintiff's total counsel fees and my fees. I informed her it is approximately $20,000. She asked my attorney for the proof of this number. He did not have it. The Judge did not like this answer and my fees are now null and void because there is no proof.

The Judge then asked my ex-wife for her counsel fees. They said $15,000 a month. I asked if my ex-wife needed proof of her fees; the Judge stated that she did not have to provide any proof.

The Judge went on that I do not have to be represented nor do subpoenas have to be sent. Judge Cynthia Myers explained that the subpoenas are unnecessary and can harm the plaintiff's case. I believe the term was "detrimental to the plaintiff's case."

The Judge argued with my attorney claiming the gifts to the plaintiff by her father & brother are financial help and do not have any bearing on the case. Judge Cynthia Myers mentioned my comments in the NJ courts letter. She was given a copy of it and it is now swaying her position against me because I complained about her behavior.

Judge Cynthia Myers mentioned multiple items in regards to my letter to the courts. She confirmed that she saw he was paid, but a few days late. I was a few days late due to me having to take out a loan to pay him.

She explained to me that due to my military service, I should understand what it is to follow orders and she is like my commanding officer and I must abide her orders regardless if I can pay them or not. "Mr. Arlotta, you must do what you are told. If I order you to pay, it whether you can afford it or not, you must find the means!"

She went on explaining that Mr. Keville and Natalie needed to get paid on time to ensure that they are prepared and paid up to successfully have a case against me. I couldn't believe this. I asked Mr. Keville for an invoice for his "interesting even numbered bill." Unfortunately, he informed both me and the court how he does not work with bills or invoices. Later, I read that this is against the state bar requirements. But he had the judge in his back pocket, so I guess that usurps law and state bar practices.

Judge Cynthia Myers and Mr. Keville explained that I make several thousand dollars a month and could easily pay $5000 in thirty days. Mr. Keville also explained that his counsel fees (in excess of $250,000) must still be paid by me. I inquired about seeing a bill or invoice. Mr. Keville explained how he does not provide invoices; I must pay whatever he verbally states.

Judge Cynthia Myers and Mr. Keville explained that they sent my attorney letters requesting they answer the interrogatories (though they could not produce the letters) and my attorney could not produce a letter in response to Mr. Keville. This is because no letters were ever sent. The Judge deemed that this was entirely my fault and screamed at me.

Judge Cynthia Myers informed me that she read my claims/interrogatories against the plaintiff, and they were extremely prejudiced against her (though this does not coincide with them not receiving my interrogatories). She said that I could not have any evidence to support my claims. I attempted to interject explaining that I do have evidence, but fell on deaf ears. She did not want to see it.

My attorney explained that the plaintiff's answers were not complete. The judge said she provided what she could. When my attorney explained that the credit card statements could be printed online, it was repeated to him that she provided what she could.

Mr. Keville explained that my interrogatories were not complete, Judge Cynthia Myers explained that I must make them complete and to Mr. Keville liking (not what I could provide) which does not make sense when I provided what I could and that's what she explained about the plaintiff's interrogatories. She said that the plaintiff must have everything she needs to ensure a strong case (against me). My attorney pressed the Judge at this point because they wanted more information from me, but they failed to provide one document for their discovery. The Judge yelled at him repeating herself, "If all they could provide is nothing that is acceptable to this court." "They provided what they could" which was nothing.

This is truly unbelievable. I have to provide documents and answer questions which I do not even know about, while they ignore our discovery requests and I am at fault. But as the Judge said, Natalie needs to be fully prepared in her case against me.

I was told that I cannot have custody of the children as I have not filed the appropriate forms. In addition, I abandoned my family by moving out of state. Judge Cynthia Myers explained that Natalie will be the primary residence and if I had any issues with that I would have to file the necessary paperwork.

She asked me if I currently had any issues with the current parenting time and I explained that it must be updated due to my relocation. She asked if I have any issues with the children being with her currently and if I was prepared to say otherwise. I answered that I do not have any issues right now (as I do not have the necessary court documents submitted). The issue of custody/primary residence must be revisited after the divorce is finalized.

Mr. Keville explained that due to my relocation from MA to NH, he explained that I abandoned the family to live with my girlfriend. He said Natalie does not have to give me visitation or meet half way as during mediation I was still in MA. I attempted to explain Natalie's harassing emails to involve my family, but per the court said that email never happened.

Natalie explained to the court I do not have any rights to the children's education or medical because I will be playing games.

Judge Cynthia Myers awarded Natalie $500 in a month in which I have to pay her directly for her counsel fees. When asked why not her attorney, as her father is paying him, the judge does not care what she puts that money towards? I told her I do not have the money, so she extended the first payment to 60 days. The judge said if I do not pay, judgments (warrants for my arrest) will be issued.

Thursday 11/19/2015: Contacted Natalie via phone at 4:30PM to speak to children. Aaron answered the phone and requested why I haven't paid his mommy. Natalie turned on television and explained that the children rather watch TV then speak to me. She ended the conversation with harassing me by asking how I felt about the court case. She threatened me stating that there are several more court motions which are going through in which I will have to pay her legal counsel (which would be easy for her).

I received another court order from Mr. Keville delivered to Judge Cynthia Myers demanding I make a payment to him in the amount of $5,000 additional.

I received an email from the financial mediator cancelling the November 24th mediation session. Apparently the mediator did something which he cannot practice law until he does some training session.

Friday 11/20/2015: Natalie sent text messages about her cell phone bill being due at this time. Re-informed her that the bill is due on 11/27 and to stop texting me lies.

Friday 11/20/2015: Continued the insurance saga which Natalie started for me. New Jersey Manufacturer's Insurance contacted me in regards to the letter of request I submitted on 11/19/2015. I called her back and spoke to another representative as the one handling my case left for the day. She will tell her to call me back. With money being so tight, I contacted Toyota about their payment, they will not grant another extension, but they modified my payment schedule by a month to help me out.

Monday 11/23/2015: In accordance with the court order, I emailed Natalie for the children's school and medical records.

She refused to provide them. I requested those documents now four times. Later on, I performed the Skype session with the children. Natalie was 15 minutes late from the start time. Eric was jumping on furniture without any pants on. Natalie explained on the video that I must be in New Jersey for visitation during Thanksgiving (against mediation agreement).

Thursday 11/26/2015: Contacted Natalie to speak with children. She informed me that she instructed my father to pick them up. She informed me that he had all three children for the Thanksgiving Holiday and they will remain overnight with him. I contacted my father and he informed me that he took the children at her request last minute and he only had Aaron and Eric. They will not be with him overnight and they will be brought back to their mother after the family party.

Friday 11/27/2015: Afternoon: Received phone call from Natalie harassing me about not going down to New Jersey as she instructed me to do. She put Aaron on the phone because he wanted to talk with me. She hung up the phone within seconds. Later in the evening, I received a voicemail from Natalie and Eric. Eric told me that he slipped on floor and he is okay. He wanted to call me.

Monday 11/30/2015: Contacted Natalie via phone to speak with children. She only put Eric on the line for a short time. She began harassing me stating she will not give me any information in regards to the children.

Tuesday 12/1/2015: I received a response letter from the NJ Courts Ethics Committee in regards to my request for an investigation and complaints for Mr. Keville's unethical business tactics and behavior.

Without any reasoning, they closed out stating it is still an open case, sent Keville a copy of the complaint, and barred me from reapplying due to the matter being closed. Wait, what? They used the following terminology:

"Notification of declination due to pending civil litigation." "The NJ Supreme Court has established policies of not considering any grievance received from a litigant in a pending civil matter, in addition, policy states that after a grievance is made, no other grievance for the same matter can be reopened."

They are claiming that the case is still open so they cannot do anything about Mr. Keville behavior and since I already made an application, I cannot resubmit. So essentially, they will not do anything and I cannot file an appeal. They will not look into the issue. I later found out this practice is done when they don't feel like doing anything or if the attorney involved is the one reviewing their own ethics complaint. Really? That's like a Judge sentencing himself to prison. Love the corruption!

What type of court system does nothing with a complaint, does not do any investigation, denies everything right off the bat, then proceeds to send that complaint to and inform the individuals you are grieving about so that their decisions can be swayed or those letters be used against you?

The answer that I received generated my curiosity as I never heard of a case like this being denied without any reasoning. Not even worth someone looking into it. So, I decided to perform some research. Google, online forums, and many phone calls later to other attorneys and law professionals, I got my answer: When an ethics report (complaint) comes in from the street, the ethic's board is supposed to review it and perform an investigation. The local attorneys in their districts make up these ethics boards.

I was informed that these ethics boards are made up with those lawyers who do exhibit unethical behavior and want that extra layer of protection. It's usually the more ethical and truthful lawyers which stay out of them. So essentially when you are complaining about an attorney, they will protect themselves by either denying it right away or making up a reason to deny it.

This now is all making sense. Why deny my complaint without any firm reasoning and then send it off to the person I am reporting so they can be informed and close out the case for good? It's because Mr. Keville is part of this board and had a chance to review it along with his criminal friends and now both he and his friends are protecting themselves and each other.

Wednesday 12/2/2015: Contacted the Family Court Mediator and requested that mediation be performed over the telephone. She emailed me a copy of the request form. I filled it out and faxed it to her office.

My attorney also sent the following letter to Mr. Keville,

The undersigned represents Defendant, Robert Arlotta in the above-referenced matter.
Please be advised that Plaintiff is in violation of numerous provisions of the November 19, 2015 Court Order. The deadline has passed for her to do the following: respond to Mr. Arlotta's parenting time proposal; complete the required paperwork to allow Defendant access to the children's medical records; and file releases/authorizations permitting Defendant access to the children's school records and to communicate with school personnel.

Additionally, Plaintiff has failed to provide Defendant with information from the children's schools and regarding their extracurricular activities. If Plaintiff does not immediately comply with the Court Order, Defendant will be forced to file an enforcement motion in which counsel fees and costs will be sought. We are hoping to avoid this and, as such, will expect immediate attention to this matter.

Mr. Keville and Natalie both ignored this letter. The court also refused to enforce it.

Thursday 12/3/2015: Spoke to children via Skype. Session lasted approximately ten minutes. Natalie contacted me via phone shortly after explaining that Aaron will be having his baby teeth cavities filled and placed under anesthesia. When asked why I was not informed earlier and why is the dentist filling baby teeth cavities (which he is losing), she explained that she does not have to abide by court orders and as long as I am paying the health insurance, she can do whatever she wants.

Saturday 12/5/2015: Received another bill for NJ EZpass. Natalie has been going to New York City almost every weekend. I wrote another letter to them requesting closure of my account and possible attorney involvement as they refuse to close my account. Natalie has not returned her transponder to close out my account. She has been requested to do this multiple times.

Sunday 12/6/2015: Contacted the Family Court Mediator via email to ensure she received the fax on 12/2/2015.

Monday 12/7/2015: Skype Session with children. Natalie was late for session again. I contacted her via phone to remind her that I am allowed to speak with the children. Eventually, she called on Skype. Aaron was in background calling me by my first name. I had to correct him. Skype session lasted approximately 3 minutes. Natalie began harassing me about more dental work for her. She wishes to do teeth whiting which is not covered by insurance.
Once again I attempted to contact the mediator to ensure she received my fax. She emailed me back stating that the request was not received, however I am still able to complete the session via phone and she will contact me on Tuesday 12/8 at the scheduled time.

Tuesday 12/8/2015: At approximately 9:45AM, the Family Court Mediator contacted me. The session was interrupted due to the court house evacuating due to a bomb threat. The session continued around 11:30AM. Natalie and I appeared via telephone. Overall the session seemed fair. Natalie continued her games with false accusations and flip-flopped on her agreements with me and the mediator. The mediator saw this and recommended that we have a pin-pointed visitation schedule. We went month by month to establish dates and a half way point for the meeting place.

Natalie attempted to get the mediator to place writing in saying that I can only have state certified personnel watch the children if I am not available during my visitation weeks. In addition, she wants only family that she approves to be around the children during those same weeks. Natalie mentioned Michaela by name as someone she does not approve to be alone with the children. This was Natalie's attempt to have Michaela removed from seeing the children or being around them. In addition, it makes my life harder if I need to find a babysitter during my visitation with the kids.

But what she does not know is that Michaela's family is all certified to work with children and her sister and mother work with foster care children. In addition, my family has nurses and state certified teachers which see the children, so we are covered there too!

The mediator explained to Natalie that I could place the same stipulations on her and that it is both unfair and impractical to have a visitation schedule moving forward with those statements as babysitters, day cares, and boyfriends and girlfriends can all change throughout the years. Natalie demanded she put it in. Luckily, the finalized visitation plan that Natalie approved did not have this writing. Perhaps it was overlooked. It did not matter though, as we had our state certified family.

Wednesday 12/9/2015: I received an email from my attorney informing me of the financial mediation session on Thursday 12/10/2015 and requesting information on the visitation mediation. Apparently, the financial mediator (the friend of Mr. Keville) is demanding I appear in his office in New Jersey tomorrow.

I cannot believe this; he said that I can appear via phone. Why is he now demanding I show into his office with such late notice? I work full time. He wants me to pay him, he wants me to settle on Natalie's terms, but decides to screw me in the process. I love this!

I informed my attorney that the visitation mediation is completed. I informed my attorney that as far as the financial mediation is concerned, the mediator did state in his letter and at the last mediation that I can appear via telephone. In addition, I have a ton of work meetings tomorrow lasting from 9:30AM till 2:30PM. The session will have to be after 2:30PM or Friday would work better. In addition, I asked how he can request I be there with only a few hours' notice. My attorney reached out to the financial mediator along with our terms with alimony, taxes, using the standard calculation for child support, and my questions involving the "marital debt" as Natalie has yet to provide a single statement.

Thursday 12/10/2015: Today had the 2nd Financial Mediation with the mediator. It started at 3:00PM and I appeared by phone. I received a phone call from my attorney. He was present during mediation. Both parties were located in separate rooms. Mr. Keville provided the mediator with letters stating that I did not want to mediate nor compromise and he also provided the letter to the governor and the NJ Bar. He used those letters I sent stating his unethical behavior and somehow was able to use them against me. The letters just explained how I did not want to compromise and had no proof with them. My attorney and I never said anything about not wanting to compromise. It was completely falsified.

Natalie was supposed to articulate a rehabilitation plan on when she will go back to work, in addition she was supposed to present evidence of her "marital debt." Her attorney wrote a letter that same day stating they refuse to provide such a document saying she will go back to work and they will NEVER provide documents of the marital debt. I must pay them the numbers they claim without any evidence.

So, with Keville claiming that I did not want to compromise and us showing the mediator that we received a HARD COPY LETTER from Keville stating that they will not, you ask, what did the mediator do about this?

I was chastised about their false claims "I need to have a better attitude about compromising." The mediator said that the letter Keville provided at the last minute was "okay" and "it's acceptable." She does not have to compromise and the letter is absolutely fine. I am the problem, not her. I am not sure about either of these things, I can't believe how one sided this mediator is, perhaps it's because he is friends with the other attorney and does not know my attorney. Whatever, I am getting used to this by now. Poor Natalie has no proof, but I am still guilty and when I have proof, no one wants to see it.

Natalie and Keville utilized the visitation order as leverage for the alimony. At first they informed my attorney and the mediator that they were not accepting the visitation order drawn up on 12/8/2015. However, later they accepted it only if I were to provide them $25,000 a year in alimony. They used the visitation order as leverage to get the money they want.

My attorney fought the good fight and apparently Natalie and her attorney reached agreements on cars, alimony, and child support. I only cared about keeping my visitation order; I want to see my kids. The mediator will provide letter of memorandum to finalize those items of agreement. Marital debt and counsel fees are still an issue and will be brought to the court. I was informed that apparently, Natalie began a "happy dance" after the mediation completed.

After the session, I contacted the children via phone. I spoke to Eric and Aaron for approximately three minutes. Natalie interrupted them and proceeded to ask about the visitation order and began calling me an idiot and stupid in front of the children. While doing this Eric began crying and she hung up the phone.

Friday 12/11/2015: Natalie contacted me via phone multiple times without leaving a message. She emailed me stating Eric has been in an aftercare program since September and she requires me to pay her $1400. She informed me that she will be filing a motion for this money and my arrest. I informed my attorney.

Scared, I read the pendente lite order and it states on #4. *"Defendant shall be responsible to directly pay on a timely basis for the parties' children's school, lessons, and extracurricular activities on the condition that he receive notice of said school, lessons, and activities and Defendant consents to said expense in writing, Defendant's consent shall not be unreasonably withheld."*

Natalie never told me and I never consented to anything. Why would Eric need aftercare if she isn't working?

Saturday 12/12/2015: Contacted Natalie to speak with the baby as it was his birthday today. Heard baby talk and giggle on phone. Natalie began harassing me about paying for child care for Eric and requests that I send her a check for $1400. I informed her I did not receive any specifics or bills from the school nor do I know what child care services she was talking about.

Monday 12/14/2015: Contacted children via phone. Session lasted approximately five minutes. Spoke to Aaron and Eric about the baby's birthday party and their rooms in the New Hampshire house. Natalie began harassing me about paying for day care for Eric and requests that I send her a check for $1400. I informed her I did not receive any specifics or bills from the school nor do I know what day care services she was talking about. I need some type of paperwork.

Thursday 12/17/2015: Contacted Natalie via phone at designated time. She did not call back until hour later. Spoke to children for approximately 5 minutes. I requested that on the 23rd she provide warm clothing and 2 pairs of nice outfits for the children. I informed her that my father will be dropping off a car seat to her for me.

Wednesday 12/16/2015: Medical Letter Issues:

I have been receiving dozens of more medical bills from dentists, pediatricians, and doctors for Natalie's bariatric surgery; most of these bills say "out of network" for services and providers. I cannot possibly pay any of these bills. I can only do one thing. I began sending out multiple letters to all of these bill collectors to let them know what is really happening. Hopefully, they will just write off the expenses:

To Whom It May Concern:

*I am in receipt of your invoice dated ----- 2015 for services performed on -----2015 for Natalie Arlotta. Please be advised, I am the primary holder of the dental/medical insurance, however per court order (attached to this letter) page two, item #5; I am not responsible for unreimbursed health expenses. For reasonable health expenses, I **did not** receive advanced notice of this expense **nor** is this an **AUTHORIRED IN-NETWORK Expense.***

You are not the only medical facility which has fallen for Natalie Arlotta's games. My ex-wife has been visiting out of network doctors and requesting out of network services to play games and drive me into financial ruin. These games have forced me out of state and currently, I am forced to pay more than I make. I am currently sitting on thousands of dollars in medical bills which I cannot possibly pay as I do not make this sort of money.

After careful consideration of the issues involved in this invoice and claim, there is no overdue balance nor any current balance due for the services mentioned above. This matter is closed and I respectfully request that you update your records accordingly. For future service, you must give me advanced notice of the expenses involved and the un-reimbursable charges which can occur before authorization. Thank you.

Friday 12/18/2015: Natalie contacted me via text to pay her T-Mobile and PSEG bills. It is always about money and harassment!

Monday 12/21/2015: Contacted Natalie via phone at designated time requesting she log into Skype. She logged into Skype half hour late. Spoke to children for approximately 2 minutes until she interrupted. I requested copies of the children's school photos. She said she requires me to pay more of her items in exchange. That sounds like extortion to me.

I spoke to Eric and it he obviously gained a significant amount of weight. I asked Natalie how much he weighs and she became irate. She did not answer the weight question about Eric; instead Natalie began to state that I abandoned the family. She requested that I move back down to NJ, in which I asked where I would live. Her response: homeless shelter. I replied that I refuse to live in a homeless shelter, she repeated herself and claimed that me living in a homeless shelter is not the point.

I asked what time she is planning on getting to Bayville, MA for the children drop off. She stated that she will not be bringing the children on 12/23/2015. "If I wish to be a father, I must go down to them." She proceeded to hang up on me. She is refusing to bring them to the half way point because of being lazy. This was the case even during mediation! I am so upset.

I sent text messages to her reminding her that by court order she is to meet me in Bayville, MA on 12/23/2015 and to bring my father's car seat, warm clothing and 2 pairs of nice outfits for the children.

I contacted her local Police and informed them of the situation. They provided the fax number and explained that to call the afternoon of 12/23/2015 the moment she is in violation of the court order.

Monday 12/21/2015: More Medical Bill Games:
I received two more medical bills; totaling $500. The statements clearly state "non-participating provider" and "non-covered charges." This brings the total for her out of network games for this month alone to $3301.

Tuesday 12/22/2015: Emailed my lawyer providing him the medical bill information and asking how the court expects me to pay any marital debt, child support, alimony, etc. As Natalie is constantly doing this. So far, the children's dentist explained that they were requested to fill cavities in teeth that my son is actually losing. I received another letter stating her bariatric surgery and all the associated doctor's visits she performed for it is "medically unnecessary." This is now her second attempt at this surgery with my new medical insurance.

She is playing these games with the medical insurance which is forcing me into financial ruin. Is there a way to inform the judge to get her to stop? In addition, can all these games be taken off the marital debt as they are against the court order and are an obvious game?

Tuesday 12/22/2015: Emailed Lawyer to inform him of Natalie's plans of not brining the children to Bayville, MA on 12/23/2015. Sent it as an FYI only, no need to inform her attorney as the police will be involved. I explained to him that I am going to wait and see if she follows through with this plan tomorrow and if she does, I will be getting police involvement.

Tuesday 12/22/2015: Natalie left voicemail message at 2:20PM requesting I contact her back for the visitation arrangements for the 23rd.

Sent text message to Natalie at 6:20PM requesting what time she is coming to MA tomorrow and to remind her to bring my father's car seat. Natalie called back at 8:36PM. I was able to return her call ten minutes later. **She proceeded to explain "once again" that she is cancelling the visitation, she does not have to follow it and if I want to see the children I must go to NJ.** I was so upset. I could not sleep; I could not do anything but cry; I want to see my children! Why is she doing this? Why do the courts allow this?

Wednesday 12/23/2015: Between 9:52 AM and 4:37 PM exchanged 14 emails with Natalie. I reminded her that she must abide by the court order and meet me in Bayville, MA today for visitation with the children. She explained that she never signed the agreement and that she was never provided my address in NH. I had to remind her that she has sent me certified mail to my address and it has been provided multiple times to her. She agreed and explained that I must go to NJ to pick up the children. Natalie listed Binghamton as a possible town that I live in. I have never lived in that town, but Michaela does. This leads me to think that she has begun private investigation of Michaela.

At 1:30PM, I faxed over copies of visitation order and emails from Natalie explaining she does not have to follow court orders to her Police Department. I contacted them later to explain to hold off until she actually breaks the order (as she is currently going back and forth).

At 2:00PM, Natalie texted me saying to check my email and that I must respond to her. She explained that she would not be able to get to MA until 6:30PM. She explained over the phone that she will not leave NJ until I respond to her email requesting the address and time of the drop off point for the 27th. I explained that it is listed in the court order but she continued that I must respond to her email if she is going to leave NJ. I responded to her email explaining "yes" and all details which are copies of what is in the visitation order.

Later that evening, received multiple texts and voicemails explaining that she left at 3:30PM and running late. She contacted me via text and phone and requested that I meet her in Hartford, CT and to provide her the address of the Cabela's Sporting Goods store to meet there. I provided that information to her and met her in Hartford, CT.

During the phone calls, Natalie was barely able to speak as the children were screaming in the background.

Natalie arrived at Cabela's at **9:30PM.** During the drop off, Natalie provided an EZpass transponder. She explained that she refuses to return her EZpass and I must do it and that I have to pay her car tolls. I requested the school photographs of the children; she still refuses to provide them.

Her mother accompanied her and lost track of Eric as he began to run into the street. I grabbed him and brought him into the car. Her mother explained that she was tired as they did not leave the house until 5:30PM (Natalie was to be in MA at 5:00PM).

I let children visit the Cabela's store and stretch their legs for about an hour. We went to the bathroom and changed diapers. We did not get home until 1:00AM. Aaron requested that Michaela read to him before bed. So with all the boys in the bed, Michaela read to them.

Thursday 12/24/2015: Christmas Eve party at Michaela's house. We performed multiple activities with the children. Arts & Crafts, cooking, read stories, playtime, etc. Kids had a great time! Eric told me today, "daddy you are my best friend." It warmed my heart! I told him that I love him.

Natalie contacted the children via phone. Aaron and Eric refused to eat the veggies and homemade food. They wanted fast food. Baby is still on formula (no solids) and Eric explained that he drinks from bottles. Eric attempted to drink out of a water bottle, but drank like it was a baby bottle. The baby crawled, but showed little signs of standing on his own. Aaron was very violent. He attempted to force-feed Eric a Chap Stick, hit Eric multiple times (and lied about doing it), kicked Michaela's mom, and began smiling while being in timeout and being punished. Aaron and Eric began questioning basic dinner items (they asked what the plate was). All three children have gained a significant amount of weight. Eric and Aaron explained that their mother does not cook and listed multiple fast food restaurants as their favorites.

Friday 12/25/2015: Christmas Day party at Michaela's house. We performed multiple activities with the children. Aaron and Eric ran outside and opened gifts. We read stories, played together, and had a lot of fun. Aaron was showing more aggressive behavior which I had to correct. Natalie called around 8:45PM (past children's bed times to speak with children.

Saturday 12/26/2015: Clean up, toy playing, multiple activities, outside parks. Aaron's aggression subsided until the early evening when Natalie called to speak with him.

Sunday 12/27/2015: Texted Natalie to request the children's school photos again (as she failed to provide on 12/23/2015). She responded to pay for her car registrations (but failed to provide any additional information).

We visited my aunt in MA with the children at 2:30PM. I contacted Natalie multiple times via phone to see if she was going to the visitation drop off point in Bayville, MA. She explained she will be there at 5:00PM.

I arrived at the drop off point in Bayville at 5:00PM. Natalie did not arrive until 5:45PM. I brought the children to her and she lost track of Aaron and Eric as they ran back over to me to give me a hug. They did not want to leave and wanted to stay with me. I embraced, kissed, and spoke to them. I brought them back to their mother's car.

Natalie was once again accompanied by her mother. She showed signs of being under the influence of multiple drugs. She was not paying attention while a car was attempting to park next to them and was oblivious of her surroundings.

I requested the school photographs of the children, she refused to provide them. Natalie began taking pictures of my vehicle (which is a friend's anyway) along with the license plate. I requested she delete them and she refused.

Natalie began aggressively looking into the children's bags for the provided EZpass transponder. She ran over to my car and blocked the driver's side door from closing. She explained that she refuses to return her EZpass and I must do it and that I have to pay. She began more harassment of bills to pay. I explained that I wish to see the bills (along with the USAA bills from financial mediation). She explained she does not have to provide them, "she gives me the number, and I must pay."

Monday 12/28/2015: Logged into Skype at 5:30PM. Natalie was not on. I texted her to see where she was and remind her of the visitation session; she contacted me back via phone explaining the children are at a function and do not wish to go onto Skype. I requested that we perform the session no matter where they are, as I would like to see them. She hung up on me.

I am getting sick and tired of Natalie scheduling events during times I am allowed to see my children. Natalie contacted me later on at approximately 5:50PM. Television was on; food was placed in front of TV. Aaron was watching TV and did not want to talk. Baby was contained in crib, but was talking to me. I requested Natalie bring him by the screen so that I can see him. I asked multiple times until she finally complied.

The baby was excited. Eric was telling me about the gifts he received. Session lasted approximately five minutes. The children (all 3) were in clothes I dressed them in the day prior.

Thursday 12/31/2015: Rescheduled the Skype session with the children due to my cousin's wedding. Attempted to make the phone call on Friday, 1/1/2016. Natalie began harassment for additional money for day care and babysitting. She is now claiming that her mother teaches the children and babysits for approximately $1400 a month which they want me to pay.

Entry #5: No End in Sight (Quarter 1, 2016):

Monday 1/4/2016: Skype session with children. Natalie was hour late to session. I had to request her to allow me access to the children via text messages to her. Eric and Aaron were eating ice cream and McDonalds for dinner. Natalie explained she is cancelling the January 2016 visitation. I explained to her that the visitation will go on as per the court order. Aaron built a Lego figure of a pilot and explained that it was "Michaela the pilot" at that point Natalie cancelled the Skype session. Aaron called me on her cell phone after Skype session was terminated to say goodnight.

At home, I received additional medical documentation from Blue Cross/Blue Shield. Apparently Natalie began the bariatric surgery predetermination process and appointments with this insurance as well. They sent three different denials stating they are medically unnecessary.

Wednesday 1/6/2016: Received Natalie's cable bill. I noticed that over the past two months that the bill was extremely high for a set service. I decided to look at both December and January bills. I noticed a variety of "On Demand" pay per view movies was purchased. I emailed Natalie and she acknowledged that she purchased the movies and I have to pay for them. These are part of the entertainment purchases I must pay for her. I paid a portion of the cable bill for the exception of the movies.

Thursday 1/7/2016: I waited to speak to the children on Skype at the designated time. After a half hour, I contacted Natalie via text message explaining I was waiting for them.

She texted me back and called me. She is not at home and will not allow me to speak with the children today.

Monday 1/11/2016: Skype session with children. Natalie was ten minutes late. Eric was begging to come up and see me. He started to pack during session and wanted to leave that moment to "come live with daddy."

Wednesday 1/13/2016: Received text message from Natalie requesting the location of the motorcycle keys.

Thursday 1/14/2016: Waited for children on Skype. I texted Natalie at 5:30PM to remind her that it is my time with the children. She called via phone and explained she needed another ten minutes as she was not home. Skype session started half hour late. Both during the phone call and Skype session, Natalie explained she requires the keys to the motorcycle. When asked if she was going to sell it, she did not answer. I informed her that I do not know where the keys are, they could possibly be in her Corolla at Harry's house and if she was going to pick the vehicle up. She explained she needed to move the motorcycle. I told her that she does not require the keys to do that. Spoke to children, informed their mother to pack warm clothes, hats, gloves, shoes, and snow boots. She explained that she will be in Bayville, MA at 6:00PM.

Friday 1/15/2016: Visitation started (MLK holiday). I contacted Natalie about the visitation time and when to expect her. She stated 5:00PM. I requested she provide the children's school photos which I paid for. She did not comply as I must pay her additional alimony under the table for her to release them to me. Later, Natalie contacted me stating she would arrive at 5:00PM.

She did not show until after 6:00PM. During exchange Natalie was inquiring whose car I was driving. It was quite apparent that it was Michaela's. The children did not eat, so I brought them into Cracker Barrel to eat something. Michaela and I expected this and we already got a table and Michaela ordered them some food. Natalie and her mother later realizing that Michaela may have been with me decided to come into the restaurant and follow us. Natalie stared down Michaela while she passed by.

Monday 1/18/2016: Visitation ends (MLK holiday). Natalie requested via phone multiple times that I drop the children off at Cracker Barrel in MA at 3:00PM. During car ride to MA, Aaron was explaining that he eats Dunkin Donuts on a regular basis. I arrived at the Cracker Barrel at 3:00PM per Natalie's request. She did not show until 4:00PM. She was an hour late. I inquired why she was pressing me to be there at 3:00PM when she wasn't going to be there at that time. She just started laughing and told me her lateness was my fault. I gave the children a big hug and kiss and left them with her.

Tuesday 1/19/2016: Natalie texted me requesting that I contact her. Later that afternoon received phone call from Aaron/Eric's school about being on lock down and that lock down is cancelled (all clear) due to a shooting/bomb threat. I contacted Natalie at around 4:00PM to check in with children. She did not allow me to speak to them and continued requesting additional money.

Wednesday 1/20/2016: Received voicemail and phone call from my attorney. They do not have my current information and are under the belief that my divorce is "uncontested." I informed them that I am fighting her attorney costs and her debt. Apparently they have not reached out to the opposing attorney yet. Sent follow up emails to correct this situation.

Thursday 1/21/2016: Skype session with children. I contacted Natalie via text at 5:30PM to remind her. She was over an hour late for the session. Children were running around and eating off the floor. I asked Natalie about their diets. She blamed their current habits on me and threatened me to come down to NJ to be a father to the children.

Saturday 1/23/2016: Natalie inquired if I had the children's sleds. I informed her via text message that I do not have the sleds. They were left in NJ at her residence.

Sunday 1/24/2016: Natalie texted at 6:30PM stating to pay her T-Mobile cell phone bill. The bill is not due until 1/27.

Monday 1/25/2016: Received letter from my attorney. The letter was from Natalie's attorney and dated the 22nd. He wrote that "after meeting at length with his client and her father, they are cancelling all visitation and financial mediation agreements." They are attacking my full salary and not allowing me to see children to maximize the child support. My attorney said it is too late to cancel the trial that is scheduled for tomorrow. He will go to trial and explain to the judge the issues.

I received a phone call and email from my attorney's office stating that I have been authorized to appear via telephone. However, looking back at the original trial request documents, my request to appear over the phone was already approved. So I don't know what has changed from that time till now.

Received another voicemail from attorney stating that we must appear in court because my ex-wife's attorney intentionally filed the letter in late so that we must appear and I would have to pay for everyone's attorney fees.

Natalie called twice via phone to explain they will be an additional ten minutes late. She began pressing via the phone calls and during the Skype session inquiring if I was going to be attending the court trial in person. She stressed the importance of me having to be present in the court room.

Children were in front of television eating Wendy's from bags. I asked Aaron what they were eating and he said "French fries, but it's okay daddy- they are healthy." Aaron was also explaining how they had hot chocolate earlier. The baby was in his normal spot confined to his crib in the living room watching television.

Tuesday 1/25/2016: Court trial began at 11:30AM (3 hours late). Judge Cynthia Myers was presiding. The following occurred: My attorney and opposing counsel had to meet and argue over child support. They did not come to an agreement and Judge Cynthia Myers ordered an intensive settlement conference in which I am court ordered down to NJ. Apparently opposing counsel requires payment beyond what I make.

Thursday 1/28/2016: Contacted Natalie via phone. She only allotted three minutes for me to speak with the children and hung up the phone.

My attorney contacted me and left a voicemail, the divorce will now go into the next step of "intensive settlement conference" due to the plaintiff not accepting her own demands and wanting more. They want to know if I would like the Judge that we have overseeing the case preside or have her authorize another judge. I contacted him back saying I want a new judge to oversee the settlement. My attorney sent a letter to Judge Cynthia Myers requesting a new judge.

Monday 2/1/2016: Contacted Natalie via phone. She did not allow me to speak with children. Asked if she will be brining children this weekend and she said she did not see that in the visitation order.

Tuesday 2/2/2016: Natalie's TV bill went from $121 a month to over $170 a month. Contacted Optimum online and they will not release any information to me or discuss the account. Emailed Natalie the following:

Natalie,

Your Optimum Television bill went up to $170 a month. Your Optimum Silver went from $65 to $80, cable box from $7 to $9. I contacted Optimum and spoke to "Brenda."

They will not release any account information to me or discuss extending their promotional offers. They will only speak to you.

Please contact them at have the bill fixed prior to payment of the $120. Thank you.

I later found out Natalie upgraded her account again!

Thursday 2/4/2016: Contacted children via phone. Natalie only allotted five minutes with them. She later left me a voicemail at 8:00PM saying there will be over five inches of snow in Bayville, MA during the visitation weekend and she is cancelling visitation.

Friday 2/5/2016: Natalie contacted me both via email and by phone very irate. She demanded that I come to NJ to pick up the children because there was a snow storm in MA or reschedule for a weekend of her choosing. I responded back to her that I understand her concern with the weather and driving and attempted to contact her earlier and left her a voicemail.

I informed her that I cannot change my work schedule around her social schedule. I had to schedule all my work and other activities around the visitation schedule and as I do not control the weather, certain circumstances may arise. I love my children, I want to see them, and whatever she does is on her. I do not wish to endanger the children and gave you an option for the last weekend in February. I cannot change my work schedule and other scheduled events this month to your convenience at a drop of a hat.

As previously stated (even during mediation) I am not available the 2nd & 3rd weekends this February. If we cannot come to an agreement for the last weekend in this month I must abide by the visitation schedule. I cannot risk going against an order because the moment this happens you will be sending it to your attorney which your father pays to ensure I get placed back into court for failure to abide by a court order. We have a court order visitation schedule and I will abide by all orders per Judge Cynthia Myers's last conversation with me.

Natalie contacted me and stated at first that Aaron had arrangements on the last week in February, then it changed to she had plans, then changed again saying she will bring the children up the last week in February. This was all during a five minute conversation. After the conversation, she emailed me stating that she is cancelling this week's visitation and that the last week in February is still not accepted by her (even though she agreed over the phone).

At 7:45PM she left a voicemail to contact her back.

Monday 2/8/2016: I was late for the Skype session due to an increase in weather related traffic from Boston. Natalie left a one second voicemail at 5:35PM and texted me saying she was on Skype. I contacted her back and she stated that she left the children unattended for a brief time, but her mother is now with the children. Natalie asked if I was alone. I said yes, then she began questioning me about Eric's development and if his issues were a delusion of hers and what my opinion was. I told her she knows my opinion on these matters and I have yet to see any classification medical records and it is my belief that both Aaron and Eric are developmentally on track and are "fine."

She was explaining that the children are both classified. I explained to her that I never agreed or seen any classification paperwork. She did not have any response.

Her request for my opinion was prompted by recent school events. Apparently she was invited to the school to have a parent-teacher conference (IEP) on Eric's development and knew of this meeting prior to its commencement. Eric will be in full-time school for kindergarten and in the mainstream classroom.

I informed her that I was not told by either her or the school about this VERY IMPORTANT IEP meeting (per court order, I must be informed prior to its commencement). She did not have any response.

Tuesday 2/9/2016: The children left a voicemail wishing me a happy birthday. I contacted them back via phone to say thank you. Eric was telling me about his day at school. He had fun. At work, I worked with my boss to reschedule a training session in Oklahoma. Unfortunately, I cannot attend now as I have trial & pretrial on March 14 & March 22.

Thursday 2/11/2016: Skype session with children. Natalie was half hour late. Once again, the children were eating fast food on the floor and exhibiting wild behavior.

Friday 2/12/2016: Received email from lawyer about the financial mediation lawyer not getting paid. The mediator (who is a lawyer) stated that he is going to make an application to the court for judgment against me if I do not pay him.

I wrote a letter to him explaining that not only did the mediation fail, but because of all these games, I cannot afford to pay him in full. I sent a check for $100 and explained I'll pay him that much each month. I informed him that Natalie and her attorney have gone back on all the items within the Memorandum of Understanding.

Monday 2/15/2016: Received email and voicemails from Natalie explaining she is cancelling the March visitation due to it being so close to the February visitation. Contacted her via phone and asked why she is really cancelling it. She explained that she is going to a wedding/party for a friend. I explained that I already made arrangements with my father to see the children during that weekend in March. She contacted my father and emailed me explaining that she will allow the visitation to continue as planned because my father will drive the children up to New Hampshire (Once again, she doesn't feel like making any effort).

Thursday 2/18/2016: Received voicemail from Natalie at 11:30AM just requesting I call her. No Skype session with children, as I was very sick and could hardly talk. Emailed Natalie the cancellation request and explained I will speak to them during the weekend.

Thursday 2/18/2016: Received email from my lawyer asking the following (even though I told them I would be away for two weeks:

I am preparing your Intensive Settlement Conference statement.

Please provide a response to the following:

Custody: You are looking for the custody/parenting time set forth in the December 8 parenting time agreement?

Debt: You want to take yours, she takes hers, and you split the marital?

Alimony: What do you want to propose? How much, for how many years? What do you want imputed? At the mediation we agreed to her being imputed 20 and you pay 25 for 6 years. Please note that we are going to include her father's contributions.

Pendente Lite Support: How much have you paid so far and can you provide me with proof, a summary and documents?

Can you provide anymore checks re: payments your wife has received from brother/father?

Saturday 2/20/2016: Received phone call from Natalie and spoke to children for approximately five minutes until Natalie hung up the phone.

Monday 2/22/2016: Contacted Natalie at 5:30PM (the agreed visitation time). She stated that she was not home. She told me to contact her mother. I informed her that I do not have her mother's phone number, in addition, I reminded her of the court orders barring me from contacting her family after she began harassing mine. She overheard the airport announcement speakers (as I was in the airport at the time) and began asking me where I was, where I was going, and needing all my travel arrangements and purpose. I informed her that my travel is none of her business. She continued with the harassing questions and commentary. I asked when I could speak to the children and she informed me that she would have them call me in 20 minutes.

I sent her a text message at 6:15 (She should have contacted me at 5:50PM) explaining that I would like to speak with my children. She called me back and allowed Aaron to just say hello. I asked if I could speak to him more and she refused. I asked to speak to Eric; she refused to let me speak to him. She stated that he was very sick with strep throat.

Tuesday 2/23/2016: Began collecting information for lawyer to answer Thursday 2/18's questions. Went to the Bank of America (BOA) website and attempted to log into my ex-wife's account to see if I can see the "marital debt" which her and her attorney fail to provide. I actually got access. The debt during April 2015 was $12,000. Currently that number has doubled. There were dozens of charges for entertainment, travel, etc. in the past few months, in addition daily (multiple) trips to fast food restaurants. I provided all the answers and documentation to the lawyer and emailed him a copy of this statement as well.

Thursday 2/25/2016: Contacted Natalie at 4:30PM. I asked if Eric was feeling better and if I should be picking up medicine for him. She stated that he is feeling a little bit better but is still on medicine. Eric was placed on prescription antibiotics. I requested that she pack them with him, but she refused.

She also stated that Aaron requires Miralax. She first stated that I needed to purchase it, but then stated he was only going to be in New Hampshire for three days, so he would be fine without it (though I would believe if he was constipated for three days that could lead to toxic shock). She stated that he was severely constipated and this is a normal aliment for him.

I asked about the baby's weight. She stated that he is going for another checkup and he is approximately 32lbs. He is still on whole milk/formula.

She began asking personal questions about my life in NH, what I plan on doing with the children, and my travel. She was harassing me once again about her having control of what I do. I informed her that my daily activities do not require her approval in which she stated that I was being a "dick." I requested a reason why she is starting a new court case stating I haven't paid her bills (which I have been). She became irate. I reminded her that the conversations must be kept about the children only. She became more irate and hung up.

Later that evening, I emailed Natalie to please pack children's school pictures, Eric's prescription, snow clothes, boots, wet weather clothing for the children as it is raining/snowing this weekend. Please provide an ETA tomorrow when she will be arriving at the Cracker Barrel. She responded shortly after saying she is leaving NJ at 3:00PM.

Friday 2/26/2016: Natalie contacted me in the morning stating she was going to be at the Cracker Barrel at 5:30PM. I left work to ensure I got there at that time. Natalie contacted me via phone at 5:15pm, 6:45pm, and 7:15pm inquiring where I was (demanding it) and requesting that I meet her in Danbury, Waterbury, and eventually Hartford. I refused. Natalie contacted me 7:45pm saying she was 15 minutes away. She arrived at the Cracker Barrel at 8:00pm. (2 ½ hours late).

She was with her mother who was smoking next to the baby. Natalie kept calling the baby by his middle name. Apparently they do not use his first name at their home. Natalie contacted me 1 ½ hours later after I left with the children. She inquired where I was and wanted to speak to Aaron off speaker phone. He was already asleep and I explained that to her. She became irate.

Saturday 2/27/2016: Visitation day with children. We all had a blast! We went on nature walks and beach runs (also looked at some ice fishing). The children have noticeably gained a significant amount of weight. No phone calls from psycho pants; thank god.

Sunday 2/28/2016: I contacted Natalie at 9:00AM to arrange a pick up time for the children. She said she will meet me at the Cracker Barrel at 3:00pm. I waited at the Cracker Barrel with the children for 45 minutes. Natalie finally showed up late as normal. While waiting for her, we walked around the Cracker Barrel with the baby and played checkers with the children to pass the time.

Natalie began taking pictures of Michaela's car. I put the children and their clothing into her minivan and found dozens of fast food kid's meals and wrappers scattered in the backseats. The car was not cleaned in a very long time and smelled. It also appeared that Natalie had a car accident as the left side of the rear bumper and quarter panel were severely damaged. Natalie was alone (not with her mother). She asked me why am I short-worded with her. I explained that everything I say is spun for court, so unless the conversation deals directly with the children, it does not happen. I informed her that I will see her in court.

Within ten minutes of leaving, Natalie contacted me asking why I am angry with her. Apparently she has forgotten everything she has done the past year and a half. I hung up on her.

Thursday 3/03/2016: Skype session with children. Natalie contacted me via text at 4:30PM. I conducted the Skype session with the children. Natalie's friend and son were present during the session. Natalie explained that my father will be picking up the children at 10:00AM tomorrow, Friday 3/4/2016. I inquired about the children's school schedule. She stated that she was not sending the children to school that day so that they can avoid rush hour traffic. On the video, Aaron had a nose bleed (which Natalie did not see) and he stated that he hates daddy and told her to hang up on me. Natalie ended session after five minutes.

In the mail, I received a toll bill from an unpaid toll on the Henry Hudson Parkway (NYC) with a picture of Natalie's car. Sent email to Natalie to pay her toll bill and remind her I am not responsible for her unpaid tolls (as we went through back in November for the EZpass.

Friday 3/4/2016: Received phone call and text message explaining there was another "swatting" phone call today. The Brendon County K-9 Unit searched the children's schools and found no threat. I received another message from the children's school. There was now another school shooting threat. The schools went into lock down. Two in one day!

My father arrived with the children at 6:00PM. I cooked and fed everyone dinner. I unpacked the clothes bag Natalie prepared. She did not pack sufficient amount of clothing or clothing that fit the children. Children's hair was long and unkempt; in addition, they gained a significant amount of weight.

Natalie texted and called me at 9:20PM. She wanted to speak with the children (however, children were already asleep) then she wanted to speak to my father (who was also asleep). I inquired what she needed, but she refused to tell me. Natalie provided cash to my father to pay her toll bill I received.

Saturday 3/5/2016: Had a blast with the children. Ran to the beach (Lake Front), gave children haircuts, Space Shuttle Discovery Center, lunch, then Bass Pro & Dollar Tree to pick up puzzles for them. Eric kept requesting a fishing pole for his birthday. I let him pick one out and purchased it.

Since children appear to gain a lot of weight, I decided to weigh the children. The following weights were recorded:
Aaron- 79lbs.
Eric- 55lbs.
Wyatt- 20lbs.

Sunday 3/6/2016: Packed up children and ran to the beach (Lake Front) again. Natalie called at 8:45AM. She did not leave a message. My father left with the children at 10:30AM. Children were crying and did not want to leave. They begged to stay up in New Hampshire with daddy. Natalie called later at 5:00PM asking what I was doing, how the weekend went and wanted to know what I was working on. I informed her the weekend went well and did not provide any additional information.

Monday 3/7/2016: I conducted the Skype session with the children at 5:30PM. Natalie stated that Aaron claimed that I am moving back to NJ. She asked if it was true and if I was moving back to NJ. I informed her that whether I move back to NJ or not, or any move in general the only concern is that visitation will have to change other than that it is none of her business.

I requested to speak to the children multiple times during the entire session with her constant refusal to answer her questions first before speaking with the children.

She mentioned multiple times that it is to the benefit of the children if I move back to her county in New Jersey. I told her that I am unable to afford anything in NJ. She began asking me how much I pay in rent in NH. She continued the harassment stating that I can speak to children more if I moved back to her county.

Eric came on the line and had red chocolate all over his face. He stated that he loved chocolate. I told him he cannot eat too much of it. Natalie interrupted him and stated that she would grant me more influence in their lives and their habits if I lived in her county in New Jersey.

Eric was begging to come back up to daddy's house in New Hampshire. Aaron came on the line with Eric and asked to come up next Friday. I told him I would love them to come up and asked their mother. She came on the line and explained that it would be too much stress for the children (even though they were begging to come up).

I inquired with Eric if he was going outside since it is a nice day out; once again Natalie interrupted him and stated that they will not go to the park or outside.

I visited with baby Wyatt. While talking with him I asked if baby Wyatt had free reign around the apartment to learn to walk. Natalie stated that she does not give him free reign (only sometimes). Natalie concluded asking me when the settlement conference is, I told her to consult her attorney.

She continued her harassment by inquiring if I was going to be physically in NJ for the divorce proceedings. I asked why she didn't give the baby free reign. What is she so busy doing, where she cannot watch the baby for a few minutes so he can walk and crawl around? She hung up with "I'm busy."

I hate this. These sessions are supposed to be with the children and me. This is not her time to harass me; it's my time with the children. She is consistently interrupting the children and my time with them.

Tuesday 3/8/2016: In addition to the fishing pole, picked up a ton of gifts for Eric's birthday. I wrapped them all up along with the fishing pole. I am excited to have him here on his special day. I already prepared the house with birthday celebrations.

Thursday 3/10/2016: Received a list of demands by Natalie and her attorney. It was sent to the judge. In it, they once again used the letters I sent to the Governor and Senators against me. They want thousands of dollars in child support, alimony, and legal costs. Each of which is beyond the amounts specified in standard calculators and well beyond my salary.

I had my Skype session with the children. Spoke to Eric and Aaron. They said they had a bad day at school. Natalie told Eric to sit down; Eric was very upset with his mother and was yelling at her.

Eric kept on saying they were going to the park. Aaron stated they were going to Van Sun Park in New Jersey. Aaron stated that he had a bad day at school. He got in trouble. He forgot what he did. I asked his mother what he did and she refused to answer the question. She began harassing me about if I was going to be in NJ for the court case on Monday, where was I staying, when I was going to be there. I informed

Natalie that these Skype sessions are for me to visit with the children, not for an opportunity for her to harass me. Natalie ended the conversation after I refused to answer her questions.

Sunday 3/13/2016: Michaela and I drove down to NJ. I showed her where I lived, where my children lived, where I grew up, and we ate at a well-renowned diner which I ate at in high school. It was really nice showing her all this. I mentioned to her that I knew this would be the last time I will ever be here in this state. It was very solemn moment for me.

Monday 3/14/2016: Intensive Settlement Conference (ISC)/ Pre-Trial Court Case. I arrived at the court house at 8:30AM.

Natalie and her attorney arrived shortly afterwards and were allowed to enter the Judge's personal chambers and conference room. They were allowed to speak with the judge before my attorney arrived. During this time, Natalie attempted multiple times to come over to me when her attorney left the hallway. I quickly got up to use the bathroom every time I saw her approach me. My attorney came shortly before 10:00AM.

We entered the new judge's courtroom while another case was going on. This case was an appeal for a father who was denied visitation and rights to his children. His ex-wife was making claims that he was hospitalized for drug abuse and was a known alcoholic and drug offender. The judge reviewed the specifics of the case and began explaining the history of this case to the court room. This poor guy lived with his children in Canada. His ex-wife took the children illegally to the U.S. where her family was. Instead of fighting her leaving the country, he decided to move to NJ to where she relocated the children. Upon him moving here, he attempted to see the children and his ex-wife refused to let him see them. He brought the case to the NJ courts and had a judge (who has been mentioned before) oversee the case and without any proof of his alcoholism and using statements by the wife's family; the judge ordered supervised limited visitation. This was now an appeal to that decision.

The woman drew up a partial transcript and provided it to the judge. This guy and his attorney had no idea where this transcript came from and it was completely falsified. His ex-wife brought her whole family to the court room (without telling the judge or this guy) to make statements on his alcohol abuse.

The woman and her attorney asked the judge to allow the "never before seen transcripts" and her family to testify that the ex-husband was an abuser and drug addict. The judge stated that this is not a trial by ambush and he did not appreciate these tactics. The ex-wife's attorney stated it was allowed by other County Judges. So the judge made a deal with this gentleman. The judge ordered a drug (piss) test right after the court hearing. If the guy came up hot, he remains with supervised visitation, if he passes, he and his ex will go to visitation mediation with no supervised visitation.

They fought the judge again now stating that the kosher food he provided to the children is not kosher enough. The judge did not entertain this and said this is a secular court and he will not even deal with that issue.

This appeal worked out in the ex-husband's favor. But what I did not understand is the statements saying that other county judges allowed for someone's word to be the proof of allegations. So if you said that the sky is purple, it is unless the Judge wants to hear anything different. This seemed really backwards. So I did some homework on both my Judge which destroyed my life along with the court house. To give you a brief Brendon County Court House Background, here is a brief synopsis of this family court:

I performed a brief internet search of Judge Cynthia Myers. She has a long history with volunteering at women's shelters and organizations with battered women. It is noble of her, but it also creates an almost conflict of interest; as she may view most (if not) all men as aggressors. This was evident in my court appearances, as I was considered a "criminal" even though it was just a regular divorce case.

The Brendon County Court house has a long history as well. Most recently, two judges have found themselves in the news. Due to legality issues, I cannot mention the cases, but you can easily Google search Brendon County court house and their current issues.

One case involves an older gentleman who had several children and was divorced. Since his divorce, the mother handed over custody of all the children to the father. The court house imprisoned him to continue making child support payments to his ex-wife even though she does not have custody of those children. The court house explained that his imprisonment is what is best for the children. His children set up a "Go Fund me" website to help pay for their dad's legal fees and basic necessities. Right now in the news, their mother who is still fighting for the additional alimony is now bringing her ex-husband's 83 year old mother to court to pay her fees. You can google it, just type in *"Father Jailed For Non-Support Of Kids Who Live With Him Gets Two More Weeks In Jail."*

Another case involves a Judge which ordered a defendant husband to pay more than he makes. The case was on video tape, and you can see the husband's attorney attempt to explain that his client cannot possibly pay what they want him to and how that court order is against the gentlemen's civil rights and the U.S. Constitution. While on the video, the Judge explained how the U.S. Constitution is null and void in his court room.

There are more cases than these two. Right now there are dozens of lawsuits against the family division of this court house, and dozens more where men have sued the judges. Unfortunately, the majority of these cases are thrown out due to technicalities or for no reasons at all. Now, you may be asking, what has been done with these judges in particular? NOTHING! There were no repercussions, no superior court interventions, or reprimands. This behavior is tolerated, justified, and legal.

Next, the judge called my case. Natalie, I, and both attorneys came to the stand. The judge asked where I lived and I stated my address in New Hampshire. He asked if I was an "A&P" and if I had an "IA." I told him I had an A&P, but no "IA." Natalie's attorney wrote this down. He began saying that he saw that the plaintiff was living in her father's building and that I had to move to MA and later NH. He said that one thing he knows well is as far as grandparents are concerned, "No" is never in their vocabulary. He asked me what I did for the government. I explained that I am an inspector and he stated he knew what that was as he owned an aircraft and was a pilot.

The judge stated that this divorce is based solely on money and finances. He explained that he did not consider ADHD a mental disorder to base child support on and he did not see any proof that they are diagnosed. Finally, I wish the other judge could see it that way. He explained that the numbers can be hashed out in his conference room. He requested the attorneys to have Natalie and I sit in his court room to see other cases and how messy cases can get. My attorney spoke saying that there is no need for that and we can discuss the case in the conference room. The judge released us.

Later, saw that Mr. Keville wrote down my conversation with the judge and my "A&P" which is a Federal certificate. He has written down previously that he can take my certificates and licenses if he is not paid. I'd be happy if he attempts to go after my federal certificate. I'm not sure how he can do that. Only the Administrator of the government (my ultimate boss) can do that. In addition, it will bring this case to a federal judge to look at all the evidence.

We entered the judge's conference room which Mr. Keville and my ex-wife were set up.

Visitation with the children was the first item the plaintiff brought up. She wants to scrap the entire program and only allow me to see my children on dates she determines and that I must travel to NJ to see them. She also requested that there will be no overnight visits (as it will adversely affect the child support).

She explained that she picks up the children at 3:00PM and does not get into MA until 7:30PM.

Her attorney asked me what time I get home at night with the children. I explained anywhere from 9:30PM to 10:00PM. He began harassing me stating that it takes me a shorter time and that due to his client having rush hour, New York City Traffic to contend with that I should change the meeting spot to NY. I attempted to explain that on my way back to MA with the children my commute is long as well (contend with Boston traffic) and that on any given day either the plaintiff or myself will have to contend with traffic. It is fair for both sides; we both must sit in traffic.

Her attorney began explaining that Bayville, MA is not the centralized geographical spot. I had to remind him that the court appointed mediator found that spot and it is a good location as the children have family in that area if they need to stretch or get fed before continuing to their house up in NH.

Natalie and her attorney also explained that the visitation order did not allow for longer visits as traveling on Fridays and Sundays are too long for the children. I explained that the court mediator looked at the children's school calendars and awarded me the long weekends where they had either a Friday or Monday off. I attempted to show them the court order but I was told that it does not exist.

My attorney asked for a proposal since they want it changed. They did not have a proposal. They requested that I go down to NJ and spend a few hours with the children and stay with my estranged father's girlfriend's house. I refused and explained I want to spend overnights with my children and I refuse to live in my father's girlfriend's house (which there isn't even a guarantee they would allow me to stay). I was informed once again that Brendon County has a homeless shelter that can accommodate me.

I explained that the court mediator said to both Natalie and I that traveling once a month is a minimum and the judge would honor that agreement. I explained that I would like to see my children more and want to increase visitation to twice a month.

They said that perhaps every other month visitation if I pick up the children and drop them off in NJ would be better for their travel. I attempted to explain that is the same as if their mother would meet me half way. They did not see it that way. I flat out said that it's not hard on the children, she (Natalie) just did not want to drive. I was told that I could not say that.

My attorney inquired about a two month interval and an interval that did not have monthly visits, but a longer stay with the children. He explained that it would be less traveling for the children and more overnights with the children. Plaintiff does not want any overnights.

My attorney asked if I could have the children on every school vacation and two months during the summer if travel was the issue. They responded again, I would have to deliver and pick up the children in NJ and no overnights.

I put an end to this stating that the visitation is not disastrous and I want to keep it as is then. The judge will now have to determine when, where, and how I see my children.

Next was finances- Natalie stated that I will be getting a $50,000 pay raise along with $100 a day in per diem travel allotments and that she wants verbiage inside the decree stating that my child support WILL be automatically adjusted every year for a $50k increase each year. I told the group this is untrue and provided documentation stating that the leadership detail I was performing for work does not give me a raise or imply as such. My ex and her attorney looked at each other and stated that the document I had does not exist.

My attorney stated that this will happen anyway, so we proposed to Natalie that anytime I get an increase in salary by $15,000 or more, child support will be revisited in court. Natalie said that even an increase by $1 she is entitled to it. Natalie said she would agree to anytime I receive a promotion in rank, child support would be revisited in the court. I asked if the same would apply if I was fired, reassigned, or demoted. She agreed but her attorney interjected stating that I must pay that amount even if I get demoted as my potential salary remains the same. I asked how that was fair, he did not respond.

As far as alimony we were all going back and forth and came to numbers of $30,000 for 3 years, $20,000 for the other 3 years. No imputation of income. Her attorney explained to her that those numbers are the same as the 25k for six years and that they discussed that I can pay more.

Due to the children having ADHD, Natalie and her attorney want both an elevated child support and elevated alimony. My attorney stated they cannot have both. Apparently, they will not impute income on her at any time because she does not have the ability to work especially with the children being at home. She asked about child care. Mr. Keville explained that I would have to pay for it.

My attorney stated that Mr. Keville explained that his client did not utilize any out of network doctors or medical procedures. My attorney informed him that we have the documents and documents don't lie.

Mr. Keville stated I was playing games with the court and cancelled mediation agreements. I provided the letter from her attorney doing those things and cancelling all agreements. He stated that the letter did not exist and I was lying (and he will make sure the judge knows I am lying).

At around 1:00PM my attorney stated to the group that we should break for lunch. Natalie stated at this time that she must go home to during lunch to discuss the divorce proceeding with her father and mother before anything is accepted. Mr. Keville stated that he was being paid by the plaintiff's father. However, the court KNOWS he is not in contact with her father and is not being paid by him. So he is lying to the court, just wonderful!

My attorney and I brought this up and he stated that anything he says behind closed doors is not to be brought up in court (but anything we say does). He stated that it was the plaintiff's father's instructions not to agree to anything in mediation and that only he (plaintiff's father) will agree to the terms and imputation of income. My attorney stated that if that is the case, her father should be present, but Mr. Keville explained that her father will not go to any court proceeding but he did invite him. I inquired why the plaintiff's father and mothers opinions are overriding and interfering with my divorce.

They stated that if their figures and demands are not met, the plaintiff's children will be thrown out to the street. Yes, grandpa will have them thrown out into the street.

Natalie brought up her marital debt. I attempted to explain how she had credit cards in her name, I had ones in mine. I explained that I have approximately $5,000 of the total marital debt. Her attorney said that my marital debt doesn't count- only Natalie's. Natalie began laughing at this point stating she paid off my credit cards prior to the divorce and she had proof. My attorney asked her for it and she could not provide it and began changing her story.

My attorney asked her how much is her marital debt and the proof. She "believes" its $18,000 along with $5,000 in student loan debt. My attorney asked for statements. We were told that we don't need to see them. My attorney explained we need them because there are cruises and expenses which we are not responsible for. They refused to provide them.

Mr. Keville brought up his exorbitant legal fees. He stated that he has yet to be paid and his bills are outstanding. Natalie began laughing and Mr. Keville had a huge smile on his face.

My attorney and I stated that he already explained that he is being paid by Natalie's father. He now changed his story. My attorney asked for an invoice and payment information. They will not provide it. Mr. Keville explained how he does not provide invoices; I must pay whatever he verbally states.

At this point I became mad and I told him that I would never pay him, and he began laughing saying that the judge already determined I will and that I have. Mr. Keville explained that my blood sugar was low and I am getting back into my criminal ways and we should end the mediation. In addition, mediation must be cancelled because he is not authorized to settle anything without Natalie's father's approval.

My ex-wife during this quick break contacted her father and her attorney asked to speak with mine. My attorney came back and explained that the mediation is cancelled. I can only assume that daddy dearest did not agree to any terms.

Tuesday 3/15/2016: Received $6,000 bill from my divorce attorney. I had to split the amount amongst several credit cards and max them all out. I am financially ruined!

Sent multiple emails to my divorce attorney:

Email #1:
As you are well aware, it is my firm belief that the plaintiff and her father are going to continue to use these mediation games to draw up my legal costs and will go nowhere as her father and mother are going to have to sign off on whatever amount is negotiated.

I would like to continue to trial and end this. We are fully prepared and documents completed along with the trial date (as long as Judge Cynthia Myers is available).

The mediation sessions are a waste of time and since Mr. Keville has enough time and resources (being paid) to draw this until I have no more money left to go to trial without legal counsel, this needs to be completed so I can get on with my life.

Email #2 (Divorce Attorney): Provided attorney with my 2015 W-2 & current bank account balance.

Thursday 3/17/2016: Saint Patrick's Day. I logged into Skype at the designated time of 5:30PM. I waited ten minutes for Natalie to contact me. I texted her twice to let her know that I was on Skype and waiting to speak with the children.

She eventually contacted me via Skype. She brought the children to Bounce U to play. Once again scheduling activities during the short times I have to see them.

I spoke to the baby; he said "dada." Aaron and Eric were unavailable. I informed Natalie that this was my time with the children and she should schedule this around my time with the children.

Natalie later contacted me via phone. I spoke to Eric and Aaron. Natalie interrupted Eric and began to explain that the other day Eric asked a friend of hers, Greg to play with him and was calling him daddy, she also mentioned that he had a "melt down" begging for daddy the other day. I asked why she was telling me all this, to make me feel bad? She said "No, I just want to let you know how you are harming your children." I hung up the phone.

Thursday 03/17/2016: My attorney wrote the following letter to the Judge presiding over my case:

Please be advised that the undersigned represents Defendant, Robert Arlotta in the referenced matter. Kindly be advised that we were told by Your Honor's staff that an uncontested hearing was scheduled for Tuesday, March 22, 2016; however, the parties have not come to any agreement. Kindly have Your Honor's staff advise as to whether trial will begin on March 22, 2016 or, if not, the date at which time trial will begin.

Apparently someone (and I think I know who) is messing around with this case and providing the court with inaccurate information.

Friday 3/18/2016: Received phone call from my attorney. Natalie and her lawyer contacted the judge and told them we have settled on their terms. The trial has been adjourned and now an uncontested hearing is set on Monday 3/28/2016. I asked my attorney how we can fight this, how can they lie to the court like this? Apparently they can lie to the court and my attorney must show on this court day. Apparently

Natalie's attorney sent a letter to mine, but no letter was found.

Monday 3/21/2016: Received phone call from my attorney. Natalie and her lawyer contacted the judge and told them we have settled on their terms. I inquired again how they can blatantly lie like this to the judge, the court, and get away with it. I was told once again that the trial has been adjourned and now an uncontested hearing is set on Monday 3/28/2016. Apparently they can lie to the court and my attorney must show on this court day.

Monday 3/21/2016: Contacted Natalie at 5:30PM via phone. She was not home. She asked that I call back at 6:30PM. I logged into Skype at that time and had to text her at 6:45PM reminding her that I want my time with the children. She called via Skype. Eric and Aaron both explained that they want to come up and see me this weekend. Eric said he wanted to see Michaela too. I told them that would be fine as long as it is okay with their mother. Natalie stated that she would not drive them. Eric picked up on this and started to say that poppy could drive them. Natalie began a tirade and started to explain to the children that I do not love them, I have abandoned them, and that I do not want to be in their lives. She hung up on me afterwards.

Fifteen minutes later Natalie contacted me via phone. She explained that the baby is being monitored having due to having a large head. His pediatrician says he may be retaining fluid around the brain. He is being monitored the next two months.

Thursday 3/24/2016: Logged into Skype at 5:30PM. Natalie was not online. I contacted Natalie at 5:30PM via text message and eventually sent a total of five text messages between 5:30PM and 6:30PM requesting that I have my court ordered time with the children. Natalie finally contacted me via Skype at 6:30PM without any excuse. Eric and Aaron were covered in chocolate. Aaron said he had a school play the other day, I requested Natalie to provide some pictures or video of it, but she refused. Baby Wyatt became very excited and was saying daddy. This warmed my heart. Eric requested that we go to the park and the "bumble bee" at the Palisades mall.

Sunday 3/27/2016:
I went to Easter dinner with Michaela and her family. I had a great time. We ordered our meals and were enjoying cheese and crackers as an appetizer. Unfortunately during this wonderful time I was thinking about my divorce.

I started not feeling well. I ran to the bathroom and began hyperventilating (I think it could have been a panic attack). My chest started squeezing and sharp pains in my chest straight through to my back. I was huddled over the bathroom toilet in pain. The pain was so severe, Michaela's niece an EMT told her to bring me to the hospital. After multiple attempts of trying to "man" it out and failing due to the severe pain, I agreed.

The hospital did all sorts of tests, EKGs, blood work, etc. My blood work showed signs of elevated cardiac enzymes. They kept me overnight to monitor me and had me on fluids, morphine, and blood thinners. I told them I had court the next day which I had to appear via phone. They were very reluctant on releasing me, but gave me orders to have a stress test performed and any sign of pain or fainting I must go back to the hospital. The prognosis- STRESS.

Monday 3/28/2016: Another Court Case:

<u>Court:</u>
Another associate attorney with my lawyer's office attended. I was talking with her via cell phone, text messaging, email, and

many times with attorneys in her office as she was losing cell phone coverage inside the court house.

She arrived at the court house at 9:00AM and informed me that my ex-wife, her attorney, and her father were at the courthouse. The judge wanted daddy there because he has his own demands that he needs from me.

She asked if I still agree with everything in the mediated Memorandum of Understanding (MOU) and current visitation schedule. I agreed and only had issues with the Child Support Calculations as it had me making $50,000 more and paying $0 in taxes. I emailed her those corrected numbers. She asked about life insurance, I sent her proof that I have $300,000 policy.

We were worried that they will be playing games today. The attorney spoke to Mr. Keville (after his private get together with the judge again) to test the waters and determine if we should end these games now. She texted me to expect a phone call from the judge. The judge called me at noon.

Judge Cynthia Myers explained to me that I will not like trial and I cannot be "entrenched in my position and must provide to my family unit" She also stated that in trial she "calls it as she sees it." She explained that today was supposed to be an uncontested hearing as I was supposed to agree to all of Mr. Keville's terms and demands.

The judge asked Mr. Keville how long of a trial does he need to successfully prove a case against me. He stated four days. She then asked Mr. Keville how many witnesses he is going to have. He stated four witnesses. Obviously she didn't even want to hear from my attorney and did not ask. Thus, she put down that the court trial will be spread across four full days (or eight half days) in April. The half days are in case there are older divorces that she may have to preside over.

The set trial dates in April are the 7th, 13th, 14th, 19th, and 20th- My attorney needed to change the 7th date and I will probably have to pay for that date change.

Judge Cynthia Myers reminded me that trial is expensive and how will I be able to afford paying counsel fees for both my attorney and hers? Wait, What???? I guess she already determined I'm going to pay for both attorneys since Mr. Keville is on loan (well, he is being paid by daddy, but who's checking his lies to the court and judge).

My attorney informed the judge that during financial mediation, agreements were made and a (MOU) was produced. She explained that later Mr. Keville and my ex-wife wrote a letter terminating all of the agreements. Mr. Keville told the judge that this was a lie and no Memorandum of Understanding was agreed upon. Apparently I terminated that mediation session.

My attorney also stated to the judge that the main attorney and I went to the court during the last Intensive Settlement Conference (ISC) and after hours of deliberations, Mr. Keville explained that nothing will be agreed to because the plaintiff's father was not there. Mr. Keville told the judge that this was untrue and I was the one which cancelled the Intensive Settlement Conference (ISC). The judge sided with him with all these points and will NOT look at the evidence, letters, or the signed Memorandum of Understanding (MOU). None of those things apparently existed.

Judge Cynthia Myers began yelling at my attorney and me about working with my ex-wife and to end the games. I cannot believe this. This is utter chaos. We have the proof, we have their signed letters backing up what we are saying, but the judge will not consider the evidence.

Mr. Keville requested a dozen more mediation sessions. Judge Cynthia Myers agreed with him and ordered my attorney to sit in Mr. Keville requested ISCs.

The Judge ordered that my attorney go through several more intensive settlement conferences (as requested by Mr. Keville). My attorney attempted to explain Mr. Keville games using mediation to drive up my court and attorney costs and cancelling them at the last moment. The judge explained that she did not care and became irate with my attorney. At this point, the judge hung the phone up on me. I texted my lawyer saying I lost signal, but she confirmed the judge hung up on me.

I questioned my attorney on why the judge did not question Mr. Keville lies with settlement and telling the judge we are done mediation and agree to all his demands, she confirmed that he lies about everything and is a "snake."

More Mediation Games:

There was numerous back and forth discussions between my attorney and my ex-wife, her father, and her attorney. There was dozens upon dozens of paperwork; but no progress was made in anything.

They handwrote a "global proposal" that deviates considerably from the terms agreed upon at financial mediation and parenting time mediation. They are being unreasonable. The following are a handful of some of the items:

Previously as recorded by my attorney, the last time I was in court, we discussed the concept of front loading the alimony. They claim now that the numbers proposed are $33k for 3 years and $20k for 3 years. This ends up being about $10k higher total. She understood and even agreed with the concept of front loading, but the numbers are a little on the high side as it ends up being a total of $160K in alimony versus $150K which would be what the 6 years at $25K would be.

They also are now introducing things like extra-curricular activities, Aaron's therapy and "special needs costs into the mix, but it was never part of my prior agreement. They want to share the cost of extra-curricular and other child-related expenses where I pay 2/3's of all costs as determined by her. These numbers are usually part of child support, but they want additional monies. As they state, Natalie will tell me how much I owe her and I must pay. $100 a month, $10,000 a month….whatever she says I owe.

She said that they introduced dozens of more outstanding issues. Issues such as credit cards, tools, motorcycles, they also want 15k in counsel fees. If I get a promotion or even a $1 raise, I must inform them and give them that money. However, if I am fired or demoted it does not count. I am still held to that high salary. They claim I took out loans against my 401(k) and that money is theirs. I never did, nor is there any paperwork stating I did. Once again their word runs the show.

Arrest & Removal of Children:
Because their demands are well above what I make, they requested that I be placed on a permanent 2 week interval bench warrant status so that I cannot go to court and file an "ability to pay" motion if I cannot afford to pay them. Normal wording in these decrees state that if I cannot pay, then the court is supposed to look at what I make, where the money is going, and get a sense of what I can afford. Mr. Keville and Natalie do not want this. They want me just to have bench warrants out for my arrest without this process.

Natalie and her attorney stated that I have to begin paying copayments for the children's therapy because of

my undocumented child abuse. They kept pressing how I continually abuse the children.

Natalie and her lawyer told the court that due to my abuse along with my residence being too far for the children to travel, they want me in New Jersey for supervised visitation.

Finally, they want to conference these issues of parenting time with the judge. They keep insisting that it is not right for the kids to be stuck in the car. My attorney agreed that this is unreasonable because we had an agreement at custody and visitation mediation. Moreover, it is end of the world for the kids to be in the car one weekend per month. However, conferencing it with the judge might actually be good for us, because Judge Cynthia Myers may agree. WRONG!

It was presented to the Judge and the court. They agreed with Mr. Keville and Natalie. They terminated my visitation schedule with the children and it was explained to me that I must be in New Jersey to see my children and I am not authorized to have them overnight. They took my children away from me. No proof, just accusations.

*Remember, overnight visits with me reduce the child support number (because it's the money that is important- not me spending time with my children).

Minivan Registration:

Within these handwritten "global proposals" there was a statement about me failing to pay for the minivan which she is driving. Apparently on Easter Sunday, Natalie was stopped by police as she did not register her car. She did not pay her car registration, and blamed it on me. The court and her attorney believe I am supposed to pay for bills which I am not even informed of. How is this possible? If I am not told about a bill, how should I know to pay it? Why am I also responsible for bills which I do not have to pay for? She knew she was driving with an expired tag? How is that my fault????

Mr. Keville kept my attorney in court for four hours waiting for me to make a payment. Later it was found out by Natalie's admission via voice conversation that she lost the paperwork, but it is still my fault and my responsibility.

I also received a letter from my attorney that they provided during mediation:

As I advised your associate this morning, an urgent situation has arisen which, if not immediately resolved, will result in the filing of an emergent application with the Court.

The marital minivan is registered to defendant. For the entire 11 month pendency of this action, this vehicle has been the sole vehicle used by my client to transport herself and the parties' 3 small children.

In what has unfortunately become his typical fashion, Mr. Arlotta has now allowed the registration on the vehicle used by his wife and his children to expire.

My client was driving on Easter Sunday, with the children in the vehicle with her, when she was pulled over by the police. Fortunately, the officer was sympathetic, and he allowed my client to drive away without impounding the vehicle, without issuing a summons, and with only a warning.

Mr. Arlotta must immediately bring current the registration on the subject vehicle, and he must immediately provide proof of same to my client, so that it can be legally used by my client to transport her and the children.

I will wait the balance of today for this situation to be resolved. In the event that the foregoing is not accomplished immediately, I will take action as outlined above.

My attorney responded with the following:

Please advise (1) if the car is registered in his name (2) when she first addressed this issue to him? How is it that she believes my client should be aware of this yet she's been driving it without any concern for this issue.

She must take some responsibility here. She could have and should have contacted him about this issue instead of incurring legal fees with these communications as well as your threat for an order to show cause. She can simply email him and be they resolve it. If she won't communicate this simply issue, how do we expect them to co-parent?

Nonetheless, I am copying my client so he can work to resolve this.

After Court:
My attorney stated that Mr. Keville will draft a letter and provide her with all their demands. Of course that never came.

Later that night, per my attorney's instructions I contacted Natalie about the car registration to have it handled. She told me that she lost the paperwork and that I must go to New Jersey and have it registered. I inquired about having the children come up and see me and informed her that my father would drive the children. She refused and told me she does not want them to see me as I am an abuser. As it was my night to speak with the children, I asked to do so. She refused stating I must pay her first, and then she will consider it.

Tuesday 3/29/2016: Another Court Case:

Court:
My other associate attorney arrived at the court house at 9:00AM. There was multiple back and forth and more demands made. He made headway with child support and alimony. He stated that it will be $1000 a week. They will not impute income to her as she is unable to work.
Whatever...I'm at my limit. My attorney went back and forth

with multiple aspects of the finances and attempting to make deals on my behalf; but unfortunately its either we meet their demands or nothing.

They had even more demands today:
1. They explained that I must provide them my tax refunds as that is THEIR money.
2. She wants $25,000 for my tools.
3. $500,000 life insurance on top of my work provided $300,000
4. As far as marital debt, mine does not count. Only Natalie's debt is considered marital. My attorney asked for a number and proof. They said they will give him a number only. My attorney asked when and they did not respond.
5. On top of alimony, child support, her attorney fees, medical, extra-curricular activities, etc. They STILL expect me to PAY HER BILLS.

My attorney attempted to fight the removal of my visitation rights with the children. The main reason behind this is Natalie's refusal to drive and their requirement of me being present in NJ to have an arrest warrant served (Bench warrant is only good within state-lines). My attorney tried mentioning Hartford, CT as a meeting spot as it was closer to her and me paying for transportation costs. Natalie refused. He attempted to send an agreement saying I will only have them during a month in the summer, she said she "may consider it" but made more stipulations stating that if I see the children, I must remain down in New Jersey and that she will never allow Michaela or any family member of mine to be alone with the children, as they may be abused. I told my attorney that I want the same stipulations on her then: Certified professionals & day care.

As far as the visitation with my children was involved, they are remaining at their resolution of having to be in New Jersey to see them. Since I abuse the children,

according to Mr. Keville, I must be in New Jersey to have supervised visitations. But during court, they brought up the whole "overnight visit number" in the child support calculations when discussing this matter- how can no one see what really is going on here? Money, that's all it is. This has nothing to do with the children spending time with me or my "undocumented abuse."

I told my attorney that the writing is on the wall. Natalie and her attorney want me to pay more than I make, they want constant bench warrants out for my arrest, and having me come to New Jersey for visitation I'm going to be arrested. He agreed. The bench warrants they are looking at cannot go across state borders and they are using the visitation to draw me into the state (the carrot at the end of a stick) so they can arrest me.

Mr. Keville and Natalie requested proof of the pendent lite support in regards to car registration, payments, and the insurance. This is a ruse as Natalie took me off the policy, got a new one, and cashed out the remainder of the one I paid for. I emailed my diary information along with all the letters and proof of this to my lawyer. I informed him that the insurance was paid up until 12/26/2015 and was purchased before the divorce complaint. I was removed off the plan in November 2015 and Natalie cancelled the policy and cashed the reimbursement check which is attached to this letter. Natalie has not informed me of any of the vehicle insurance information or requested any payments. I have no idea what is going on with it or have any access to the accounts.

It was explained to me that the judge (as she already stated previously) expects me to pay for my ex-wife's attorney and his lies. I was informed to give a number such as $10,000. Even at $10,000, the court is pulling $1000 every week out of my paycheck (I only make $1100) which leaves me with $100 a week for rent, food, water, car, everything. $100 x 52 weeks is ONLY $5200, never mind paying state and federal taxes, I inquired how am I expected to pay her attorney $10,000 in 30 days? My attorney explained that my ex-wife and her father are hell bent on having me incarcerated. My attorney told me to start protecting myself, only communicate with her via email.

I was briefed that I am going to have to pay all her attorney fees for anything that she determines to be divorce related from now until I die. If I owe $1 to them, they will bring me to court. I was prepared for dozens of bench warrants and thousands of dollars in legal fees.

My attorney left at 3:00PM and it he stated that the Judge ordered him to go to another mediation session (per Mr. Keville request) to discuss more demands that they have.

After Court:
My attorney stated that Mr. Keville will draft a letter and provide him with all their demands. Of course that never came.

Contacted the NJ Driver Motor Vehicle Agency (DMV) and attained the necessary information to register the vehicle for the exception of car insurance information. I informed Natalie of this via email and told her I would send her a check. She agreed.

Natalie called me later requesting my NJ and NH license numbers and my past NJ addresses. I provided this information to her via email. She stated that she will register her vehicle and I must provide her the check.

Natalie explained that none of the medical bills are out of network (even though they clearly state it on the bills) and that instead of her being responsible, I am responsible for that debt in addition, I must pay her that amount. I don't understand how I am responsible for the debt and now have to pay her. She explained that she went to the doctors more and I am responsible for all co-payments and travel fees associated with her medical visits even if she decides to go out of network.

Natalie explained that she will deal with my friend who has the Toyota Corolla directly and she will contact him via Facebook to arrange a pick up. She again stated that she will process her minivan registration.

At midnight, I received an email from Natalie reminding me to process her minivan registration. This is against what was agreed upon via email and phone. She changed her mind last minute, like usual.

Natalie and her attorney requested that I make arrangements to have Natalie's car (which she attempted to call in stolen) brought back to her. I called my friend about the car. He took a look at it and saw that the registration and insurance both expired and obviously had issues driving it to her because we did not know if it is in fact registered, insured, or if they were just playing games like last time he attempted to deliver it. He started looking into it getting towed to her; I contacted my attorney to see how we should proceed.

My attorney reached out to Mr. Keville and he stated he will see if it is registered and insured with his client. Natalie did state that it was registered and insured via phone to me (but provided no proof).

Wednesday 3/30/2016:

I received a voicemail from my attorney. He spoke to Mr. Keville yesterday about the status of Natalie's car insurance and registration. He received a letter from Mr. Keville explaining that it is not insured or registered (once again my fault) and now they are going to court about it....Wonderful, love the lies.

Bills are piling up. All credit cards are maxed out and I am about to get another $6,000 bill from my attorney which I will not be able to pay. I am losing my sanity, my will, and ready to leave everything behind. Michaela is the only thing keeping me sound.

I paid the registration on Natalie's vehicle and emailed her the receipt and the following:

Natalie,

Last night you requested my driver's license number along with my address which the car was registered under. You do realize I have previously provided this information to you multiple times. You explained that you will attempt to register it with that information online. Once again, you are changing your mind at the last moment and blaming me for your changes.

I'm not sure where this request was made in December as my attorney and I received your attorney's letter this week.

Since you did not allow me to speak with or see my children on Monday, am I allowed to see them today?

You informed me yesterday that you will be making arrangements directly via Facebook to pick up the Corolla as well. However, this does not coincide with your attorney's letter. Are you still making arrangements directly or am I?

She responded quite quickly providing her text message from December just stating to pay a registration (without any information) and failed to answer any other questions. I love these games.

I forwarded this payment information to my attorney and received the following letters (3) from him:

1. He requested that the Judge change the April 7, 2016 trial date to the 20th due to his wife's medical procedure.

2. A letter from Mr. Keville demanding that I deliver the Toyota Corolla by tonight and pay for the Toyota Minivan by tonight as well- giving Natalie both vehicles for her convenience. In his letter he also stated that I have been holding the vehicle from her and she requires it. Wait a second; I attempted to give it back to her back in October because she was going to call it in stolen. Apparently though, this never happened.

2. My attorney responded to Mr. Keville explaining he is lying:

The undersigned represents Defendant, Robert Arlotta in the above-referenced matter. I am in receipt of your letter dated March 29, 2016. Your letter regarding the vehicles and registration is inaccurate. We never discussed or agreed that my client would provide the Toyota Corolla to your client registered or insured. This is your client's vehicle and my client has no knowledge as to whether the vehicle is registered and/or insured. As you are aware, my client, upon demand of your client some months ago, attempted to provide the vehicle to your client; however, she refused to receive the vehicle. Since that time, the vehicle has remained in New Jersey at a third party's home.

Moreover, I personally contacted your office yesterday, prior to your letter being faxed to our office, advising you that according to the sticker on the Corolla, the registration has lapsed and the third party is unwilling to drive the car over because of the lapsed registration. I also inquired as to whether your client had registered the vehicle, as my client would have no way of knowing this, and whether your client would be willing to pick up the vehicle or whether it should be towed, in an effort to solve the vehicle issue. I have yet to receive a response.

Please advise whether the vehicle is registered and confirm that the vehicle is insured, and how your client would want the vehicle to be exchanged.

Please be further advised that the vehicle is in working order and my client provided your client with the DMV information and pin on March 29, 2016 at 1:26 PM via email and will be sending her a check for $71.50 for the registration fee for the Sienna.

Car Drop Off:
Since my friend who was storing the Corolla and I did not know if the car was registered, insured, or any other information. With all the lies from Natalie and her attorney we could not take any chances. My friend checked to make sure it was running and I paid $70 to get the car towed to Natalie. The tow truck provided a receipt and delivered it to her at 6:30PM. I forwarded a copy of the receipt to my attorney. However, this will not matter as they are going to be bringing me to court for not providing either vehicle (more lies to the court), plus the court will not allow me to show any of my proof. I told my attorney that I love how I have to give her all cars, pay for everything, and the court will still blame me for things I did not do. How is this fair? How can there be no due process?

My friend called me later this day, apparently Natalie and her mother attempted to block the tow truck driver from delivering the car to them. They stated they did not want it. This is completely against her own attorney's threatening letter. I AM DONE WITH THEIR GAMES!

Family Calls:
My cousins and aunt found out about my recent hospital stay and everything going on with this divorce. They urged me to schedule my cardiac stress test and to seek a therapist to discuss these matters.

Thursday 3/31/2016: My lawyer emailed me asking how many vehicles my ex-wife now has possession of. I told him the truth- all of them. Minivan, car, and motorcycle- not sure why she needs all, but that's what they want or they will bring me back to court again.

My friend who had the Corolla dropped off left me a message. He checked at the house and saw the car parked out front in fine shape. So she has the vehicle. He also mentioned that he spoke to the tow truck driver today. He saw him at an emergency call (my friend is an EMT). Apparently Natalie and her mother told the tow truck driver that they did not want the car and tried to refuse it. Tow truck driver dropped it off anyway. I can't believe this. This is against their own attorney's demands of me? Why the games? Why, why, why? They want the car, now they don't? It had to be dropped off or I would be going to prison that night if I did not comply. Is that why they denied it? So they can claim it never came and off to prison I go?

Entry #6: Close to the End (Quarter 2, 2016):

Friday 4/1/2016: Received an email from my attorney with a letter from Mr. Keville. This attachment was the adversary's most recent settlement proposal. They have regressed and are stating we have agreed on certain items. This is incorrect of course.

I read through these six pages of lies stating we agreed to higher counsel fees, more alimony, more child support, and additional costs and fees. Apparently, I agreed to take on all debt even without them giving me numbers and I gave up all my rights to anything owned by me. In addition, apparently I still have to go to New Jersey to see my children (even with their bench warrants against me). In addition to this, they stated that I have not been paying any of her bills or rent to her father. I HAVE THE CASHED CHECKS!!! How can they blatantly lie about this?

I called my lawyer to discuss the various items and told him about my financial inabilities to keep this up. I just want to be divorced. He agreed and asked for me to provide him a written statement under each point of Mr. Keville's letter on how to proceed, as it is in my best interest to fight all these terms (which means more money which I do not have).

My attorney told me that Mr. Keville stated under his breath about their plans on continuing the court cases and wanting me behind bars.

Saturday 4/2/2016: I went through line by line addressing each item. Of course, my main concern is seeing my children. How is this possible that I can only see them in the State of New Jersey? I am willing to give up everything to see them.

I asked why we can't show these letters to the judge to show her the games that they are playing with all these ISCs? How can the Judge say that her own grandchildren cannot go from New Jersey to New York in a car without at least one of them throwing up? My children have been fine during the past few months with coming up each month. I believe it is unfair that the Judge is using her grandchildren as examples instead of actual evidence or any scientific backing.

It is unfair for them to make me go to New Jersey and other months to the half-way point. Where am I supposed to stay? Hotel? How am I going to afford that? What does this show the children, this is not exactly providing them a stable environment? This whole issue should be about the children and what's best for them not what's best for her and having their father in their lives in a stable environment is what's best for them. What about these 2 week permanent bench warrant statuses as well? The moment I enter New Jersey, I am arrested. That seems like the agenda here.

In addition to above, there is a more pressing factor. As discussed with my attorney (along with whatever comment Keville said to him under his breath), the plaintiff has already threatened that they are planning on stretching this out along with brining me back to court for anything she wants (believe she said for $1). Anyone can see this with the ISCs, this recent car thing, their request for 2 week bench warrant status, prior counsel fees, and they are preparing cases for the car insurance and rent which you already know the issues with (plus, her daddy's rent has been always paid).

They know how much I make and all these numbers FAR exceed what I make and the plaintiff has explained she will get as many bench warrants as she can on me. So it is my firm belief that they are utilizing my love for my children to rope me into coming to NJ when there is a bench warrant out for my arrest. As it was threatened, daddy is paying for the attorney and they will never stop.

I emailed my attorney to put me on a payment plan. In addition I sent this letter to my other attorney:

As we discussed, please see attached responses to all points in Mr. Keville's letter. My responses are colored red and are under each point.

As I mentioned, this case really has nothing to do with money. The plaintiff and her father will continually pay for Keville to bring me back to court over and over and they are hell bent on bench warrants and having me arrested and imprisoned. As they have mentioned Mr. Keville is being continuously paid by the plaintiff's father and he can greatly afford all of this.

The children to them are the carrot that will bring me back to the state. Unfortunately, I cannot return to NJ. As the moment they know I am down there, she will contact the authorities and have me arrested. Thus, I don't see my children regardless. This is going to happen as I do not have the credit or funds to even pay Mr. Keville attorney fees (and they KNOW IT).

This needs to end now because after this week I will no longer be able to pay the large bills that they are causing your office to generate. Your office knows how much I make, and I am going to need a payment plan as I do not make enough to pay the $5000 & $6000 bills when they are due.

If they continue to play their games and this cannot end soon, please contact me to explain the possible repercussions if I do not show up to anymore court sessions or have an attorney present. What can the court do? Even moving forward with the court motions they are preparing to file for bills/expenses I do not even know about yet?

As long as I pay child support and whatever I can afford in alimony, as long as I do not step foot in NJ, what are my options?

Saturday 4/2/2016: I am at the end of my rope. I am constantly crying and cannot sleep at night. I am having suicidal thoughts. My girlfriend began reaching out to Father's Rights Movements for help.

Monday 4/4/2016: Another Intensive Settlement Conference (ISC), as requested by Mr. Keville. The new judge was presiding today. This one mainly dealt with the parenting-visitation time and debt.

Natalie changed the amount of the marital debt three times within the mediation session. In addition, she wants me to now pay her credit cards and debt as it stands today. My attorney refused, so she said the complaint day, and then changed it to the date of separation (due to the fact that the same date would go for my debt). The debt number is approximately $23,000 this minute. However it is subject to change. They are still hiding the debt and continuously refusing to show proof. What is there to hide I wonder?

Natalie gave up on wanting me to have an additional $500,000 life insurance policy on top of the $300,000 I currently have.

My attorney requested I send him my 2015 taxes because Mr. Keville requests them. I did and now Natalie is entitled to the full refund. It's her entitlement (or icing on the cake) of course. My attorney did what he could with their demands. She now gets a portion because she gets ALL Assets. All of them!

After eight solid hours, my attorney contacted me back via phone and text. Finally he called and said that they have settled. He said that Keville attempted (multiple times) to get him and Natalie out of the courtroom without signing any agreement stating he had his daughter's medical appointment to go to. The judge urged him to stay to get the divorce agreements to be placed on the record with the court.

My attorney stated that I will be divorced today. The decree will only have the basic outlines. The settlement agreement will be an amendment to the decree and will be done in May. He gave me the phone number of the Judge to call into.

I called the Judge's chambers at 3:30PM. The Judge patched me into the courtroom at 4:00PM. The judge asked the attorney's their names and firm addresses and stated the "Cause of action" Both Natalie and I had to answer many questions with either "yes" or "no" which were pretty basic. Then Mr. Keville's got into the agreements:

I will only see my children during a one week long school break (either winter or spring- alternating each year) and three weeks in the summer (not consecutive). I lost my children! Four weeks a year I get to see them. That's it. I know the attorneys were going back and forth with visitation and it became so convoluted and complicated. At least the meeting spot is still Bayville, MA.

I am allowed to speak with them on Mondays and Thursdays, but the visitation and the phone calls can be cancelled at any moment, any time if their mother wants. I know what that means. It's over....I lost my children!

But hey, as it can be cancelled at any time my official "overnights" which is calculated in the child support remains zero, so in essence; it maximizes their child support. I cannot see my kids because of money. I LOVE the family court system.

Then Keville went into the New Jersey "equitable distribution," and all other monies and debts.

The final divorce decree & property settlement (even though I have no property) lists 53 pages of demands I must meet. $23K of her debt, $15k counsel fees, and additional fees if they want to bring me to court again, alimony, child support, extracurricular, medical expenses, and the list goes on…

So out of two cars, motorcycle, and personal tools (which I still don't know how they are an asset) along with debt, here is the breakdown:

- **Assets:** Her- All. I know what you're thinking, she gets everything? She sure does. Remember, the judge already agreed that she needs two cars and a motorcycle to survive.

- **Debt:** I have to pay the majority of the debt. Really? How is this fair and equitable?
    - Rest assured; in New Jersey this is what is fair.
    - They don't have to produce any documents to prove the amount.

- They wanted $10,000 cash for my work tools. Really? First, I need them for work; second they aren't worth that much. Not even $500. So I told my attorney give them the tools. So they took them. I still have no idea what they are going to do with those tools. They do not know the difference between a screwdriver and a wrench. So, I have to make arrangements to get them to her.
    - These tools are my livelihood. I need them to perform my job. I am an aircraft mechanic. Why would they possibly want them? I was told that this is to ensure that I get FIRED! Lovely…

- Child Support will be determined by "Harold Keville's Guidelines."

- I must pay daycare, pre-care, after-care, special needs, etc. Whether the ex-wife is working or not.

- I pay all extra-curricular expenses.

- I pay 2/3, of all non-reimbursable and out of network medical expenses

- I have to pay 60% of Natalie's $23,000 debt (mine doesn't count as marital somehow)

- I pay the children's College

- Three years of $30,000 each and three years of $20,000 in alimony (Six years total)

- I have to amend my 2015 taxes to married and lie about spousal support to give Natalie the big refund that goes with it.

- Whenever I get a new job or increase in my income I must disclose it and pay Mr. Keville to take me back to court.

- I have 120 days from today to pay Mr. Keville an initial payment of $15,000 towards his outrageous fees.

Mr. Keville made the claim that apparently I have not been paying my "pendente lite" support. So since I have not been paying the ex-wife's bills; I must repay her rent, car insurance, van payments, etc. up to March of this year. Apparently my receipts for paying all of these do not count. Love the lies!

At the end the judge asked if either Natalie or I were either coerced or on any medication or substance which could inhibit our thoughts or comprehension. I said no. Natalie stumbled. She began asking what type of medications, so the judge repeated himself. There was silence (as she was thinking) and then she stated "no." I was laughing to myself.

The judge asked Natalie if she can maintain or exceed her standard of living with all these figures. She was ecstatic and said "Yes, Yes, Yes." He asked me the same question, I laughed and said no. I informed the court these numbers are well beyond my income.

Natalie requested to change her name back to her maiden. It was approved.

Mr. Keville decided to use this time to make up more false statements. Now it is my address. Apparently I falsified my addresses. The judge asked what my current address is, I told him and it was the same one that was on the record the last six times I have been brought to court.

I was asked a magnitude of questions so that the court and "pick me up" when I fail to deliver these thousands of dollars they are looking for. They asked me my employer's name and address twice along with my New Hampshire driver's license number. Apparently they were having issues entering it into the computer as it does not have the same amount of characters as a New Jersey license.

At the end, the Judge said it is always nice to see "Harry" Keville as he is a regular in the court.

May 4th the lawyer has to go back to finalize the numbers (child support). I have to provide him a ton of documents tomorrow. I eventually now have to make arrangements to drop off my work tools to the ex-wife, amend my taxes, and show proof to the court that I have been paying all the ex-wife's bills (because I refuse to repay what I already paid for).

But one thing is done. I am finally divorced, but at great cost financially and losing my children.

Michaela and I discussed how to go about bringing this case to a New Hampshire judge for protection. We need to bring this information to the state to see what they can do (if anything). My attorney did not know about NH law, but he said that bench warrants are only enforced within the state they are issued, for the exception of support payments. I checked online and found the NJ law and it is correct.

Tuesday 4/5/2016: It appears I will not have the children on their birthdays. I am going to miss so much. I went to the house today and just stared at all the birthday stuff I hung on the wall and the gifts I got for Eric. I just sat there…crying.

I called the pediatrician and dental offices to get a statement of what I owe them.

I received multiple letters from the court and my attorney in regards to trials for April. I guess my attorney just sent those letters prior to yesterday. I began sending my attorney all the documents that they need to defend me from Mr. Keville's current lies and to fight his "personal child support guidelines."

I sent the following to my attorney for processing:

1. The child support calculations using the correct numbers & children's insurance information.
2. My medical 1095-B's showing that I am fully covered under the VA medical plan (free)
3. Current Pay Stubs (3)
4. The Car Insurance fiasco binder- for the pendente lite proof (as they more than likely won't send me anything/nor can I pay it)
5. The binder including my marital debt.

I informed my attorney that I did not notice (or remember) the issues of the QDRO or sharing the children (dependents) for taxes. Those issues were not stated for the record. If I remember right, the QDRO would be split 50/50 and the children for taxes was one each and alternating 3rd child (Me- Even year filing, Natalie- Odd year filing). I asked if he could let me know if these items are still the case.

I requested that he forward the divorce decree from yesterday to me so that I can update the insurance companies with Natalie's removal. I mentioned to him that I still owe him the rest of the pendente lite proof and that this Friday I will be going to HR Block to attempt to amend the taxes.

Wednesday 4/6/2016:
I began all of my paperwork for the divorce to prove my innocence. I printed and sent off all the pendent lite proof to my attorney and told him I'll let him know what HR Block says about the taxes. He acknowledged this and will look for my email. I completed payments toward the Minivan, deleted my checking account from all of Natalie's payment websites (so she doesn't pay her bills with my checking)

My attorney sent the divorce decree. In it, I received another divorce decree date in May and got my alimony payment information. I ran the numbers and between the $300/week child support I am currently paying and the now $577/week in alimony (as the decree stated), I am left with a whapping $696 to live on every two weeks. WOW. Live off of less than $350 a week. That's not even enough for gas or a car or even food. Maybe this is why the NJ courts want me to have life insurance. It seems they want me to pass away.

This amount left over will not cover the plaintiff's "marital" debt or her "counsel fees" in which I have been asked to pay. This number does not include ANY of my expenditures or 401(k) contributions. If I am left with no money for food, shelter, car, gas, or any items listed under the CIS I am subject to termination from my job which will result in no money going to the plaintiff.

The decree states that my wages are to be garnished the full amount. Really? I have never missed a payment: never missed, never late. But they want to ensure that I am garnished because I am a deadbeat (or that's what Natalie and Mr. Keville claim). So, if they garnish me, am I going to still get my weekly child support payment reminder phone call?

Michaela and I did the numbers again and saw that this is REALLY unfair. She found the Dept. of Labor laws with wage garnishment. They can only dock me up to 60% of my net pay. That's good news. So just in case they pull out more I can bring this handy law to my Human Resources Representative.

I began getting more bills through my online health insurance alerting system. Natalie is apparently going to the doctors even after the divorce (on my insurance). I immediately contacted the health insurance providers and removed her from the medical and dental benefits. It's part of the little print, once I get the decree I have to remove her or I am liable for everything she does.

Began reaching all the medical bills Natalie charged up. I went through each Blue Cross Benefit Form and called each individual provider to see if they were paid, how much I owe, and if they went to collection. So far I've called thirty doctors (that's her medical visits in the past month- That's one doctor a day).

After work, on my two hour drive home I received a voicemail, four phone calls, multiple Skype voice calls and text messages from Natalie (I guess she really needed to talk with me). I never called her back. It was about "her tax return money." I love this. I am burnt out, broke, heartbroken, missing my children and this bitch will not stop with the money she is "entitled to."

Thursday 4/7/2016: More and more paperwork. I hate this. I am beyond burnt out. I hate that Natalie and her attorney just have to pick up a phone and it means hours and hours of work for me. This is affecting my job, my life, me!

Got another child support payment reminder phone call. These come once or twice a week. It's just a friendly reminder that if I do not pay, I'll be a deadbeat and it will have legal repercussions. These calls are harassment!

I have been attempting to research father's rights and divorce. Finding resources and information on being a father in the family court system is a very difficult process. All of the resources online seem to be directed towards women and the maximizing of their child support and alimony. Finally, I found the Father's Rights Movement and websites. I must commend them on their page and dedication.

There are hundreds of other father's out there with the same or other issues. These websites and groups are very difficult to find, but they are out there. It's very interesting how many of the father's just want equal rights; not more or unfair treatment- they just want things to be fair: 50/50. There should be a book on Father's Rights and how the system is broken along with resources to help father's get through this.

Thursday 4/7/2016: Continued…
With my questions if amending the taxes was legal due to Natalie and I living in two different states and the fact that I am paying her alimony, I decided to visit the local IRS for those answers. They were very nice and explained that it was legal, but the numbers would be a wash. But, I'll do what I am told. So, I emailed Natalie stating that I will be amending the tax return tomorrow and to please have her phone or email available during the morning in case HR Block needs to reach her.

When I got home at 5:30PM, Natalie contacted me on Skype. I began my normal recording. Eric and Aaron had chocolate all over their faces and loved talking with me. They want to come up with daddy so badly. The baby was stuck in his crib "prison" but managed to see me and kept saying daddy. I miss them so much. Natalie's step-sister came into the room and Natalie began apologizing that I am on the line. Natalie began begging me to take the children this weekend and next weekend. I told her that this weekend was no good as plans were already made, and I really need more than 12:00 hours' notice. She began quoting the original visitation agreement. Wait, the one that they had removed from me? I reminded her that it was her and her attorney which had that removed due to my "abuse." But I agreed to have the children next weekend as I miss them. But I was very careful; I told her I need this request and agreement in an email. Of course she hesitated at this point. This just shows that they know I am not an abusive father, this is just a way that they were able to maximize their child support number (overnights=zero). Hopefully she'll email me the agreement and I'll be able to see my children.

Friday 4/8/2016:

Tax Fiasco:
I went to HR Block and began filing the taxes. The tax preparer knew exactly what to do and offered to do them later on that day. So I went home and checked the mail. Every time I check the mail, I cringe. It's either a bill of the ex-wife's, a creditor, or threatening court documents. Today was no different. The minivan registration came in. Not sure why New Jersey sends their registrations to a NH address, but whatever, have to send that down to the ex-wife now.

Got another exciting letter too! Apparently, Massachusetts Dept. of Revenue is auditing me for a $200 refund. They require a whole bunch of documents, pay stubs, back taxes, and of course; copies of the children's, my ex-wife, and my social security cards.

I called them up (multiple times) and a pleasant gentleman who could not speak a lick of English answered (after hanging up on me a few times). No email, no calls, send "male" to them. Right! I inquired should I preemptively send the amended return as well. "What is amended, send anyway male?" was his answer- Right! He eventually stated that they need the amended return along with copies of everyone's social security cards (including wife and children).

So I called Natalie to inform her that I need a copy of her social security card. Oh boy. Someone forgot to take their medication today.

I contacted Natalie to inform her that I need a copy of her social security card (as I am in possession of the children's which she still hasn't realized yet). Once again- this for that. Give her $25,000 cash and "maybe" she'll send it in herself. Wonderful!!!

Then, when that was not good enough; not only did she refuse to provide her social security card, but she refused to sign the amended tax return. What? This was their request, their demand; they swore to the court that they will sign? Why? What?

So I emailed Natalie the MA Audit letter and the following:

Natalie,

I've been attempting to work with you with the now court ordered 2015 joint tax return. Your continued bad faith and games are not appreciated.

As I already informed you, the State of MA is conducting an audit of the individual return (and after today the joint return). Included in their request, I must provide copies of each individual's social security card. Thus, to process the amended return, I require a copy of your social security card. Your outright refusal is not appreciated.

I require by COB today a copy of your social security card to satisfy this audit. You can scan and email it to me.

In addition, if you DO send your card and the taxes are able to be amended, I will REQUIRE a copy of the tax return YOU sign.

Failure of this will result in no refunds being generated as stated within the State of MA letter attached.

Thank you for your cooperation.

Attorney Update:

Back and forth, back and forth we went emails, calls, cc'ing lawyers, providing the audit letter, etc. Natalie eventually sent a copy of her social security card. Finally! It was a terrible picture of her social security card, but whatever, it will have to do.

I informed my attorney of what was going on with the taxes and I also had some concerns in regards to Mr. Keville's hiding language in his letters and previous demand letters, so I needed some clarification:

1. Just out of curiosity, do we get a copy of the finalized decree Keville's is writing before it goes to court? Just wanted to make sure he doesn't hide anything. Plus, we need the QDRO & tax dependent items included (Even Years-me, Odd Years- Natalie).

I noticed that Mr. Keville sneaked in extra wording and non-standard language stating they want the State of New Jersey to issue bench warrant statuses on me whether I am in compliance or not. This was placed in last time as well.

My attorney informed me that, yes; we will review it beforehand to make sure Mr. Keville does not sneak in additional demands or threats.

2. In addition, if the plaintiff fails to provide any documents for the marital debt that she is claiming, how do we move forward with that? Do I still assume responsibility even though they keep breaking the agreements and the decree? I need a number and proof, as the number has changed drastically each time we ask. My attorney reminded me that we included language on the record that she had to provide you with proof.

3. As a note, HR Block is working on the amended return now. In addition, MA is doing an audit of me and will require a copy of the signed amended return and everyone's SSN cards. However, during a phone call with the plaintiff (to get permission for the joint return) she outright refuses to sign the taxes or provide a SSN card. Not sure what she is doing here as this was their request.

My attorney informed me that if Natalie does not cooperate, I don't file.

Natalie contacted me multiple times via text message and phone throughout the day. She inquired about the tax refunds. I informed her that I didn't know the specifics while I was driving, but she is getting a refund back from the Feds, MA, but now New Jersey is owed money. I also informed her that the filing costs were about $200. She began her threatening saying how she doesn't have to abide by court orders or decrees and that I must pay any monies owed along with the filing fees. In addition, she is entitled to the full refunds (which were apparently mine per the court order), and will now be taking the motorcycle along with other items. I hung up the phone. I should have known better than answer her call. Leave it to voicemail. I have to work on that!

Late on Friday, I completed the amended return at HR Block. The original refund total (NJ, MA, Federal) which is mine is: $9455

The new numbers are as follows:
Fed: $3030 (additional)
MA: $98 (additional)
NJ: I now **owe** $328 (Due to the increased double state taxes)

The cost of the filing is $220. Thus, I will add the two refunds are: $3128. Per the agreement, she pays the differences after my original amount plus the filing fee, so with those deductions, the final number she will get is: $2,580. She will have to sign the returns and mail them. The envelopes are included in the package being sent to her.

I emailed my lawyer this and attached the documentation to this email. I will be forwarding the amended returns to Natalie via certified mail along with the check for NJ taxes. Once I get the refunds, they will be sent to her.

As I am currently being audited, the tax refunds will be delayed unfortunately. The plaintiff has been notified (as he saw in the rash of emails).

My tax accountant received a phone call on Friday, April 8 from Natalie. She classified the phone call as aggressive and harassing. Natalie was demanding that she gets a refund of $16,000-$25,000 and requesting personal information about my exceptions, salary, and other associated numbers. She began explaining to the accountant that I lied on my taxes and that they did the taxes wrong. (Not sure how this is possible as I have yet to send her a copy). Due to HR Block policy, no information was released, but this is what I am dealing with.

Stress Test: I performed my stress test. I ran on the treadmill, up and down, faster, slower. They cleared me. They asked what started my chest pain and I told them a brief story. While doing this, they saw my blood pressure increase and I was shaking. The doctor even said this was killing me.

Sunday 4/10/2016: Natalie texted and called around 4:30PM. Apparently it was an emergency. I called her back. Her emergency was that I had to speak with the children right that instant for only two minutes because she is cancelling tomorrow's Skype session with me and the children due to her going out with some friends. I inquired why her going out to party affected my time with the children. She did not have an answer; she just stated that she is cancelling it. I spoke with Aaron for about two minutes until she interrupted and began harassing me about the taxes and her refund. She was telling me that the taxes are all wrong and the amended return needed to be fixed. I asked once simple question- How does she know their wrong when she does not even have them? She hesitated and hung up.

Not even five minutes later, another "emergency call." This time was if I plan to stay in New Hampshire and my relationship with Michaela. I informed Natalie that it is none of her business and I am done with the harassment under the pretenses of "emergency children." She stated that her phone calls are not harassing and my relationship with Michaela is her business as it deals with the children.

Monday 4/11/2016: Received the zero balance statements from Quest Diagnostics and the children's pediatrician. It is unfortunate that the pediatrician had such a large balance, that they required Natalie to "pay up" before they performed any more work on the children. I scanned and filed these reports for future court appearances.

I completed the packages for the MA tax auditors and Natalie's amended return. I included the check for the NJ taxes, amended taxes, and the car registration for the minivan. I took pictures of everything and emailed my lawyer the same.

Monday 4/11/2016: Continued... I checked online with my dental benefits and saw that they still have not removed Natalie off the benefits yet. So I emailed and called the dental benefits people. I informed them that this was my third time trying to fix this issue. The woman over the phone did not even realize I had an account though she had all my information and knew my address without asking it of me. I requested her supervisor, so she decided to hang up on me. Why is this so difficult to accomplish?

Natalie called twice; once at 3:50pm and again at 4:15pm. She wants to know if I would like to meet her in Bayville, MA this Thursday for visitation. I told her that I need the request in writing (as mentioned to her multiple times already).

I headed down to Bayville, MA to stay with my family for the next few nights. I had a work conference down in Hartford and needed a place to stay close. I had dinner with my family in MA today. It was nice to see everyone and to hear all the support. Glad my family is here today.

Tuesday 4/12/2016: At noon, Natalie sent the written visitation schedule change in an email. However, instead of Thursday, now it is for tomorrow (Wednesday).

I requested guidance from my lawyer since this is against the visitation agreement now (as I still am a threat to the children) can I see them without any repercussions, or is this another game of Natalie's? I asked that under the current situation and decree, is this allowed? Can I schedule this?

He told me that there is nothing stating that I can't have the more time with the children. If she offers it, I can take it. Under the agreement, there is not mention of these long weekends. However, if I do it, make sure it is all in writing.

So I got the green light, but I had to confirm the days and times as she changed her mind a lot already. I told her that she mentioned Thursday the other day. Did she mean Thursday or Wednesday for the children? I asked that she clarify and tell me what time to meet in Bayville as well via email. Either day was fine with me.

She only confirmed that it is for Wednesday. She did not give any times. So I had to press (love these games- especially when I am attempting to get work stuff done).

I emailed her back stating:

You have failed to inform me of the time. I will meet you at the Cracker Barrel in Bayville, MA at 3:30pm tomorrow. That will give the children enough time and breaks during the drive and you will not meet with any traffic at that time. Thank you.

She confirmed the time and date and agreed. After that she called and left a voicemail at 7:45 to begin changing times around. I did not return her call.

Wednesday 4/13/2016: Early in the morning Natalie called twice (but no message) - probably another harassment call. I called the dental insurance again to see why they still have not removed my ex-wife from the account, as she is continually utilizing the benefits and I am still responsible (even though I am divorced from her). They still don't have a clue what is going on.

Natalie called at 2:00PM to let me know she was on her way. She also mentioned to me about payment to her psychiatrist stating I must pay, but failed to tell me how much. So nothing has changed here, I am responsible for her payments, but she refuses to tell me how much and her psychiatrist will not talk to me. They are just going to send everything to collection. Peachy!

I worked out these impromptu visitation days with my employer. They were very agreeable and worked with me even though it was extremely short notice. After work I went to the visitation drop off site in Bayville, MA. I got there at 3:30PM and Natalie was already waiting for me.

She began questioning me about finances and weight loss surgery, I did not respond. The children were ecstatic to see me. They gave me HUGE hugs. The children gained a significant amount of weight. I will be weighing them tomorrow morning.

The children were begging to go out to the park and play outside as they do not do it often. Aaron said he was off from school for the past week and he has been bored. I asked him what he has done. Has he been to any museums, parks, Lego Experience, etc.? He stated that Eric and he were at home watching TV every day.

Aaron was saying he was able to call his mother and grandma by himself. I asked him how. He began showing me his brand new Apple iPad with 3G phone calling capability. He showed me the calling App along with a handwritten piece of paper with his mother's and grandmother's phone numbers written in crayon. A six year old with a tablet phone, I'm curious how much that cost.

Aaron was talking about his metal tooth. He later showed it to me (all I have to say is wow). I asked him if he brushes his teeth everyday so he does not get any more cavities and takes care of his teeth; he stated multiple times that "mommy doesn't like me brushing my teeth" and that the last time he brushed was with me during the last visitation (which was in the beginning of March). When we got home, Michaela and I had him and Eric brush their teeth but they had severe difficulty. I do not know of any six year old who does not know how to brush his teeth.

Michaela did a food shop for us and cooked tacos. Eric refused to eat as he does not like tacos (he wanted a hamburger) and Aaron refused to eat the tomatoes. Michaela and I mentioned dinner with cauliflower. Eric and Aaron asked what cauliflower is.

Thursday 4/14/2016: I was able to work from home today. During the day Michaela and I took the boys to parks, played outside, and we did some indoor activities to stimulate brain power by using puzzles and Legos. I took a picture of Aaron's metal tooth for my Aunt. She wanted to see it. This is unbelievable. This is child abuse.

In the morning, weighed the children:

Aaron weighed 80 lbs. (+1 lbs. since March 5)
Eric weighed 60 lbs. (+5 lbs. since March 5)
Wyatt weighed 20 lbs. (No difference since March 5)

At night time we celebrated Easter and Eric's birthday. The Easter bunny came over and left various toys for the children and I gave the stuff to them. We celebrated Eric's birthday early and had a cake with his name on it and had a pizza party with the children and Michaela's family. Eric opened all his gifts from Michaela and I; he had fun and a great birthday! After the birthday party, the children played outside. Eric continues not to run. He says he can't. He started to, but due to his increased weight (5 lbs.) he is having issues with getting out of breath and dry heaving.

Michaela and I bathed the children and showed them how to brush their teeth. They stated that they do not do this with their mother and do not know how to brush their teeth. Aaron and Eric did not like their baths at all. Aaron was flailing around while having his hair washed. Natalie called at 7:00PM wanting to know about Aaron and if he was sick.

Harassment:
Just like the interrogatories and discovery being sent to me with a 24 hour time frame for me to answer after Natalie dropped the children off to me; now I am in another situation just like it. I received another letter from Mr. Keville today where I had to respond within minutes or the court will interject.

Mr. Keville stated the following:

I am in the process of revising the parties' Property Settlement Agreement.

Toward that end, I ask that you please provide me with proof of the cost to Mr. Arlotta of the children's portion of the health insurance coverage provided to them through Mr. Arlotta's employment.

Please also provide proof that Mr. Arlotta has $300,000.00 of life insurance coverage, as required by the parties' Agreement.

Finally, as you know, the parties are pursuing a possible amended tax filing for 2015. My client advises that she contacted the local accountant near Mr. Arlotta who prepared the existing returns. My client advises that the accountant was not very helpful, and that the accountant essentially took the position that she had already provided all documents or information for the amended filings to Mr. Arlotta, and that Ms. Arlotta should take the matter up with Mr. Arlotta. Therefore, we ask that you forward copies of all proposed amended returns, worksheets, schedules, etc., to this office for review.

While taking care of the children (thank God I had Michaela's help), I was able to compile all the information and emailed my attorney the following:

Here are the answers & attachments:

1. *Please explain to Mr. Keville that the total medical ($448/month) is for the children as I am fully covered under the VA.*

If he wishes, the plaintiff can cover the children's medical if they are only going to give me a portion of what I pay for them. I have included my VA information along with the medical differences paperwork. But I really would like this full amount credit, especially since they are not going to impute Natalie's $20,000.

2. *Life Insurance Information is attached.*

3. *Amended filing is attached. I now owe NJ money since I was only a part-time resident, and now due to adding Natalie, I am a full time resident and owe NJ State more. My accountant was not helpful to her because of Natalie harassing her stating that we lied, coerced, and we owe Natalie anywhere from $16,000-$25,000 return. Obviously, no HR Block representative is going to accommodate her with her attitude. She will be getting around $2500 return once I get the money. I will be providing her the amended return this Sunday (child drop off) along with the attachments I sent to you earlier.*

There are four (4) attachments total. Hope this helps. See what you can do with crediting me the $448 full medical and seeing if they used MY REAL PAYCHECK to calculate child support, as they made up their numbers out of thin air last time. Thanks.

Friday 4/15/2016: I was able to work from home today. I continued pushing the children to clean up after themselves, cloth themselves, and show good behavior. We set up Eric's birthday presents, including a portable inflatable ball pit. The baby and Eric loved it. Aaron and I threw the Frisbee around. But he was showing aggressive behavior to his two little brothers. I had to put him in time out a couple of times. Natalie called at noon asking if the children were sick.

Michaela and I brought the children to the supermarket and the park where we played for hours and Aaron, Eric, and I ran around playing tag. Eric is still having issues with running around. We walked on the walkway around the river. It was a beautiful day. Michaela was explaining her fears that the ex-wife will soon be making up lies about her and bringing her to court as well. Natalie called in the early morning explaining that she was sick and the boys were going to be sick. After the children brushed their teeth, and after bed, Eric started to run a small fever. I gave him a little Tylenol and put a fan on him. He felt better and went right to sleep.

Saturday 4/16/2016: Natalie called at 7:45AM. She was asking about her attorney's letter and still on this "kids are sick" thing. I continued pushing the children to clean up after themselves, cloth themselves, and show good behavior. The baby is doing amazing with learning to walk and run around. He loves the free reign he gets up here. The house is fully baby-proof and from the moment he wakes up to when he falls asleep, he is on the run. Natalie called again to "check on the children" along with harassing me about money. After the children told her how they are having fun, I hung up on her harassment portion of the phone call.

Today was a long-great day. Eric was begging all day to fly his birthday gift kite. We flew it around the local softball field, went to the park, played outside, etc.

I emailed Natalie with specifics about the drop off times with the children. I explained to her that for the children pick up, tomorrow Sunday, April 17 she has not given me any times. I told her that I will be at the Cracker Barrel in Bayville, MA at 2:30PM to ensure the children get to her home so they can prepare for school the following morning. She confirmed this time and concurred.

Lawyer bill arrived, another $4,000. I looked at the invoice and saw the dozens upon dozens of letters, emails, and other items they received and responded to from Mr. Keville. Apparently they have been shielding me from a lot of his bullshit while I had the boys here with me. Natalie and her attorney LOVE to bombard me with this while I have the children. You just have to love the harassment.

I received dozen more insurance explanations of benefits forms (EOBs). Apparently Natalie has brought all three children to doctors multiple times this week.

Sunday 4/17/2016:
In the morning, the boys and I packed up and got dressed. The children and I left our house and went to pick up Michaela's to drive her to the airport. We had breakfast at her house and used the bathroom/diaper change. Natalie called at 9:00AM asking were we were. I told her we began driving to get down to the drop off point. She said she would meet us there at the designated time. We dropped Michaela off at the airport and she gave the boys goodbye kisses. We continued on to Bayville, MA to visit the family.

Around noon, I received a text message from Natalie asking to change the drop off time to 3:00PM. I called her asking why she is delaying it. She began explaining that she did not even leave the house yet. Just wonderful!

We were a little bit early and my aunt was not home yet. So, the children and I went for a quick shop at Walmart before heading to my aunt's. When she got home, we arrived shortly afterwards. My cousins were there and the children had fun with puzzles, games, and outdoor activities. We celebrated Eric's birthday and he received a bunch of fishing items. He loved it as he has been talking about fishing nonstop for the past two visitations. We played hide & seek, and I showed Eric how to cast his new fishing rod.

During this time, Natalie called again to continue delaying the drop off time, stating that she will not be there until 4:00PM; she called later stating 4:30PM. She also stated that I had to meet her in Hartford, CT. I asked if I wasn't at my Aunt's; why would she wait last minute to leave and make the children wait for over two and a half hours for her to show? She only responded with "not my problem." Thank God we were at my family's and the children were able to have some fun, run around, and took some well needed naps.

After lunch and nap time, my family cooked dinner. At around 4:45PM Natalie called saying she is almost at the drop off point and that I have to be there IMMEDIATELY. Funny how she can be two and a half hours late, but I still have to bend over backwards for her. So the boys and I packed up and headed out.

While driving to the drop off point, I started saying my good byes to the children. Eric started to cry and kept saying "Stay with daddy" and Aaron said he wants to stay with me. I asked why and he said that he likes the way I make him feel and that he likes to "do stuff." He explained in more simple terms that he likes that I give him small responsibilities to do on his own (become more independent), and he likes that. I told him that I would love for him and his brothers to be up here with me and I will always fight for them.

Drop off Antics:
Natalie arrived at the Cracker Barrel at 5:00PM. She was accompanied by her mother. Natalie looked disheveled and had snot stains all over her shirt. Natalie parked her vehicle perpendicular across three RV extended parking spots and was standing in the fourth. I began moving the children's coats and suitcase in her car.

Natalie was asking the children if I bathed them and brushed their teeth. After I secured the children and gave them all a hug and kiss, I gave Natalie the following documents and had her sign a receipt for all these documents to protect myself when she claims she hasn't received them (like everything else in this case):

1. 2015 Amended Tax Returns and envelopes for signature and processing (3 total).
2. HR Block Receipt for $220 of Services for Amended Return
3. Personal Check to the NJ Division of Taxation to be mailed with the NJ Amended tax return.
4. 2016-2017 Toyota Sienna Minivan NJ Registration

She started looking inside the envelope and was arguing over the taxes, claiming items were missing, and explaining that she will make sure she gets her $25,000 refund. While she was having her temper tantrum, an RV came into the parking lot looking to park in the spot Natalie was standing in. I moved to the rear of the car and informed Natalie that she should do the same.

She refused to move and the RV driver became annoyed and started going into the spot. He was inches away from hitting her. She continued looking at all the documents, harassing me more and I just explained to her she is signing a receipt for the items, not if the items are to her liking or not. She explained how she was sick and decided to cough all over the receipt before handing it to me. My aunt was nearby watching all of this. She couldn't believe her eyes. I entered my car and Natalie ran up to me. She began more harassment about money, refunds, and she said that I gave Aaron treats but not Eric. I didn't respond to her.

After Hours Harassment:
Later that evening Natalie left me a voicemail demanding I call her back to discuss her tax refund. Of course, I will not call her anymore. I am done with this harassment.

Michaela and I are worried that Natalie is going to continue her games using the children as weapons. Once my money runs out, she will start suing my family and Michaela with frivolous lawsuits with making up lies like she has been with me. Either stating harassment or child endangerment. We also know that the moment the bench warrants are issued, she will not show up to pick up the children and request I bring the children to NJ (where I will get arrested) or call the police saying I kidnapped them. Either way, the end result is the same.

Monday 4/18/2016: Checked the dental insurance online. Natalie was finally removed. Sent out the following emails and Bcc'd my attorney on all of them:

(Email #1): Emailed Natalie the following letter to end her games with last minute changes and plans:

This weekend with the children went very well and the children love spending this additional time with me, as I do with them.

However, both my employer and I would greatly appreciate more advanced notice than your typical 12-24 hour notice. Providing me only a day or half-day notice does not give my employer or me enough time to reschedule my many activities. My employer was fortunate to grant me a modified work schedule on such late notice and your constantly changing plans during this week's impromptu visitation.

Thus, moving forward, we would greatly appreciate at least a week notice before sending an unscheduled child visitation request/offer as I have to schedule the applicable annual leave and reschedule work activities and work related travel. This is completed more effectively with at least a week's notice.

Thank you very much for your cooperation.

Monday 4/18/2016: Email #2: Received voicemail from Natalie requesting I fax over a copy of the Toyota Bill to ensure it was paid and requested what I am going to do with the motorcycle. I responded back via email. It read as follows:

Natalie,

I received your voicemail from today, April 18, 2016 in regards to the status of the Toyota Sienna minivan payments and your request to have the motorcycle removed from the property.

The minivan is current on all payments per the pendente lite order and all documentation has been sent to your attorney.

As far as the motorcycle is concerned, you are in possession of all the motorcycle keys which were left inside your Corolla (about 3 sets). Please place all these keys in the right hand saddle bag on the motorcycle. I will begin making arrangements to have a tow truck company come and collect the motorcycle from your premise.

Monday 4/18/2016: Email #3: Sent a follow up email to Natalie about her constantly showing up late for visitation (either drop off or pick up):

Natalie,

In regards to yesterday; I do not appreciate your continued games and bad faith, especially when it deals with the children.

Within this Visitation Email String we had a set arrangement and we spoke at 9:00AM when you were informed of and knew the children and I were on our way and were going to be at the meeting spot at the designated time you agreed to at 2:30PM.

You called and texted me at 12:00PM explaining that you had not even left your residence. You again called and continued to delay the time. Having the children and I wait over two and a half hours for you is inexcusable. The children should not be waiting for that long and then having a shortened time to be prepared for school the following morning.

In addition, you agreed to have the meeting area be Bayville, MA. Your request to have it changed to Hartford, CT was not part of the written arrangement within the email that you confirmed and concurred.

This is not the only time you have been excessively late (either drop off or pick up). This continued behavior must stop for the best interests of our children.

Monday 4/18/2016: Email #4: Emailed my attorney the 2015 amended receipt letter that Natalie signed on 4/17/2016. I informed him that she is in possession of the amended return along with the minivan car registration. I inquired with him if Natalie and her attorney provided her debt statements which I am expected to pay.

Monday 4/18/2016: Natalie called at 5:20PM and left a voicemail stating it is "imperative that I call her, it's an emergency with the children." So, being a worried dad, I called her back. Big mistake! Apparently, the three children, including the baby all have bronchitis along with her. I thought this was interesting as I just had them the past five days and they were not sick at all. She told me that they are all going to the doctors tomorrow and "I must pay."

She stated that she is extremely ill as well. She told me she went to the doctor's office and found out she is no longer covered by any health insurance. She told me she is entitled to health insurance and that I must contact my employer to have her covered by both Cobra and normal health insurance. I informed her that I have no access to that information, but being divorced, I cannot legally (per my federal benefits program) cover her. I told her she is welcome to call them herself. She did not like that answer.

She informed me that she and her attorney will now seek court intervention to have me cover her with FULL medical and dental insurance, cover all her copays, cover her out of network medical, etc. In addition, I will have to pay her attorney fees and she capped it off stating I am required to pay her a sum of $5,000 in addition to everything else. She also cancelled my Skype Visitation Session with the children until I pay her demands. I hung up the phone. I should have known better. I hate that she is continuously utilizing the children as weapons. Now when there is a really an emergency with the children, I'm not going to even know with all these bullshit lies.

Tuesday 4/19/2016: Natalie sent a Facebook friend request to me. Really? Is she serious? After everything she has put me through? What possible reason does she have to send this? I ignored it. Today, I also received the Bank of America (BOA) Cancellation Release Forms for removal of me from Joint Marital Accounts (2 Letters).

Thursday 4/21/2016: Filled out the Bank of America (BOA) release forms and got them notarized (as required). I called BOA about the children's custodial accounts. The woman on the phone said that I do not get a letter for those accounts; only the main checking and savings. So I completed the two forms, mailed them to Natalie (with tracking information), and emailed her the following:

Natalie,

Moving forward, I have mailed you the required documents for Bank of America (BOA) to split the marital accounts. You will remain on the account. This authorization only removes my name from the accounts. The originals must be signed by both of us. You must sign next to your name on Page 2 of each request. There are two total (Savings & Checking). They have been mailed to you along with the prepaid postage envelopes. Once you are in receipt of these documents, please sign them and mail them to BOA. I have attached courtesy copies to this email. However these copies cannot be used. Only the originals must be, as they are notarized. Thank you.

Thursday 4/21/2016: More collection phone calls. More and more bills are piling up, but I can't afford to pay them. All my money must go to Natalie first, then my lawyer to fight all these allegations which just keep piling up.

Natalie called my cell and left a message asking if I am going to Skype with the children. I responded back that I was. I waited over 20 minutes for her to log into Skype. She finally did. She did not let me speak to Eric. I spoke to Aaron and saw the baby. The baby was stuck in his crib in front of the television and Aaron was just asking me where I was and where I was living (looking at his mother the whole time). I just told Aaron he knows where I live and where I am. The session was short as Natalie began her harassing money remarks again. I hung up.

Monday 4/25/2016: At least a dozen more creditor phone calls. Money, money, money. At around 4:00PM, Natalie called me and left a message. She is taking the children out to Chuck E Cheese during my visitation time and she is cancelling the visitation. I emailed my lawyer the following message along with the saved voicemail but to no avail. Unfortunately, since the court determined I am an abuser without any evidence, Natalie does not have to allow me any visitation. I hate this.

Please find a voicemail message attached to this email. Natalie is consistently cancelling Skype visitations. Not too sure if this will help in court or not.

I still have yet to see any statements or "martial debt" information from her. We are a week away from court.

Have you received the typed up divorce decree or child support information? I want to make sure that the numbers on the Child Support Worksheet are the ACTUAL numbers (which I have previously provided you) and not the made up numbers Mr. Keville claimed on the last one.

Tuesday 4/26/2016: Received an email back from my attorney. He will contact the adversary in regards to the parenting time and marital debt statements. He has not received anything from the adversary. His office has followed up on it and received no response. However, my documents were provided to them.

Friday 4/29/2016: My lawyer contacted me to follow up on Natalie cancelling the Skype sessions; I informed him that she cancelled the session on Monday and again yesterday as well. As far as the marital debt or any other documentation, I have not seen a thing. I do not know what we are going to do in court next Wednesday, as they still haven't provided her portion of the marital debt (statements, etc.) or the finalized decree.

I also received an email from Aaron's school about an initial IEP meeting later in the week. I guess Natalie is getting him classified.

Friday 4/29/2016: At least a dozen more creditor phone calls. Money, money, money.

Friday 4/29/2016: At around 6:00PM, I received an email from my attorney. It contained the child support numbers that Natalie came up with. Obviously, they did not use any realistic numbers. They did not use any number from my pay check. I apparently make a million a year and don't pay for healthcare or taxes. I resent my attorney the real numbers along with copies of pay stubs to prove what I pay for taxes, income, medical, etc.

They changed most of the already agreed upon (and stated on court record) items. From visitation, to counsel fees being "voluntary," to not being able to seek relief if I am in financial ruin, alimony can be changed at any time, etc. Went through all 40 pages of demands I must obey and sent back my comments to my attorney. How can they go back on what was already stated for the record? How can Natalie and her attorney determine what child support is? Doesn't the court determine that? Why isn't ANYONE LOOKING AT MY DAMN PAYCHECK?

Monday 5/2/ 2016: Received an email and phone call from my lawyer's office. They wanted to discuss the continuing saga of child support calculations being bogus, the ever changing visitation schedule, and the sneaky inclusions inside the divorce decree. We went through the divorce decree notes I provided the other day.

In addition, apparently Mr. Keville had the court case scheduled for May 4th cancelled. My attorney does not have a new date. But he is going to send a response back along with another (5th request) for them to provide copies of Natalie's marital debt statements and the child support calculations they are using. This may go to trial anyways because of their constant changing minds and games, even after agreements were made on record with the court.

Monday 5/2/2016: Skype Session Fiasco:
Logged into Skype at 4:30PM. I waited for the children for over an hour. At around 5:30, I emailed Natalie to remind her of the Skype sessions, as she keeps on cancelling or not showing up for them. I informed her that I have been logged into Skype today at our scheduled time to speak with the children. I explained that I cannot see her online and she did the same thing last week. I requested that she please stop these games and let me speak to my children. Her bad faith is not appreciated.

Later that evening around 6:00PM, Natalie left a voicemail explaining that she will not log into Skype until I contact her. I sent a text message explaining that I have been on Skype. I have been on since 4:30. I informed her to check her email and her bad faith is not appreciated.

Natalie responded to my original email claiming that she is not playing any games and that I neglected to celebrate Eric's birthday with him (though we did when he was up in NH). She blamed me for her not allowing the children to speak to me. I still don't understand that either.

Natalie finally agreed to log into Skype and let me speak to the children. However, she included in her email how I will not be logged into the Skype system (another personal shot which I still don't understand).

During the Skype session, I was only allowed to speak with Eric only. The baby was placed in front of the camera for only a second with his mother holding him in such a way that he could not see the screen nor could I see his face.

Eric was happy and wanted to go to the park. He was saying that he wanted to go to the park by Michaela's house and fly his kite. He was talking about fishing, playing, and flying his kite. I asked him if he was going to go to the park with his mommy today. She interjected and said no because Eric had a "well visit" at the doctors today. I still am not sure why a well visit would disqualify Eric from going to the park on a nice day.

It was apparent that both Eric and Natalie gained a significant amount of weight (again). I inquired with Natalie about Eric's checkup and if the doctor had concerns about his weight. She refused to answer any of my questions. All I had to do was "send the check."

Natalie was requesting where I was, if I was at Michaela's house, the visitation plan, along with what my plans were for the children during Father's day weekend. I simply did not answer her questions and reiterated to her as I normally do, "this is my time with the children, not your time to harass me." Eric started talking to me again and Natalie was interrupting him. I asked her to stop and let him speak to me. After he was done, Natalie continued her harassment and I ended the call.

Tuesday 5/3/2016: I was copied in two letters from my lawyer to the court house. The first one was to confirm the cancellation of the court case tomorrow; the second was the rescheduled court case for the divorce terms. Apparently I now have to be in court on Wednesday 5/11/2016 (next week). Well, unless Mr. Keville has another personal meeting with the judge and the court. Love the games. Also love the 20 phone calls a day from these creditors. They are definitely relentless.

Thursday 5/5/2016: I called the children at 6:00PM to perform our Skype session. The baby was saying daddy and Eric was talking up a storm. Natalie was asking Eric if I was at Michaela's house. I asked to speak with Aaron multiple times and she was leading him stating "Aaron, you don't want to talk to daddy, right?" She followed up after each leading statement explaining that Aaron concurs and does not want to speak with me. After about five minutes, Natalie began harassing me about divorce related items. I ended the Skype session and saved the recording.

Saturday 5/7/2016: Received several Blue Cross/Shield claims via email. Apparently Natalie is continuing to use her medical benefits, which I cancelled after the divorce. I called Blue Cross and of course, they are closed till Monday.

Monday 5/9/2016: Called Blue Cross about all the claims this weekend. Apparently, even though I am divorced, Blue Cross feels I need to cover Natalie. She is covered for another two months. After that they retroactive the coverage to the date of the divorce, from there I (yes, me) has to repay

Blue Cross for all of the coverages with Natalie going to the doctor. This is absolute insanity.

I logged into Skype to speak with the children. Natalie was only 15 minutes late to this one. I saw the baby for a short time. Natalie had the TV on and Aaron and Eric did not want to talk to long. They wanted to play their game. Aaron said he had a bad day today because he called a girl and his teachers "shit" to their faces. I attempted to see why he did that, but Natalie interrupted to talk about divorce related items.

Tuesday 5/10/2016: Received a voicemail from my associate attorney. He explained that he will be at court tomorrow and that he sent everything we had to Mr. Keville. Of course, after dozens of attempts to reach out to Mr. Keville, their office received no response or paperwork.

Wednesday 5/11/2016: Amended Decree Court
The associate attorney arrived at 8:30AM for the 9:00AM hearing. My attorney did not even know why this court appearance was necessary. If Mr. Keville was actually forthcoming and honest about this whole decree, this court appearance did not even have to happen. My attorney knew that Mr. Keville would be late in his normal fashion, or may not even come today.

Eventually, Mr. Keville appeared (late as usual- which is my fault as the court likes to claim). I was in constant contact with my attorney via phone and discussed every bit of what was going on. Mr. Keville handed my attorney a new decree proposal with even more changed demands. I asked my attorney if he had any excuse why he did not provide this earlier and why he was not working with their office. He said that Mr. Keville did not say anything about it, it did not matter, and Mr. Keville gave his devilish grin while handing it over.

My attorney reviewed it. Apparently, now we are going back on issues which were already agreed to and on the record. It was brought to the attention of the judge. The judge made Natalie and both attorneys' fight it out.

Visitation:
The children visitation schedule was the first issue that was discussed. Back and forth, back and forth the attorneys went. Natalie wanted me to have no overnight visits as it would affect her child support payments. The more overnights with me means less money in her weekly support payment. She did not want this at all.

Natalie and Keville prepared a list of holidays where I would see my children for only a few hours in a day. My attorney explained that the visitation they proposed does not make any sense. It was they who pressed long weekends to reduce the driving times for the children. My attorney was able to change some (not all) of the holidays to this thinking.

However, Father's day I still only have the children for five hours. They are fighting tooth and nail. Eventually my attorney and Keville reached a deal. Natalie would not budge anymore. I saw the visitation date listing and was extremely upset!

I only get to see my children about four weeks total a year! This is terrible! I started to cry. I asked if there was any way to see the children more, but Natalie and her lawyer would not allow it because the judge was counting up the overnights with me and they wanted to maximize their child support numbers. This is so sad.

Alimony:
The next issue was the verbiage in the alimony section of the decree. My attorney asked that death, remarriage, and cohabitation be included. Natalie and Mr. Keville did not want the verbiage of cohabitation. My attorney attempted to

get this included, as it is standard language used in divorce decrees. But we lost that battle. Natalie does not have to inform me or the court if she cohabitates with someone else. I must pay a private investigator and bring her back to court to have it looked into. This was done as her boyfriend is currently living with her. **I have to pay $577 per week in alimony, final number.**

In the decree, it states how at any time Natalie can request the court for an alimony extension. New Jersey does not have lifetime alimony in one shot, they have it in pieces. So after the six years of getting alimony, she can go back to court, cry, tell them she needs more money and more years and have it granted. She can continually go back to court and have it extended each time, which would make it lifetime alimony. I asked what type of things she would need to accomplish this. Since the burden of proof is on me, she doesn't need anything. Just a lawyer, some tears, and a good backstory. If they do grant it, guess who pays her attorney for bringing it to court again? Yup, you guessed it- ME.

Child Support:
The next issue was child support. Now that overnight visit issue from above came out. Mr. Keville and Natalie provided their calculated numbers which included zero overnights and made up numbers (i.e. I don't pay taxes or medical insurance). My attorney fought them with the dental and medical insurance along with the proof. He explained that we will gladly go to trial if they don't use them.

As it was explained to me, child support will always held at the highest salary, even if I lose my job or get a reduction in pay. If I do lose my job, Brendon County no longer has "ability to pay" court cases and I have to pay the highest amount they deem- period.

For future Alimony/Child Support, I learned more information about my future alimony and child support.

Apparently, as alimony decreases, child support increases. It was explained to me that it will be another court case and another fight. If I do not show to it, the judge will default to what Natalie demands. If she wants a million a week, she will get it since the burden of proof of a paycheck is on me and if I am not there, it is defaulted.

As far as the overnights, my attorney calculated that I have a minimum of 43 overnights with my children. Mr. Keville explained that they don't count (I have no idea why they wouldn't). My attorney showed Mr. Keville the law where the 43 overnights are to be counted towards the child support number. They backed down.

Now, in another attempt to increase the child support, Natalie stated that my federal retirement and union participation were not mandatory. My attorney requested that I get him some documentation stating they are required and mandatory. I quickly searched through work documents and Google and found the union contract and congressional mandates about the retirement. I emailed them to my attorney and he presented it to the judge and Mr. Keville.

I asked my attorney why is it that Natalie can make any claim she wants without proof and the burden of proof lies with me or I am just found guilty. It is common knowledge that as a government worker I am automatically in a pension and must contribute to it. The pension is mandated by congress. He explained that he knew this, but the court system is set up this way. "The accusation is the proof."

Natalie and her attorney now reverted back to the old calculated worksheet which was seeking $241 per week in support. My attorney ran the numbers from my pay check and got $198 and offered it to Natalie & Mr. Keville. Of course, they did not buy it. My attorney explained that Mr. Keville and Natalie's father (who according to the court has no involvement) want ten times that amount. I explained to my attorney that the worksheet they now want to use still does not have me paying taxes, insurance, and has a 14% increased amount because my children are over the age of 14. This is the worksheet I had to respond to months ago with all the erroneous numbers within it.

The court saw that we were going nowhere with this issue. They offered to perform the calculations, both with my pension/union dues and without. The numbers were $207 & $192 a week. Mr. Keville and Natalie flipped out about the court calculated child support.

They were sticking to the $241 number, since they "gave me" a higher salary than I made and made concessions stating that I paid for the medical insurance (which even confused my attorney). I am court ordered to pay them, how is that a concession?

My attorney stuck to his guns and I discussed with him that if they continue to battle for this $241 and make claims that my pension is not required, tell them we will gladly go to court and I will also file a motion against Natalie for lying to the court about pensions not being required (as I have the documents stating that I must contribute). Eventually, after an hour, Natalie agreed to the **$192 per week.** Lower than what we offered originally.

Retirements:
Natalie automatically gets 50% of my 401(k), 50% of my pension, and 50% of my social security.

Even if she gets remarried, she still gets my retirement. Looking online, there are apparently lots of women who marry and remarry to gain two and three pensions so they are set for retirement. I fear for the next schlub who marries her. Hopefully he has a good pension to give to her.

Emancipation:
The next issue was emancipation of the children. Natalie wanted child support whether the children were with her or not until the children's 24th birthdays. My attorney fought this and had it changed to 23rd birthdays, but if Natalie shows "good cause" when the children do not reside with her, I still must pay child support. The children are emancipated at 23 unless ordered by the court to extend it due to other issues (like medical).

Marital Debt:
Here we go. Marital debt went up again. Now it more than doubled. My attorney asked for proof. No proof available. So, with no proof, Natalie went back down to $23K. My attorney asked for that proof, they said they will "think about giving it" but nonetheless, I have to pay whatever they claim and something about binding arbitration. Apparently, this debt includes her luxury furniture and cruises she purchased last year. I remember her saying how I would have to pay for them. Whatever!

Insurance:
I have to claim my ex-wife as the sole beneficiary to "cover" the children with my life insurance until children are emancipated.

Natalie's COBRA is paid by her unless otherwise ordered by the court (which Keville's wrote in, I think I know the next court case coming up).

Other Fees:
I must pay additional services and extracurricular activities for the children. I have no input to this. If Natalie tells me that she took them to the mall and purchased pretzels for $100, I must pay.

I pay for college, but have no input on where they go or informed of anything related to that. My attorney fought this.

Now, I have to be informed, but have no input on what they do; I just provide the check.

Emails from attorney:
My attorney emailed me confirmation of the following:

Let this confirm that you have had an opportunity to review the amended property settlement agreement with the handwritten changes and have agreed to the terms set forth therein.

Additionally let this confirm that we have had an opportunity to discuss all changes and all revisions made to the property settlement agreement and you agree to such changes. Let this further confirm that you have received a copy of the agreement from the court in which you will sign and have notarized and will initial on every page in which a hand written change has been made.

Court Finalization:
My associate attorney went through the amended decree to make sure Mr. Keville did not hide any additional demands or modify already set ones (since he is just such an honest guy). Everything seems fine. I still have to split the costs of the QDRO; taxes are the same, and the standard language.

The Judge called me on the phone in open court and asked Natalie and me a bunch of standard questions and went over each and every item in the divorce decree. He asked a final question to both Natalie and I about living the next few years. He asked Natalie first if she is able to maintain her lifestyle with the stipulations in the decree. She happily said "yes" and began thanking him. He asked me the same question. I started laughing. I told him "no" and explained how all the items in the decree FAR exceed what I make. He made a record of my response and I got my normal "I have to find the means" speech.

My lawyer called me and told me that the judge had Natalie, Keville, and him sign the finalized decree. The decree is backdated to April 4, 2016, so I will be already late with the child support. The judge ordered me to print, sign every change and sign the back pages in front of a notary or he will not release my attorney. He wanted it done right then, right now.

I received an email with an upside down copy of the 43 page list of demands (also known as a decree) from the court. So, I ran home, printed it out, went to the bank to get it notarized, Michaela came over to sign the witness block, and the bank was really nice and faxed it to the court house, instead of me having to scan in 43 pages by hand. While this was all happening, my attorney was waiting at the court house.

On my way back home, my lawyer texted me. It is finally done. May 11, 2016 at 3:30PM, it is done! He has the finalized decree signed by the judge and will send a copy to me tomorrow via email. All he asked was that I mail the original to my attorney's office, so I did.

So now total, I have two divorce decrees which total 53 pages of demands I must meet over the next 23 years. After court, Natalie and her attorney were ecstatic over the outcomes. Apparently, Natalie did another happy dance after court like she did during mediation.

Thursday 5/12/2016: Last time I was ordered to pay child support, my account was created the next day. So, I figured today would be the same thing. I checked the child support website for the $192. Nothing yet, however the $300 has been going to spousal support which is paid by the same system. I hope to God they don't combine child support and alimony together.

I started running the numbers and to see where I stand with paying these monthly bills and my spending ability. It does not look promising. More creditors are calling. It's up to 12 times a day, and now they are calling my work line and main office numbers. So with all this going on; I started realizing more and more that I am financially ruined. How can I survive? How do I get out of this?

After I got home from work, I called the children on Skype and started the video recorder (as I always do). Spoke to all three children. Eric was being the most talkative. He was begging to come up and be with daddy. He wanted to go outside to the park and go fishing. I expressed my love to them and explained how I missed them so much.

The session ended premature, as Natalie wanted to explain divorce related items. She wants her tax refund money. I asked if she mailed in the amended taxes. Apparently, she says she did. She also received the Bank of America requests to remove me from her accounts, but has not yet processed them until her attorney reviews them. I requested again to have the motorcycle keys placed on the bike. She said she couldn't find the keys. I informed her again where I last placed them in her car.

Friday 5/13/2016: I resent & mailed an updated NJ Courts District Ethics Committee complaint to the Brendon County Courthouse in regards to Mr. Keville's unethical business practices and behavior. Let's see if they process it this time.

I emailed Natalie about an offer made by my father. The other day I received a phone call and text messages from my father. He explained to me that he has vacation during Father's day weekend and wanted to bring the children up for that weekend. I informed him that it must be approved by Natalie, as I only have the children that day for a few hours. I emailed Natalie the request and copied him into it as well:

Natalie,

Per the court order, I only see the children from 10:00AM-7:00PM on father's day. This does not coincide with the agreements made about reducing travel times for the children.

With this in mind, my father has extended his offer to pick up the children at your residence on the Friday before this holiday and drive the children up to New Hampshire to spend the holiday with me to extend this trip.

Please email me back if you approve this and please make all travel times/dates with my father. Thank you.

She replied shortly afterwards that this was acceptable. I replied back to her to please make the arrangements with my father.

Harassment: Natalie called multiple times and finally left a voice mail at 11:45AM and begged me to call her back as it was about the children. I called her back; she began harassing me about the children's health insurance and child support. I told her all modifications must be made by the court and hung up.

She contacted me later this day to inform me that since the court order only allows for a few hours with the children on Father's Day, she wanted to remind me that these additional overnights are not to be counted in her child support number. Here we go…it's all about the money again!

Natalie called me again at 12:30AM and left a voicemail to call her back about the children. This time, I wasn't foolish enough to call back.

Saturday 5/14/2016:

Garnishment: Did a lot of cleaning up, reorganizing my stuff (3 moves in a year tends to destroy everything). After a days' worth of cleaning up, I decided to check the mail. I received a letter from the federal government payroll garnishment office explaining that starting immediately; my pay was to be garnished the $577 a week in alimony. I also saw memo's and letters from attorneys I know within the office.

I have multiple questions: What happens when child support hits? What takes priority? What about 60% maximum garnishment law? What happens if my pay drops? How much money am I left with to survive myself? (Remember, I can still go to NJ and admit myself to the Jail operated work release program as New Jersey's answer to all of this). I am so upset about all of this. I told Michaela what I received, she too is very upset. This garnishment went very quickly. Luckily, there is a contact name on this letter that I can email.

Harassment: Natalie called multiple times and finally left a voicemail at 8:15AM in the morning. She inquired where her Toyota Corolla title was. I called her right after the voicemail and informed her that I do not keep track of her documents. She claimed I stole it; I informed her that I will look for it within my paperwork, but I am pretty sure I do not have it. I asked her about the motorcycle. She did not know where the keys were to it (again).

She then began her harassment about the children's medical and dental health insurance. This is a BIG deal with her as she has been harassing me about it since the child support number came in my favor. I decided to hear her out and placate her.

So she began explaining that her "salary" also known as alimony is non-taxable and un-claimable so she qualifies for welfare and Free State paid health insurance. She said that she wanted to cover the children's health and dental insurance and it can be easily done out of court.

All I have to do is show up at her attorney's office and fill out forms he is preparing for me. She continued to explain that she is "doing me a favor" so I do not have to cover the children and "save some money."

I never knew anyone, especially someone so vindictive and evil to call me at least ten times in a day to do me a "favor." There is something else at play. I did some research and of course I found my answer. It is quite obvious that she is upset with the child support number and she wants it changed. Her harassment about this came right after that number was produced by the court.

I am a firm believer that she thinks I'm stupid. I know that she wants a higher child support number (it's obvious with this whole years' worth of games). She wants to remove the health care credit from the child support calculation.

If she really wanted to help with health care expenses, why would she go out of network? Why would she go for unnecessary surgeries and medical procedures for both her and the children? Why wouldn't she tell me about her welfare and state provided coverage previously? I think I know, because she claimed that she did not receive any welfare on the child support calculations sheet; essentially lying to the court.

Monday 5/16/2016:

Garnishment:
I was doing some budget number crunching after receiving the garnishment letter this weekend. I went through all the numbers. They do not look good for me. I need a few part time jobs.

I emailed the federal government payroll garnishment office contact that was listed on the letter from this weekend. I attached multiple documents and explained my case. I showed him (with math) how the child support and alimony exceed the 60% maximum garnishment law. I also emailed him my list of questions:

1. When you begin garnishments of both child support and alimony, what is the order of priority? Meaning do you pay the child support in full and the remaining portion of the 60% out of alimony?

2. If I receive more or less than my standard amount within my paycheck (bonus, or demotion), are my payments automatically adjusted to pay out my obligations within the 60% law?

3. If I get remarried, does the garnishment cap of 50% come automatically, or do I have to contact your office and request the change?

Financial Ruin: I cannot possibly afford payments to my divorce attorney, Natalie's mystery debt, her attorney, my bills, etc. How am I supposed to pay Natalie's "marital debt" and counsel fees? They only gave me to the beginning of August to provide everything in one lump sum. This is not happening to me, how the hell am I supposed to come up with this sort of cash? How do they expect me to come up with this sort of money? Are they stupid? They know how much I make. The writing is on the wall. They want me to fall behind and then seek their warrants.

Children Phone Call: I called Natalie on her cell phone at the normal Skype time of 5:30PM. I spoke to the children very briefly. Natalie interrupted as she normally does to ask if I have looked for and found her Toyota Corolla title. She also informed me that the motorcycle was ready to be picked up. I told her that I can only look for the Corolla title during weekends, as weekdays I have a long commute and do not have the energy or time to look for it.

Natalie began asking me about Michaela's house in Binghamton (not sure how she knows, because I never told her). She explained that I am at Michaela's house in Binghamton during every Skype session and inquired if I was living there. I told her I live at my address in Freeport which she has. She began asking how much rent I paid, my utility bills, etc. I told her it's none of her business.

She became irate and demanded that I tell her as it is her right to know. I told her again it is not her business and she is not a friend or family member- she is an adversary (as defined in the legal paperwork). She began threatening me stating that she and her attorney will do anything in their power to find it out and make sure she gets the money that she is entitled to. I asked if that included lying to the court. "He represents me and we will do whatever we want" was my answer. I hung up.

Tuesday 5/17/2016: Email Day:

1. Received an email back from the federal government payroll garnishment office. They stated:

The payroll system is automatically setup to ensure that the not to exceed 60% percentage is not exceeded. The first priority is child support then alimony. As far as the 50% goes, that only applies if you are paying on a second child support order. The child support and the alimony will be a prorated percentage based on your disposable pay. The child support will be entered into the system at 16% and the alimony will be entered at 44% to equal the 60%.

2. Received an email, phone call, voicemail, text message, etc. from Aaron's school. This was to inform me that the school went into a shelter in place, at approximately 10:00AM this morning, due to an alleged threat to their security. The police were contacted and conducted a thorough search of their school. They confirmed that there was no threat to our safety. Students and staff are safe and they have resumed a regular

school day. **This is now the fourth incident this year! Tell me again how NJ schools are safer than NH?**

3. I received a news article from my employer about my federal retirement accounts. Apparently the QDRO process normally conducted does not work for federal accounts. I forwarded this information to my divorce attorney. In addition, now that my divorce is complete; I thanked him for everything and inquired about when my retainer will be issued back to me.

Wednesday 5/18/2016: Yesterday, I called up an old friend who I used to ride my motorcycle with. He offered his help and said he could pick up the motorcycle from Natalie on Friday or Saturday this week. I emailed Natalie the specific times he is available and she responded via email offering Saturday afternoon for him to pick the bike up. I let my buddy know and he will pick the bike up on Saturday.

Later today, Natalie texted me stating she was in a major car accident and my middle guy was in the car. I called her frantically to check on his condition and if he was hurt. She told me that he was alright and was not hurt. She just wanted to inform me of the accident (she crashed into a parked car) and since the car is in my name, I am responsible for the damages to both that car and the poor bastard she smashed into. Of course she blamed the accident on me and the parked car. She explained that multiple body shops and insurance companies will be reaching out to me. I hung up the phone.

The good news just kept coming today; I went home and found a letter from Visions Federal Bank. Apparently now they are going to be suing me for the money and they too want me to pay for their attorney costs. I forwarded this letter to my attorney. He contacted me the next day, this letter is apparently a standard threat they use. That puts my mind at ease (I think).

Thursday 5/19/2016: Contacted Natalie via phone. Spoke to Aaron for only a minute. She said Eric did not want to talk as he was playing a video game. I inquired about father's day visitation and the motorcycle. She said that she has not spoken to my father yet but they (Natalie and my father) are planning for the children to come up on the Friday before Father's Day and leave that following Monday. Natalie said she was going to pull the children out of school for those two days. Natalie also inquired with my about July 4th weekend. I told her that we will discuss when I have the calendar in front of me.

So against court orders, for father's day, Natalie will allow me to have the children for the weekend instead of the few hours as listed in the order. But she told me when she approved it that I am not allowed to calculate those overnights with the children against her child support numbers. You got to be kidding me; this is all she thinks about. Money, money, money. I'm just glad I get to see my children.

I reminded her about the motorcycle being picked up on Saturday and to ensure that the battery is still plugged into the wall. She began playing her games saying she never agreed to this and didn't know if the battery was still plugged in. I reminded her of her email and that I have everything in writing and hung up.

I texted my father to ask about the arrangements with the children for Father's day. He said that Natalie has not make contact with him yet (she is waiting till last minute) but he will be seeing them this Sunday to get them their weekly exercise.

Friday 5/20/2016: Received a text message from Natalie at 2:38PM requesting a copy of the Toyota bill. I also received a

Progressive Insurance statement today about the damages to the minivan which she incurred on Wednesday 5/18/2016.

Saturday 5/21/2016: Motorcycle Pick up. My friend texted me at 10:30AM. He is at work but will be at Natalie's house at 11:15AM. I texted him back and confirmed arrangements with him. I also told him about the motorcycle cover, extra keys, and trickle charger for him to pick up. After speaking with him, I then called Natalie to remind her again about the pick up today. More games from her, and now she needed to "do a vetting" with whoever was coming to the house.

I was very nervous what games Natalie was going to play with the motorcycle and my friend. It was silent from 11:45AM when my friend said he was on his way till 1:15PM when he finally texted me back saying everything went well.

Monday 5/23/2016: I logged into Skype at 5:00PM to speak with children. 5:30PM came and went. I texted Natalie to remind her that I am allowed to speak with the children today.

Natalie finally called me on Skype (late as usual) and I began the recorder. Aaron spoke very briefly and wanted to play in the other room. The baby saw me and was yelling my name. After a brief visit, Natalie moved him to the other room saying right now is a bad time for him because he hears my voice and wants to see me which she does not want (isn't this the point of seeing my children and show that they miss me????). I inquired why she will not give the baby free reign in the apartment. She first stated that he does, but then stated he does not due to the apartment having electrical outlets.

What is she so busy doing, where she cannot watch the baby for a few minutes so he can walk around? While seeing Aaron and Wyatt; Eric was jumping into the camera view to talk with me. As normal, Natalie was standing behind the children interjecting.

Eric wants to go fishing and was asking about "flying with Michaela." I told him that I am going to see him on father's day and we will go fishing and maybe a campfire. Eric was ecstatic and said his normal "okay, let's go." Eric continually said to "come over quick, play with us" and he wants to go to "daddy's house" and that I am his best friend.

Eric asked his mother to come up to see me this weekend. I said that was fine, but Natalie became upset with Eric. Eric was begging to come up and stay with "daddy" and Natalie began telling him that he cannot come up to daddy's this weekend because I have abandoned him and that I do not love him. Eric became furious and started yelling at her. She ended the Skype session.

Soon after, Eric restarted the Skype session and called me back. Eric began playing with a toy by the computer screen, and just wanted to play near me. He wanted me to watch him. Natalie began her normal harassment and hung up on me. Natalie left me a voicemail shortly after she hung up on me, as Eric wanted to speak with me again.

Monday 05/23/2016: This weekend, Natalie left multiple voicemails and texts requesting my password information for Toyota. In addition, I received a letter from Progressive Insurance explaining my insurance policy deductibles and rights for my recent claim which occurred when my Toyota minivan was involved in an accident on 5/10/2016.

Tuesday 05/24/2016: I received an email from Natalie requesting that I provide her my user name and password to Toyota. In addition, she requested that I take the children on the following days:
Friday 07/01—Sunday 07/10
Friday 08/05—Sunday 08/21 (She is going on a cruise)

Wednesday 05/25/2016: I received an email from my attorney about the QDROs. I called him back and told him whatever he has to do to get them complete. After work, I called Natalie to let her know that I will be at a prior engagement tomorrow and to reschedule the Skype session with the children for Friday at 5:30PM. She inquired about the minivan again, and I informed her again that she must call Toyota to get the title and finance information sent to her. She asked about the children visitation and demanded that I give her an answer as she already made plans. I told her that I must schedule it with work, but she demanded that I visit the children on the dates she sets.

Thursday 05/26/2016:
I emailed Natalie to follow up in writing about the conversation we had yesterday about me calling via Skype at 5:30PM this Friday to see the children and as far as the minivan is concerned, she must contact Toyota Customer Service. They will direct her on the paperwork she must fill out and she will have to provide a copy of the divorce decree to them listing her as the new owner of the vehicle. I also provided Toyota Financial contact number.

My attorney's office bombarded me with paperwork for the QDRO. Of course, it is late as normal and I now have to rush to get it all done. I will send it out on Friday.

At 5:45PM, Natalie left a voicemail stating that she is changing her mind and that I cannot speak to the children on Friday. Once again: bad faith. She knew I had a previous engagement today as we discussed on Wednesday, and we rescheduled the Skype session for Friday. I love how she just ignores agreements & decrees and makes up stuff as she goes.

Friday 05/27/2016: Signed QDRO forms, compiled all the requested information, and forwarded to my attorney.

I contacted Natalie via Skype at 5:30PM. I called her three times until she answered. She was not prepared for the session. The children and she were driving in the car, eating ice cream. The session only lasted two minutes.

Sunday 5/29/2016: Natalie left a voicemail at 7:00PM. Eric wanted to talk with me and was pressuring her to call me.

Monday 5/30/2016: Texted Natalie to remind her of the Skype session at 5:00PM. Natalie texted me back twice demanding that I agree to her dates & terms for the summer visitation schedule with the children. I spoke to Eric on Skype. Once again, he was begging to come up and stay with "daddy." Natalie did her normal interjections while he was talking, and at certain points, you can see him look at her before he spoke (she was out of camera sight). Aaron did not want to talk; he kept going back to their room to play. The baby was taking a nap. I asked Eric if he played in the park or water sprinklers today- not surprising the answer was "no."

Wednesday 6/1/2016: Received a text message from Natalie requesting that I provide her with the visitation schedule for the children for the entire summer. I have already informed her that I cannot give her the entire summer as work does not approve my leave months in advance.

Thursday 6/2/2016: In the morning, I responded back to Natalie's email about visitation with the children. I confirmed the dates of: Friday 07/01—Saturday 07/09.

After work, I waited at the normal time to speak with the children on Skype. Natalie was 30 minutes late to the session. I was speaking with Eric. She gave Aaron a video game and then asked him if he wanted to play or speak to me. Obviously, he said that he did not want to speak to me. Natalie in her angry voice stated "he does not want to speak to you Robert!" As I was talking to Eric, Natalie began her harassment stating that Eric needs his baby teeth filled and dental work performed. She demanded that I pay her more money and pay for this additional dental work.

I inquired why Eric's baby teeth need to be filled, due to him losing them. She just yelled saying she will do as she pleases, and I must pay regardless. I reminded her that this Skype time is for the children and me to see each other, not for harassment. She began yelling at me saying that it's not harassment; rather it is her reminding me of my obligations. During her yelling, Eric sat at the computer looking at me with a distressed look on his face, extremely sad.

I asked to see the baby, Natalie yelled at Eric to move away from the computer, he did not move. He said he wants to stay with daddy. She yelled at Eric and placed the baby into a carrier toy barely in camera sight. Natalie ended the session with more demands.

Natalie later called and emailed, responding back to the visitation email about July. She stated that she already knew my answer for July (guess she is psychic), but demands that I take them in August and to confirm the dates.

Friday 6/3/2016: In the morning, I responded back to Natalie's email about visitation with the children. I confirmed the dates of: Friday 08/05—Saturday 08/20. However, this is contingent upon me finding a babysitter, as I do not have enough vacation time.

Friday 6/3/2016: Natalie sent an email and called multiple times to change the dates of visitation. She specifically wanted to change the drop off date from Saturday the 20th to Sunday the 21st. I informed her that I must still seek work arrangements along with child care as I did not have enough vacation time between the July and August vacations. She became irate and explained that she already booked a cruise for those dates. I did not confirm dates with Natalie or respond.

Sunday 6/5/2016: Natalie emailed and called me again stating that she will be traveling on her cruise during August and that I must abide by her demands (per court order). I reminded her that per court order I get the children two weeks in the summer, but it does not state which two weeks or provide specific dates. I reminded her again, as I have multiple times that I am looking into day care and child care for the dates she requested as I do not have enough vacation time and the children deserve the best care possible. I did not confirm dates with Natalie or respond.

Monday 6/6/2016: I received more emails and calls from Natalie in regards to the summer visitation. She informed me that I must make August a priority over other dates and that I must take off work (she claims she does not care if I get fired or not). Minutes later, she sent another email explaining that she cannot wait for me to make arrangements for the children, and that she will be sending the children up to me on August 14-21 because she already scheduled a cruise to Bermuda during those dates. I'm still curious how she can afford that since she tells the courts she is dirt poor. I did not confirm dates with Natalie or respond.

She is being adamant about these dates as she already booked her cruise without checking my schedule first. I have to make some arrangements at home because after the first two weeks of visitation this summer, I will be completely out of vacation and sick time.

After work I had my Skype session with the children. I got home early at 4:00PM. I attempted to contact Natalie on Skype, but she did not answer. She finally picked up at 5:30PM. Spoke to Eric, Aaron (briefly) and the baby. Eric was telling me that they were ready to play in the sprinklers outside, which Natalie set up, but right after she set them up she cancelled their playing so they could speak to me. This is a deliberate action to get the children upset with me. Aaron barely spoke to me (as he was mad at me for cancelling his sprinkler session). Eric was upset as well, but still spoke to me.

The baby was saying "ena"- for Michaela and Dada clear as day. The household looked severely messy and the baby was in his pack/play prison. Natalie began harassing me about the visitation stating that I have already agreed to her terms & dates. She also said I must abide by the court order which includes her demands. I ended the Skype session.

Tuesday 6/7/2016: Received two emails from the children's soccer league which contained a confirmation of payment. Received another email from Natalie explaining that she would like to sign the children up for soccer and I would have to pay her $310. She explained that she wanted to confirm with me before signing them up. However, she did not realize I received emails that she already signed them up.

Natalie demanded more money. She wants me to pay for her cruise, more extracurricular stuff, more out of network medical, and alimony. If I want to see my children, I will pay up. Funny how she can use the children as weapons. I am still waiting on the invoices for the extra-curricular.

Thursday 6/8/2016: Contacted Natalie three times from 5:00PM till 5:30PM. Natalie called my cell phone and stated that she is cancelling the Skype session. I was not allowed to respond as she hung up.

Friday 6/9/2016: As the tax return check has still yet to arrive, emailed Natalie to inquire if she changed the address on the taxes and if she received any refund check. Reminded her that she still owes me for filing the amended return and the now (owed) payment to NJ State. As per the court order, I would keep the $9455.

She did not answer the questions, she explained that she is entitled to additional refunds from Massachusetts, explained that I owe her $1360 ($450- Eric Dental, $600- Aaron Dental, $310- Soccer), and she refuses to pay for the amended return.

Sunday 6/12/2016: Emailed Natalie about visitation stating that I am able to take the children from Friday, August 12 through Sunday, August 21st. Pick up/drop off at Bayville, MA Cracker Barrel. Natalie quickly responded and explained that I did not inform her about the July visitation or the status of her tax return. I had to remind her about the emails dated June 2 & 9 which we agreed and discussed both those matters. I do not understand why she is continually asking questions she knows the answers to. I am also getting pissed that she is cancelling Skype sessions.

Monday 6/13/2016: A friend who has been following Natalie's Facebook shared with me a recent post of hers along with a picture of Eric. It appears Eric gained a significant amount of weight. The picture had Eric sleeping with a video game controller in his hand and pen marks all over his face. The posting stated, *"I thought drawing on someone's face was mostly reserved for the first person that went to sleep at a sleepover or in his case the person that fell asleep while playing a video game. It's nice to see the sibling camaraderie has been established early between them. Now I just have to clean it up before he realizes what his big brother did to his face while he was sleeping."*

After work, I contacted the children on Skype. Aaron was playing a video game, standing directly in front of the television. Eric was playing with his toys, and the baby was in his prison crib. Eric initially said he did not want to speak with me, but came around. Aaron did not want to talk long as he was playing his video game. Natalie muted the Skype session via her phone for a short period while I attempted to speak with the children.

When she called Eric over to talk with me, he did not come over. She then yelled out "cookie" and he came over thinking there was a treat for him. Like a dog.

I inquired about Eric's weight as he looked like he gained more weight this month. Natalie stated she thinks he weighs 56lbs. I asked her what he is eating. She stated that he could be eating better, but his significant weight gain is because of me. Apparently I am a terrible father and making the children gain weight because of my move to New Hampshire, according to her. She hung up the phone right after this.

Shortly afterwards, received an email from Natalie requesting an answer regarding if I will be sharing the soccer expenses, swim lessons for the summer and Eric's dental bills. This is the first time I heard of swim lessons, and as far as soccer and dental bills; Natalie has yet to provide proof of these expenses.

Tuesday 6/14/2016: Emailed Natalie the following: *Please ensure that you pack adequate swimming gear, hot weather gear, pool shoes, and long pants for the children for them to play in the woods. Thank you.*

Friday 6/17/2016: I called the children on Skype. Natalie was fifteen minutes late, as usual. She asked me if I got her emails regarding additional money. I kept on being focused and requested to speak to children multiple times. She kept on pressuring me asking "if she could ask me an additional question."

Eventually, after repeating myself to speak to the children, I informed her that it is my time with the children, not her time to harass me. Natalie moved the phone camera and kept the camera pointed at the ceiling, not the children. I was able to speak with Eric and the baby. Eric asked if we are going fishing soon and if we are going to go swimming. Both children had chocolate cookies all over their faces: from ear to ear. I asked them if they were going to run around outside and burn off some of that chocolate, their mother interjected, she said "no."

I asked to speak with Aaron. Natalie yelled at him a dozen times and told him to talk with me. He eventually did, but he only said, "Hello daddy."

In addition to chocolate cookies, Eric had chocolate pudding in his hands. I told Eric he should be using silverware or a spoon for his chocolate pudding. His mother interjected with "they don't need spoons."

At this point, Natalie took over the conversation to continue asking questions. She asked me if I was satisfied with my bariatric surgery. I told her it was none of her business and hung up. It's been three months since I have seen my children, and I miss them so much. But I am also done with their mother's games.

Friday 6/17/2016: Began receiving more medical bills for Natalie for her "therapeutic care." The notes on the bills state that these charges are post-divorce and she is no longer covered under my medical plan.

However, the bills state that I AM RESPONSIBLE for them. This is completely against the divorce decree. I called her and asked her about it. Her answer, "You must pay it; I don't care." This is driving me into financial ruin! I love how we are still playing these medical insurance games. Isn't this insurance fraud? Shouldn't the doctor see this? What is therapeutic care anyway?

Friday 6/17/2016: The children and my father arrived at my home at 6:00PM. I had dinner waiting for them. They left New Jersey at 11:00AM but hit lots of traffic in NYC. The boys ate their dinner and the baby was running around the house. His walking was a bit clumsy at first, but since he has free reign around the home; it quickly got better. I set up a campfire for the children and I taught them how to roast marshmallows. Aaron and Eric loved roasting them and learned about fire safety. We all had a blast.

I received several bills today which appear to be more medical games. I need to include these in the financial ruin list.

1. The first bill is from the dentist for work performed on me in 2015 (which is odd, because I did not go there in the past year). The total is $90.

2. The second bill is from Natalie still utilizing my medical benefits, even after the divorce. The bill is for "therapeutic care" and the note within the bill even states this, but explains that I am responsible for the bill. The total is $150.

3. The third is a bill from Natalie's Hospital. I contacted these people months ago to ensure my balance is at zero. But apparently now they are billing me $555 for services performed on 10/22/2014. I haven't received any bills for this until now.

Saturday 6/18/2016: The children and I had a fun filled day. Aaron and Eric went fishing in the brook at Michaela's sisters and caught two little trout. However, they did get bored at different times. Eric kept reeling his fishing rod in. The baby was given free reign around the yard and was running all around. We finished the evening with the children playing at Michaela's parent's house, dinner with the family (the children had trouble eating the good food, but the baby ate all of his potato/regular salads along with mine), and Michaela's mom gave Aaron and Eric haircuts. The baby was able to run around the wrap around deck and made a game going up to Michaela's mother and giving her hugs & kisses.

When we arrived home, my father opened my mail and saw threatening letters from creditors and their attorney's. He told me I need to curb my spending and learn how to budget better. I went off on him. I explained everything going on with my divorce, since he failed to even check to see what has come about or transpired. He still thought I was married to Natalie. He didn't realize lawyers cost so much money. He didn't know that I have to pay Natalie's attorney. He requested a copy of these new threatening letters I received from the creditors.

Sunday 6/19/2016: Early morning, Eric got sick in the morning and vomited in his bed, the hallway, and living room. He wanted cereal and milk, but I gave him a lighter breakfast- which was good, because he vomited it up as well. He eventually felt better. The baby ran around while Aaron got dressed. Eric is still having trouble dressing himself, Aaron is fine. We went to Walmart to pick up some small odds and ends and made our way to Michaela's sister's house. We swam in the pool all day. The water was low enough where Aaron could stand, Eric needed only swimmies, and the baby needed his baby tube. The whole family was there and enjoyed taking turns with the kids and baby. We had a BBQ, along with lobster and steamers. Lots of pictures and videos were taken of the children, especially when Eric was using the hose to spray Aaron. The boys are still afraid of going under water and jumping into the pool. We left once the baby became very irritable because he was tired. Once we got home, all the boys and I snuggled up on the couch to watch Toy Story movie.

Monday 6/20/2016: Eric woke up before everyone in the house. He woke up around 6:00AM while I was teleworking. I set him up with some puzzles to build quietly before his brothers woke up. Eric has been extremely needy and is craving attention. He cannot play on his own and needs constant attention and entertainment. Whether it was fishing, swimming, playing ball, or playing puzzles; he consistently requests help and wants others to play with him. I gave him all the attention and love he wanted!

I fixed a couple of Eric's toys which broke this week. He was ecstatic when I fixed them. I loved it when he was telling me that he loves me and that I am his best friend.

For breakfast, Eric asked several times for chocolate. He explained that he is allowed chocolate for breakfast at mommy's and wants to go back to her. He refused to eat his eggs and toast. Natalie called around 9:00AM. She wanted to speak with Aaron alone. I allowed it and hung out by the door to listen. Natalie asked Aaron if I was away from him and began asking leading questions. "How many times did daddy hit you, you're not having fun, right?" Aaron complained to her that I did not allow him to play with his tablet this weekend. She told him how terrible I was because of that and said it is "okay, you're coming home soon."

The children cleaned up after themselves for the weekend and left at 10:00AM. They were very sad to go. Aaron and Eric stated they wanted to stay and live with daddy. There was crying and sad faces when they left.

I contacted Natalie and informed her of the bill I received for her therapeutic care inquired about the bill and her that I am not responsible for her medical. She stated that I must pay regardless of the court orders, as she is above them and I must pay whatever she tells me to.

She also began having a tirade about how she promised Aaron that he can play with his tablet at my house. He is accustomed to playing with it often and going to bed with it. I requested that she leave it at her house next time as I do not allow tablets in my home. I want the children to develop an imagination and play outside.

During this weekend, the children were good overall. Aaron had some stints but time outs worked for him. We all had a lot of fun and the children and I enjoyed spending father's day together. I can't wait to see them again. I am sad and solemn right now, as I normally am when they leave. I wish I could have them all the time and not just be a "visitor" in their lives.

Tuesday 6/21/2016: Natalie left a voicemail explaining that the children are deathly ill. I called her back and of course, she was "crying wolf." She explained that Eric had a cough and she must bring him to the hospital for it. She began harassing me stating I did not take care of the children and Eric got sick because of me. She began roping Aaron into the conversation asking him if Eric was sick at my home. Aaron at first said no, but she began yelling at him and his story changed. She informed me that she'll send me the bill.

Later on in the day, Natalie called back and explained that Eric wanted to call me to tell me how sick he was. She put him on and instead of doing what his mother wanted, he began begging to come back to "daddy's house" and said he wanted to go fishing and swimming again. Natalie hung up the phone.

Wednesday 6/22/2016: In the evening, Natalie left two voicemails stating there was another important matter involving the children. She followed up with an email. It had nothing to do with the children:

1. *Can you let me know when I can expect the money for the credit card debt? How do you want to handle the Toyota Sienna? Do you want me to take out a car loan for it for the remanding amount? Or can I sell it? Please respond to this email as soon as you can. Thanks!*

I responded back to her with:

> 2. Per the divorce decree, you are to furnish all statements and invoices of the debt to determine the amount. Once you provide all the information and give me and my attorney time to review, we will then revisit that question. We have been waiting for you to provide this since the interrogatories.

Despite what you claim, you must follow court orders as well.

Natalie responded quickly stating that they were already provided to my attorney and she is going to forward my message to her attorney to bring me back to court.

I was now forced to do the same. I forwarded the emails to my divorce attorney:

> 3. I received this request from Natalie about the marital debt. I have yet to receive any proof of her debt. She says that she sent it to your office?

I can only assume that they are planning on bringing me to court again soon. Please advise.

Thursday 6/23/2016: Received an email back from my divorce attorney. He explained that Natalie is incorrect. His firm never received these documents. He checked his emails and their cloud service. There is no proof of debts.

Thursday 6/23/2016: I called the children on Skype at the normal time. I called multiple times and texted Natalie to remind her that it is my time with the children. Natalie finally called me back on Skype ten minutes late. Aaron didn't talk much; Eric did the majority of the talking. He wants to go fishing again; he also saw an alligator at Van Sun Zoo today. Natalie said the baby was sleeping and hung up quickly. She pushed Eric out of the way and was yelling at him while he was talking to me. When she called Eric over to talk with me, he did not come over. She then yelled out "cookie" and he came over thinking there was a treat for him. Like a dog.

Tuesday 6/23/2016: I checked my mail today and received a response letter from the NJ Courts District Ethics Committee for my second attempt to bring my grievances about Mr. Keville's unethical behavior and lying and make it known what he did. The letter is dated June 17.

Apparently, they say the case is still open (even though it's not) and once again, they will not process anything I give them and they provided all the evidence and letter to Mr. Keville to let him know about the grievance. Why is everyone in that state SO CORRUPT?

Okay, so the Ethics Committee is refusing to process my complaint. So they like to go against their own procedures and policies. They forwarded my complaint to Keville again, whom I later found to be one of their "investigators." So, apparently, he is allowed to investigate a complaint about himself.

The answer that I received from them generated my curiosity as I never heard of a case like this being denied without any reasoning. Not even worth someone looking into it. So, I decided to perform some research. Google, online forums, and many phone calls later to other attorneys and law professionals, I got my answer: When an ethics report (complaint) comes in from the street, the ethic's board is supposed to review it and perform an investigation. The local attorneys in their own district areas make up these ethics boards.

I was informed that these ethics boards are made up with those lawyers who do exhibit unethical behavior and want that extra layer of protection. It's usually the more ethical and truthful lawyers which stay out of them. So essentially when you are complaining about an attorney, they will protect themselves by either denying it right away or making up a reason to deny it.

This now is all making sense. Why deny my complaint without any firm reasoning and then send it off to the person I am reporting so they can be informed and close out the case for good? It's because Mr. Keville is part of this board and had a chance to review it along with his criminal friends and now both he and his friends are protecting themselves and each other.

Tuesday 6/23/2016: I also received the federal tax return check today. I deposited it and sent Natalie her amount per the court order. I also included a letter with the check that read:

Dear Natalie,

Please find enclosed your tax return amounts per the divorce decree.

As you already know, the amended return numbers are as follows:
Fed: $3030 (Difference)
MA: $98 (Difference)
NJ: I now owed $328 (Due to the increased double state taxes)

The cost of the filing is $220, plus I have spent $10 for mailing all these items and packages to you for signatures and mailing to the tax entities. Thus, I added the two refunds and it is: $3128.

Per the agreement, you get the difference after my original amount ($9455) plus you pay the filing fees. So with those deductions, the final number you get is: $2,570. ($3128-$220-$328-$10).

If there are any questions, feel free to contact me or my attorney.

Monday 6/27/2016: In the morning, I received another $500 out-of-network dental bill for the children. It appears that Natalie is up to her old games again. I'll just add it to the pile.

Monday 6/27/2016: Received another letter and bill from the medical insurance company. It is for a claim regarding an ambulatory surgery center in New Jersey. It says that I must call them back with information regarding the claim, or it will be denied in full. Wonderful!

I went home after work and started up the computer to talk with the kids. I called Natalie on Skype a total of twelve times along with calling her cellphone. I received no phone call back, no email, and messages went straight to voicemail. At 6:00PM, I emailed Natalie the following:

Natalie,

Tonight was my night to speak with my children. I contacted you on the phone and on Skype multiple times with no answer from you.

This behavior is uncalled for and the children are suffering because of it.

In addition, I received a bill in the mail for an ambulatory surgery. You are supposed to inform me of any medical issues with the children.

Your continued attitude of the decree and court orders not applying to you is not the case and now I am forced to seek legal representation for access to my children. Your bad faith is not appreciated, and when the children are older they will resent you for keeping them away from me.

An hour later, Natalie texted me explaining she is not available and she will attempt to have the children's babysitter get a hold of me via Skype. She blamed the cancellation of Skype on me.

Three hours later, Natalie then emailed me the following:

Robert I told you I was not available to Skype and if you wanted to Skype let me know I would have the babysitter set it up if you could not wait. I also did inform you that Eric needed Dental work and you never responded to those emails. That is the bill you are referring to I guess. I can't let our children's health wait until you decide to respond. I also talked to you about it and you refused saying he was just going to lose his teeth anyway why fix them. His doctor, dentist, and I had a different opinion. That is the bill you are referring to.

Tuesday 6/28/2016: Early in the morning, I received another email from Natalie. More lies, harassment, and deceit! Apparently, she contacted me well in advance for the Skype session (which she didn't) and demanded more money. In addition, I guess I am behind in child support, even though it is garnished. Love the lies. I think she is beginning to believe them herself.

Robert: I did not keep you from the children! You moved to New Hampshire to be with another woman. When the children are older they will resent you. I was not available to set up a 5 minute Skype phone call this evening. I said I was not at home to set up the Skype I should have told you in advance I responded when you called me and said I could have the baby sitter set it up for you. YOU DID NOT RESPOND! I have always acted in good faith. In addition Aaron's CCD class is $100 are you going to help contribute to that or are you going to ignore this email as well? You also have not paid me any child support speaking of court orders. You are about over $4000 in arrears in what you owe. But I take it you assumed it was getting paid so I won't blame you for it. It should be taken out of your paycheck shortly. It's easy to speak of a 5 minute phone call as if that is what is keeping you from your children. You can call your children any time you want. If I was not there to set up Skype and you chose to not have the babysitter do it for you why not call your kids latter? Just curious I guess.

Tuesday 6/28/2016: I had to follow up on the medical bill I received yesterday. I called the medical insurance phone number listed on the letter in an attempt to provide them more details on the new bill. I also wanted to know what surgery my son went through, as I am kept in the dark. The website of the surgeon's office states how they perform all these intensive surgeries such as bariatric. I explained the situation over the phone to the woman, and the billing code used was not a valid code, so we decided to call the NJ doctor together on a conference call. We wanted to call together for two things; first, for me to learn what happened with my son, and secondly, for the insurance to pay their bill.

The woman over the phone called three different phone numbers; all numbers were disconnected. She went ahead and did more research on this company and called me back a few hours later this day. She found out that the surgeon was a woman named "Patricia." I was told to give her a call as I am the subscriber and have full rights to the information to what the surgeon did to my son. I made the calls and it was a dead number.

With Natalie's claims with me being behind in child support, I now had to contact the NJ probation office to see what Natalie's friend (my case worker) was doing to my account. I called several times with no answer. I finally got through and spoke to a Middle Eastern woman who was extremely hard to understand. Apparently, I am in arrears for $350 for child support and $3,000 in alimony. I inquired how that is possible as they garnish me, but she did not understand my question. She explained that I should seek other avenues to pay my support (e.g. loan).

Later on in the evening, I received an email from Natalie. This time, she has begun her games with stalking me. She explained that she sees that the house I am living in is for rent and inquired to where I was staying and where the boys will stay while they are in New Hampshire. I can't believe she is still stalking me. Doesn't she have anything better to do with her time? Or am I paying her the "alimony salary" to just stalk and harass me. Michaela read the email too and was livid! I responded back to her with the following:

Natalie,

It is not a current listing and is none of your business. As normal, I will be bringing the children to my residence in Freeport now and every time they come up. However, I am more curious on how you have the time to be stalking me and gathering research on New Hampshire real estate when you should be looking for a job.

If you keep up these stalking games, you will leave Michaela and me no choice then to file the applicable restraining orders and begin private investigation on you as well since these are the games that you are playing.

Wednesday 6/29/2016: I received a voicemail from my medical insurance company. They keep calling up the surgeon and out of network medical center Natalie went to the other day. They still cannot get a hold of anyone there and left dozens of messages. They told me not to worry, and they are going to handle it from their end.

I could not keep up with all the creditors, the court ordered payments, and just everything. I have been getting harassed by creditors, courts, and Natalie. With all these newest games with the medical insurance I had no choice. I have been forced into financial ruin. I had to officially declare bankruptcy today.

Thursday 6/30/2016: Saw Natalie cashed her tax refund check. I sent her an email asking if she could send the children's extra bikes up with them so they can ride their bikes up at my house for the weekend.

*Just a little background on this, I purchased and received donated bikes throughout the years. In total, there were about six of them. Essentially two different types if bikes for each kid.

Natalie responded telling me she wants them back after I am done with them. She does not want me to have them as they are still "her asset." Later on during the Skype session, she explained that she will not send any bikes at all. They are "hers" not the children's.

During my two minute session with essentially just her and Eric; Eric said he is ready to go swimming and I noticed the baby still locked up in his "pack n' play" prison. Someone knocked at the door and Natalie asked Eric to open the door…not even knowing who was on the other side. The session ended abruptly when Natalie's ex-stripper sister came into the house.

Entry #7: Post Divorce Games (Quarter 3, 2016):

Friday 07/01/2016—Saturday 07/09/2016: I had my visitation with the children. I used up my vacation time at work to take off this week to spend time with them.

Each day, Natalie continued her harassment of me by contacting me either by phone, Skype, or email. She requested to speak with the oldest, Aaron alone.

Overall, each time the children went into the car, it was a catastrophe. Aaron would pull and twist on his seat belt, which is now completely broken off its base. The two older children cannot pick up after themselves, and as far as getting ready; Eric cannot dress himself at all and Aaron cannot tie his shoe laces. Michaela and I were continually tying them for him. Eventually, Michaela picked up a set of good shoe laces.

All weekend Aaron used his manipulation skills by saying to other's what they want to hear. For example, he went up to Martha saying how beautiful she is to get snacks and other items. In addition, there was a case when I was out of the room (but could still hear the children) Eric was crying saying he wanted to go to mommy's for McDonalds, Aaron told him that he misses mommy too and cannot wait to go home to her. I entered the room to put clothes away and Aaron then began saying how he wants to stay with me and "eat healthy."

For Eric, we had multiple times of him not listening to directions. I had to repeat myself three to four times until I received a response. On occasion he did yell at me with a "no" which I had to parent him on. Eric also had issues utilizing the toilet. Each time he went to pee; he would press his body into the toilet (toilet seat down) and pee all over the bowl. When he had a bowl movement, he would put the toilet seat up and sit on the toilet bowl itself (completely opposite toilet bowl usage). In public restrooms, Eric attempted to sit down in a urinal. Aaron explained that this behavior was because they don't have a clean toilet bowl or a seat at mommy's house.

Friday 07/01/2016: I picked up the children after work to start the week long visitation. I was supposed to pick up the children at 5:00PM in Bayville. Natalie did not show until 6:45PM. When I picked them up, both Aaron and Eric were covered in chocolate from head to toe. I asked Natalie to clean them up before they went into my car. She poured a half empty water bottle on her hand and smeared the chocolate on their faces and said "are you happy, they are cleaned." She then threw the children's bags at my car.

On the way up to New Hampshire, Eric was explaining that he went to the school nurse today because he wet his pants in school. We stopped at Walmart in Tilton to pick up some food on the way home, as the children explained they did not eat since 1:00PM that day. While taking them out of the car, Eric's pants were wet along with his car seat. He wet his pants. I changed and cleaned him up. We had the discussion about peeing in his pants, and holding it in. He also needs to tell me when he has to go to the bathroom.

We got home late as there was a strong thunder storm on our way home. When we got in, we had no power, so with just a cell phone in hand, I got the kids changed and in bed.

Saturday 07/02/2016: The children woke up early. We had our normal breakfast, got changed, and brushed our teeth. Before we left the house, I unpacked and sorted through the children's clothes to put them in the dresser draws. Unfortunately almost half the clothes provided by their mother were fleece and winter clothes. Love the continued games!

We stopped by Walmart to pick up some supplies and snacks for the week. Afterwards, we went over to Martha's house to use her pool. The whole family came by and a small get-together became a large one. The children had a blast!

After the pool, we started to head home and decided to go to the local park by the bank. Aaron and Eric were playing with other children and the baby was running around. I had some issues with Eric listening and Aaron having temper tantrums. Unfortunately, at the park, my eyeglasses broke, so have to get those fixed tomorrow.

Sunday 07/03/2016: Aaron was up all of Saturday night into Sunday. He was screaming bloody murder about sunburn. He was screaming that he was having a "heart attack" and "had to go to the hospital." I gave him lotion, aloe, and wet clothes and none worked. This morning, Michaela's mother came over with some more sunblock and aloe along with checking out Aaron. The baby & Eric's faces had more sunburn then Aaron did: and they were fine. Aaron was barely red. His actions were surprising since when he was at the pool yesterday; all three of the kids were covered from the sun.

After we put sunblock on the children and got them ready for the day, the children and I ran over to the local mall to get the eyeglasses fixed and went over to Martha's house to play in the pool. The family came over again and we all had a great time! Eric would ask for his "friend" and Carlos and he would play their football game.

In the evening, I put all the children to bed, but over the lake, the neighbors had loud music and a fireworks party. Eric and Aaron woke up and wanted to see them, so I quickly dressed them and they sat in the car trunk (opened of course) and watched the fireworks from the house.

Monday 07/04/2016: I quickly got the children ready for the town parade. At 10:00AM, the town had a 4th of July parade. My friends at the Masonic lodge saved us some seats in front of the lodge. We parked, got ready, and watched the show. Aaron and Eric stayed down by the road because all the organizers and marchers were throwing candy out for the kids and Batman was there giving out small prizes. The baby sat in the shade and was interested in all the colors and noises.

Afterward the parade, we went to Martha's house to play in her pool some more. The kids were begging to go to the pool. They are my little fish. Took more pictures of all three in the pool along with baby Wyatt running in the yard. Well, until my phone broke. I think it overheated and now will not turn on. I set up portable crib for the baby to take a nap there as well.

Michaela came home from work today and greeted the children. She missed them so much! They missed her too! We went to Michaela's mother's house for dinner. Natalie contacted me on Skype there and demanded she speak with the children. The kids spoke to her on Skype, but had their reservations about it. They were more interested in playing outside. Skype session was recorded, as usual.

Tuesday 07/05/2016: Natalie contacted me in the morning with more harassment. I let her speak to the children and then hung up. The boys and I went with Michaela to the airport. She had to finish up a quick meeting, so the children and I walked around the ramp. The boys were looking at all the aircraft. Eric wanted to go into the maintenance hangar. We did and he started to point at all the aircraft saying that he owns all of them and wants to fly.

Michaela treated the boys and me to the Hobo Railroad ride. They served us lunch, gave the children balloon animals, gifts, and other items. Before we went on the train, there was a railroad park next door which the three kids played in. Eric refused to eat his lunch. He only wanted McDonalds. Michaela told him that he needs to eat his lunch or he will not have s'mores later on after dinner. He still refused.

After the ride, we went home and had dinner. Eric still only wanted McDonalds. After the children took baths and went into bed, Michaela started up the fire to make s'mores with Aaron. I put the baby and Eric into bed. Eric did not get any s'mores because he was bad today and refused any meal except McDonalds. Aaron had s'mores and played with some sparklers.

It was a long, exhausting day. After the day's activities; it was apparent to both Michaela and I how the children were not appreciative whatsoever.

Wednesday 07/06/2016: Today we went to play mini-golf and go on some water scooters. I attempted to show the children how to hit the golf ball and play; but it was to no avail. Aaron and Eric did not listen, as they already know what they are doing (apparently) and on the water scooters; Aaron was on his own, Eric & I were on another, and Michaela was with the baby taking pictures. Afterwards, we had lunch at a local diner but it was interrupted by baby Wyatt having a complete melt-down. I took him outside and he fell asleep in the car.

Since I did not have a working cellphone today, I used Michaela's to contact Natalie to make sure that the pickup time for the children was still on for noon on Saturday. Calling her is never easy. Instead of just confirming the time; Natalie continued her harassment and began telling me that she called Toyota and they voluntarily told her about my bankruptcy and that she will be providing me documents I have to sign to get the minivan released to her. I informed her that I cannot sign anything without my attorney looking at it first.

With the children's behavior, I decided to call their pediatrician. I spoke to a doctor within the office, since their normal pediatrician was out on vacation. She explained that both Eric and Aaron were diagnosed with ADHD, but were on no medications and that Eric was diagnosed with obesity and requires specific vitamins (which Natalie did not inform me of).

Later that evening, I received more harassment from Natalie. Now she emailed my attorney along with hers. I apparently now have to go through loops and bounds with the children with me to get her paperwork filled out. I love it how every time I have the children, she pushes these games on me. The email read:

I attempted to pay off the Toyota Sienna and I was informed that you had filed for bankruptcy. In order for me to proceed with obtaining the vehicle and paying off the debt on it, I need you to sign an authorization for third party payoff. Or I need you to be available to talk to any dealer if I decide to trade it in instead. They will only give the authorization for third party payoff to you because you are on the account. Please get this form signed for me by this Saturday when I come to meet you to pick up the boys. As requested I am notifying your attorney as well. I hope you get it done soon because I don't know what legal right I will have to the vehicle since you filed for bankruptcy.

Thursday 07/07/2016: My friends from the Masonic Lodge invited the children, Michaela, and I to go to the New Hampshire Lake Science Center. It is a hiking trail/science center/zoo all wrapped into one. We saw bobcat, lions, and other New Hampshire native animals. Aaron also got to feel a snake. There were outdoor play areas for the children as well. The kids had a blast there. Later, we all had lunch with my friends and spent the rest of the day watching movies and playing outside at Michaela's parent's house.

Friday 07/08/2016: I received an email from Natalie in the morning to make sure the children contact her; they did. Afterwards, we all went to the mall to walk around and played outdoors. We went to the beach on the lake and Michaela, the children, and I played in the sand and swam in the lake. We went to a local amusement park and played mini-golf and Aaron, Etic and I went on water boats which had water guns on them. We had a water fight on boats! We had a great time! Even today, Eric tells me how he wants to do it again.

Saturday 07/09/2016: Prepared the children to go back with their mother. Michaela, the children, and I visited with my family in Bayville. The children were playing and eating their lunch. I called Natalie as she was ½ hour late. She was going to be later and wanted to know if she could stop at my family's house. I told her she is not invited there.

Since my family and I expected her to be late, we began feeding the children lunch anyway. So at around 12:30PM, we dropped off the children at the meeting point. Natalie introduced herself to Michaela. I asked Natalie for the documents she wants me to sign; she said that I have to do the research and provide her the documents. I inquired about what the doctor said about Eric's weight and being classified with obesity. Natalie just stated "So what? Anything else nice you want to say?" She still blames Eric's obesity on me. I am still not sure how this is possible as I only see him a few weeks a year.

Monday 07/11/2016: Another big computer/paperwork day. I received an email from the children's schools about more lead found in their school drinking water; I also received the certified mail receipts from more letters I sent for all these bills.

I followed up on the Toyota payoff issue that Natalie created. I filled out the paperwork and forwarded it to her. I emailed her the following:

Natalie,

You did not attach any document to this email. In addition, per our conversation last week, you stated that you would give me the form on Saturday and never did. I have since did your homework on this and received this form attached. However, this form is not required as you have the same divorce decree that I do and all you need to do is present it to Toyota.

But per your request, I have attached this and mailed you the original.

In addition, have you mailed out the Bank of America documents I provided to you two months ago to remove myself from the marital accounts? I had them signed, notarized, and certified mailed to you to confirm receipt.

Thursday 07/14/2016: Received more good news in the mail today. First was another letter from the Department of Interior. They are now garnishing me a total of $1,538 per pay period (every 2-week) per the additional court orders. I did learn though, they garnish me this amount until the State of New Jersey tells them to stop, not by the divorce decree. I looked this process up online. It seems like the New Jersey State Courts do not follow up and many fathers overpay for years without any reimbursement. They have to pay a lawyer and go back to court just for the State to stop the garnishments; just another thing to look forward to the next couple of years.

I emailed and spoke with the lawyers in my division inquiring about this process and if it is true that they will continually garnish me this same amount until New Jersey tells them to either reduce it or end it. I provided them a copy of my divorce decree showing the reduction after three years, but they did not care. Unfortunately, the garnishment orders that New Jersey sent to them did say to garnish me until "further instruction." While speaking with them, I felt an underlying tone that they thought I was a deadbeat I have encountered this tone before and heard the line of "only deadbeats can garnished" at least a dozen times already. I guess in New Jersey, as they garnish most men; we are automatically deadbeats, even if we are paid up.

I called the New Jersey Probation Services about them informing my employer in the future to modify or terminate my garnishments. I learned that the case manager is ultimately responsible for informing my employer. However, it is up to them if they order my employer to have it changed. If they choose not to enforce it, I will have to bring the State of New Jersey to court to have them enforce their own court order. In which time; Natalie can actually fight it and have the alimony increased or have it remain the same. So this will more than likely have to be the case since I have already went through games with these people and Natalie's interference.

So, my question is why even have this in the decree, if it is just going to be another fight and not even enforced? I'm curious if Natalie and her attorney knew this process and were hell bent on the alimony to be set this way (higher then reduced lower). I have so much to look forward to!

The second was a medical bill from an Eye Care Center in New Jersey. The bill was for Eric. Apparently they tested Natalie and the kids and billed my non-existent vision insurance. When I called them about the bill, they explained that they attempted to bill Natalie multiple times, but she refused and on their forms she wrote down to bill me. I asked how I am responsible for the bill and they explained that I just am. I tried to make a reference stating how I can just put down anyone's name on a form and have them be billed for my medical work is illegal. They did not understand. They said it will go to collection if I refuse to pay.

I also wrote a strongly worded letter to the Eye Care center; as I do not have any vision insurance and the invoice even stated that they are out of network and it is an out of network service:

To Whom It May Concern:

I am in receipt of your invoice dated June 15, 2016 for services performed on May 24, 2016 for Eric Arlotta. It appears that these services are not covered as I do not carry vision insurance on this patient.

Please be advised, I am the primary holder of the medical insurance of this patient, however I do not have vision insurance. These services you provided are NOT covered by a medical plan, and are a non-covered service, as it is indicated on your invoice.

Per court order (attached to this letter); I am only responsible for providing medical and dental insurance for this patient. My ex-wife must only use "in network" health care providers and use "in network" services. This was not an emergency situation nor did I provide you written consent prior to this treatment.

Natalie Arlotta, the patient's mother knows this information and knows that the children are not covered under any vision plan. You are not the only medical facility which has fallen for Natalie Arlotta's games. My ex-wife has been visiting out of network doctors and requesting out of network services to play games and drove me into financial ruin.

After speaking with your office on July 14, 2016; it is apparent that your billing services and business practices need revision. Sending a bill to an individual which has no insurance or ever been to your practice for services they did not authorize is not only unethical but possibly illegal. I am forced to copy my attorney into this.

After careful consideration of the issues involved in this invoice and claim, and the fact that not only do I not cover vision insurance and have not authorized this; there is no overdue balance nor any current balance due for the services mentioned above. This matter is closed and I respectfully request that you update your records accordingly. Thank you.

Friday 7/15/2016: Received a letter from the QDRO company through my attorney. The letter stated there were two issues with the processing of the court ordered QDRO. First was the marriage date was incorrect, the second was Natalie's portion of the QDRO has not been paid. I wonder how much money it just cost me for my attorney to review this letter and forward to me?

Anyways, I called the company up and they were very helpful. I corrected the marriage date with them and inquired about Natalie's portion of the QDRO. They are charging me this week with my $500 portion, but Natalie and her attorney are outright refusing to pay their portion. The woman handling my case can't believe this; she never dealt with this before. She said that she never had to deal with someone refusing this; it's only in Natalie's best interest to do so. After the QDRO is done, Natalie gets half of my 401(k), so she was confused. I informed her briefly of the issues with my case.

Unfortunately, this is another tactic they are using. If they fail to pay and the QDRO gets held up, this will unfortunately be my fault as the QDRO has not been completed and it would be seen as not following the divorce decree (contempt of court) even though it is really them. Another thing I can look forward to.

Wednesday 7/20/2016: While I was down in Oklahoma City for training, I received more homework in regards to my divorce and more games by Natalie:

1. Bank of America Games:
I received mail at home with Bank of America Statements. Natalie made $12,000 in deposits not including my child support or alimony in cash deposits (wonder where she is getting all that money) and withdrew over $10,000 in expenses

for herself. I believe $5,000 went to her upcoming cruise next month.

I received emails about her over drafting the savings account and how I am responsible for the overdraft payment. Apparently she has not removed me yet.

I wrote the following to Bank of America and provided them with their forms which Natalie refuses to sign along with the email I sent to Natalie to have them signed, and full copies of my divorce decrees.

RE: *Court Ordered Customer Removal Authorization*

In accordance with my divorce decree and court order, I am to remove myself from all the accounts listed below. I have attached my divorce decree and the court orders to this letter.

On April 13, 2016, your office sent me the following forms and in accordance with your policies, I have filled out and notarized the Customer Removal Authorization/Modification Agreements to remove myself (and only me) from the following accounts:

Case/Request Number: Account Number: Type: Savings
Case/Request Number: Account Number: Type: Checking

These forms were provided to Natalie Arlotta (the account holder) on Thursday, April 21, 2016 for her final signature and to provide them to your office. Unfortunately, Natalie refuses to sign these forms in an attempt to have me placed in contempt of court order.

Please reference all the attached documents and remove me from all Bank of America accounts. Please update my account accordingly. Thank you. If you require any additional information or have any questions, feel free to contact me or my attorney.

2. **QDRO/Pension Games:**
The QDRO company which is dividing up my accounts emailed a copy of my receipt for their fees. They explained that they reached out to Natalie and her attorney multiple times without any response. Unfortunately, this is another tactic of theirs from my understanding. They are going to inform the court that I have not done the QDRO even though we are waiting on them for their part of the decree. Whatever, it will be my fault once again, I'm used to it by now.

The QDRO company needs to know which account to split; pension or 401(k)/TSP. I called them up as I do not know which one they should split since Natalie and Keville are playing games again, they told me to have my attorney call them.

I reached out to my attorney. I spoke to him and he will get a hold of the QDRO company to determine which one to split. He asked if my entire 401(k) is marital. I told him about the military buy back and the money I rolled into the account was premarital, but it is way too complicated and will cost too much in legal fees to have it researched, so just process it as is. He is thinking about splitting the 401(k) first until Natalie pays her share of the QDRO. He will inform the company and take it from here.

Something so simple becoming so complicated. If she would just pay her half of the QDRO as the decree states, all these phone calls, letters, emails, writing, legal costs would never have happened. Once again a prime example of when she decides not to do what she is required to means hours, days, even weeks of heartache and headache on me. I hate how she can give me all these hours of aggravation and stress, just because she can.

Friday 7/29/2016: I have begun getting my paychecks with all of the garnishments and arrears payments taken out. So now with all the garnishments; I now take home less than $350 a week. I have just enough to pay for my car and gas. I did the calculation; I make $8.75 an hour now after all the payments.

After I saw my paycheck and became even more depressed; I received a voicemail from Natalie. She is going for a personal loan for the car. She requires my signature to cosign it. Is she serious? She also informed me that I must pay her a few thousand dollars a week for additional "babysitting" costs for the children. This is funny as her mother babysits the children. I remember she did this before.

With me making only $8.75 an hour, I'm still not too sure how she and the courts expect me to pay all these additional costs, her attorney, and all of her out of network medical games. I guess I just have to find the means, as the courts told me last time. As far as seeing my children more, I cannot even afford an attorney to fight for more custody or visitation!

After the last visitation in July through my next visitation in August 2016, Natalie denied me seeing the children on our Skype sessions each week. Without fail she would cancel the sessions on the last minute and find every excuse under the sun.

At times, Natalie would not show up on the session at all, and other times would call me demanding additional money in exchange for me to speak with the children.

She explained that the children do not want to talk with me unless I give her the money she wants. More money, more extortion; but this is the behavior that New Jersey Courts allow.

Friday, 8/12/2016: Summer Visitation. I was excited to see my children this week. With Natalie's Skype session games, I haven't been able to see them. I picked up the children for visitation after work. Natalie stated previously on the phone that she would be at the meeting area in Bayville at 4:00PM, she also confirmed this time in the morning. I waited and waited at the meeting area. Eventually she showed up at 6:00PM, only two hours late, but who's counting. Her mother was present during the drop off.

Natalie was telling me that Aaron did not want to come with me because I did not give him enough snacks or his required 4-5 glasses of milk a day. She demanded that I give him this amount of milk and more snacks. While she was making these demands, her mother began telling me how terrible of a father I am.

Natalie boasted how she will be in Bermuda on a cruise during the next week. She will be on another cruise later this year and demanded that I provide her a copy of my work schedule, training schedule, and both Michaela and my vacation schedules so that she can schedule her cruise (on our schedule). She explained that she is entitled to this information and if I do not comply, she will get a court order for it.

I attempted to explain that if I am at work or work related training, it would be hard to schedule a visitation during that time. She just did her normal evil laugh and said I had no choice and I would only see the children when she allows it, even if she schedules it during those times. Now I see why she wants that information.

She also began demanding where I was living. She explained that she did significant research on Michaela and wanted to know if I was staying at her home in Binghamton or Freeport. I told that I live in my home in Freeport. She demanded the same information again saying it is for the children. I told her that the children would be in a safe, comfortable, loving home with me. Later on during the week of the visitation, she would harass me with the same questions.

Once the children were moved into my car; Natalie gave Aaron and Eric their brand new iPADs and Nintendo game systems for the ride. I attempted to remind her about my rule of no tablets or game systems, but it fell on deaf ears. I tried taking them away from the kids, but they became extremely upset. I figured I would let them have the electronics until we got home.

Not soon after we started driving, Natalie called me up saying that she wishes me to have the children next week as well, for Labor Day. I reminded her that she stated to the court that too many visits (especially back to back) are too much travel for the children. I'd be happy to take them, and love to see them, but I'm curious why she now wants me to have them next week as well; another vacation possibly?

During the car ride home, I caught up with the children. Aaron said something weird about the divorce. He was telling me that I stole thousands of dollars from mommy and said that "mommy's lawyer has a gift for you." He thought it was an actual present and wanted to know if I got it and what it was. He had no idea that a lawyer's gift is a bad thing. I am not sure how he knows this or why Natalie is drawing him into our divorce. A six year old should not know about any of this!

Saturday 8/13/2016: The boys slept in and woke up in the late morning. I cooked them breakfast, brushed teeth, and we got ready for the day. It was a rainy day today, so we decided to go to some stores and do indoor activities. We started to look for some birthday gift ideas for Aaron to celebrate his birthday this week since I will not see him for his actual birthday.

Sunday 8/14/2016: The weather held up nicer today. Eric has been begging to go to the pool at Aunt Martha's. So, the whole family got together and we played in the pool and had outdoor activities. When we arrived at the pool, Eric automatically set up his football game and he, along with his "friend" Carlos played their game.

We played outside and the baby played in his inflatable ball pit which Michaela purchased for him. There were a few instances when Aaron and Eric began fighting with each other, but it was quickly remedied with having them run laps around the house and do pushups. We are still working on getting one push up done.

Monday 8/15/2016: Because I used up my vacation time on the last visitation, I had to work in the office today. The children needed to be watched. Michaela and I researched day cares and found them to be way too expensive. Plus, having all three at the same time is too much for anyone. So the family pitched in to watch all three. Eric and Wyatt were with Michaela's mother and Aaron spent the day with a family friend. All three boys played outside, ate, and had a full day of adventures. When Aaron came home, they all played in the yard, ball pit, played in the garden, and picked blackberries. When Michaela came home from work, she treated them to ice-cream.

Tuesday 8/16/2016: I was able to work from home today. Michaela had to work at the airport. Aaron requested that he go to the airport with her to see the airplanes. Eric said something funny telling Aaron not to touch the airplanes he owns (last time he was there he picked out airplanes and said he owns them). Michaela was nice enough to take Aaron with her to work. They had a fun day at the airport and other airport workers played with him, entertained him, and purchased Frosty's for him. At home; Eric, Wyatt and I played while I finished up some work and later had cupcakes they made with Michaela's mother.

Wednesday 8/17/2016: I worked from my office today. Michaela watched all three children. She called in the morning to let me know that the baby learned how to take off his diaper and proceeded to pee in his crib. It is now time for potty training!

At work, I received a letter from Toyota Financial. The minivan that Natalie has been awarded is now completely paid in full. About $6500 paid off in one lump sum by her. This payoff along with a cruise to Bermuda; I'm still not sure how she is desperate for money.

I also received my "gift" from Natalie's attorney which Aaron told me about on Friday. My attorney received a bombardment of legal paperwork which consisted of letters stating how terrible of a person I am. The letters were written by Mr. Keville.

My attorney has never seen this type of letter before. It explained how all my children are under the age of six (untrue), how my ex-wife is completely financially dependent on me, and how I have not been paying child support or alimony (even though it is garnished and I am paid up).

As in all bankruptcy cases, Mr. Keville is supposed to just state that he objects to my proceedings and file the objection electronically. Apparently, not only did he not file electronically with the court system, but the letter did not follow their guidelines for the objection. Instead of just saying he objects and follow the rules, he used his unethical tactics within his letter.

Thursday 8/18/2016: I had to work at the office again today. Michaela gave me consistent updates with the children. She and her family were able to watch the children again while I was at work.

They attempted to give the children milk, but the kids did not want any and drank their juice and water instead. This was a daily occurrence. We wasted a bunch of milk trying to give the kids the amount their mother wanted us to. At least their mother would be happy to know we attempted to comply with her demands.

Aaron was corrected after failing and refusing to listen while climbing a rock wall. He was placed in time out. In time out, he began biting himself leaving teeth marks on his arm. He told Michaela that he wanted to hurt and kill himself. Much like his mother did when she did not get her way. She inquired why he wanted to do that and attempted to defuse the situation. He said *"I can go into the kitchen and just take a knife out and kill myself."* This behavior is completely new and we did not know where he heard this or started doing this. We did not say anything like this last month.

Later, Michaela came to the office and greeted me after work. Her family watched the children when she came down. We met with a divorce strategist to help protect ourselves from further onslaught by Natalie and Mr. Keville. He had a lot of good ideas, but our options are limited as everything must go through the New Jersey court system and they are renowned to be corrupt and the "wild west." Afterwards, we shopped for Aaron's birthday gifts.

When we came home from shopping, I laid in bed with Aaron and Eric to hang out and talk. They both explained that they had good days. I spoke to Aaron about his behavior and the incident involving him biting himself. He lied saying that he was not on the rock wall and stated that he was mad because Eric was hitting him and he got in trouble for it.

Friday 8/19/2016: I took off from work today. Michaela and Wyatt went to the store to pick up birthday party supplies. Michaela was telling me the stories of how Wyatt was flirting with women at the store and saying hi to everyone.

I brought Eric and Aaron to a local metal foundry to watch copper being melted. It was an interesting experience watching the foundry and metal workers move around liquid metal. The workers set up the area so the children could enjoy themselves. Aaron did not enjoy it, and while he was "bored" he explained again that he wanted to hurt himself.

Natalie called a dozen times and I eventually answered the phone. She demanded that she speak to the children alone. I gave Aaron and Eric the phone and walked a small distance away. Eric was telling her how we are celebrating Aaron's birthday today and explained how excited he was.

She started asking Aaron leading questions. She asked him how bored he is and told him he would be safe at her home soon. Aaron repeated her answers that said he was bored and wanted to come home. He said that New Hampshire does not have city parks and he misses them. I guess he does not want to have his birthday celebration or enjoy everything I have done with him so far this week.

At 1:00PM, Michaela, the boys, and I went to a large amusement park with friends from the Mason lodge. When we arrived, our friends greeted us at the door with tickets and food. They are so nice and treated us to a fun filled day. They spent in excess of $100 just for the tickets!

The children ran around the various park areas and rode a train. During the train ride, the children onboard were to scream at a train robber to go away. Aaron began screaming "Go away you bitch." I slapped his arm lightly and told him we do not say that word. It is just another thing which Aaron has been saying, which I do not know where he learned it.

Eric and Aaron saw water bumper boats like the ones they were on last month. The bumper boats move around and have tiny water cannons on them to spray other boats. They both wanted to go in them. So, Aaron, Eric and I waited in line to go on the ride. After the safety briefing which the employees told us the rules, not to run, and wait for their assistance to enter the boats; Aaron decided to go against each rule and run, put himself into the boat, and doing so, almost fell into the water. I rescued him before he fully went over the dock and the attendants screamed at him for not listening to their instructions.

I apologized to the employees and they allowed Aaron to enter his boat. I went into Eric's boat. The ride started and all 30 boats went into the water and everyone began spraying each other. Eric had a wonderful time. I looked over at Aaron; it did not look like he was. He was smiling when he sprayed another child with his water cannon, but when he was sprayed back; he crossed his arms, and began to have a temper tantrum. He did not want to play anymore because someone sprayed him back.

So while watching him crossing his arms and not move at all, his boat just stayed still. Eric maneuvered our boat and Eric fired his water cannon directly onto Aaron which made him more infuriated! Eventually Aaron softened up and started to play as he was squirting more people.

The ride ended and everyone got off the boats. Aaron saw a water slide and wanted to go on it. Our group wanted to go to the last Bear Show which was showing that day. Michaela and I told Aaron we will go on the water slide after the final Bear show.

Because he wanted to go on it right now, Aaron decided to throw the temper tantrum of the millennium. He began throwing himself on the ground, not moving from his spot, saying foul language and screaming at our friends who treated him to such a day. I got him up and started moving him with the group towards the Bear Show and told him to behave. He began walking in a way that looked like an old German military march along with having a sour puss on his face.

During the Bear Show, he was crying and complaining the whole time how he could not see unless he had a front row seat. He made such a scene! Michaela found a front row standing area for him to go to. He went over to it and had even more temper tantrums! An older woman in the front row saw this and gave him a seat next to her to enjoy the show. He was ungrateful to her and informed her of such. This was so embarrassing!

Michaela and I were at our wits end and decided to leave. While leaving, Aaron had no remorse for his behavior. Michaela asked him what would he want to do instead, his answer was "In New Jersey they have bounce houses and video games." Instead of an amusement park, he wanted to play video games.

During the ride home, Aaron was begging for his video games. Once we got home, despite Aaron's behavior, we decided to continue having his birthday celebration. We had cake, singing, balloons, gifts, you name it. During the week, Aaron picked out many toys while we were shopping. Michaela picked up those extra gifts he pointed out. She also picked out small goodies and Slinkys (per Aaron's request) for goodie bags for the other children. Aaron opened up those gifts and started playing with them.

During his specially made dinner, Aaron was telling the family about his video game at home in New Jersey called "Grand Theft Auto" and how cool of a game it was. I am still in shock that his mother allows a six year old play that game.

Saturday 8/20/2016: We all went to the town "Old Home Day Town Celebration." There were local vendors, a parade, army trucks, soldiers, book fairs, and food. During the parade, candy was being thrown to the boys from the marchers. Michaela purchased ice cones for the children and tried to teach Aaron and Eric how to throw rocks into the pond. Michaela's niece, Emma was there and we all had a good time.

After the town celebration, we all went to Martha's pool to play. The rest of the day, we all played poolside. The whole family and I played with the children. Eric and Carlos played their football game.

Insurance Abuse:
When I got home, I received good news in the mail today. I received a medical insurance Statement of Benefits for Natalie. She is still using my medical insurance!

This letter is just like the others I have received:

These charges were incurred by your spouse after the date of divorce. They have been removed as a covered dependent under your blue cross and blue shield service benefit plan. For this reason, no benefits are available. **You are responsible for these charges.**

This letter looks just like the one I got from the same doctor back in June. However, this one is for $600 in therapeutic care. I researched who the doctor was. It is her psychologist. I contacted him previously, but he still refuses to talk to me about his billing practices.

I called the medical insurance antifraud hotline. They explained that I am not responsible for the payment, but cannot do anything about the abuse of my benefits.

Bank of America letter:
I received another letter from BOA still refusing to remove me from the bank accounts unless Natalie signed the forms. They provided another copy of the forms for Natalie's signature.

Sunday 8/21/2016:
Natalie stated that she would be at the drop off point at 4:00PM (as agreed on 8/12). Michaela, the children, and I went to my aunt's house in Massachusetts at 2:00PM for a quick visit and lunch before dropping the kids off. She along with my family wanted to see the children. The kids played with the dog, toys, and had lunch.

The moment we went into the house; Aaron began asking my aunt for presents. He expected her to have gifts for him. My aunt and I still do not understand why he now just expects gifts whenever he goes there. He never exhibited this type of behavior before, nor have we provided gifts each time for him to warrant that type of behavior.

My aunt had some spare puzzles in the back room and gave them to Aaron and Eric to play with. Aaron did not want to play with the puzzles, so he began to have a temper tantrum and act up. I instructed him to play outside. Eric and my cousin went outside with him to play.

Inside the house, I was able to catch up with my aunt and grandmother. We talked about many different current events and watched baby Wyatt run around and play with a tiny shopping cart full of fake food.

My aunt prepared a huge lunch with various dishes for all of us to eat. She also provided lots of fruit as well; apples, mangos, and strawberries. Eric and Wyatt eat all of the fruit they could fit in their mouths. Aaron on the other hand did not eat a single piece of fruit. He explained that he does not have to and does not like it. This is quite a change since he was little. He used to love fruit.

Natalie called up and showed at 4:15PM. I attempted to have her sign the Bank of America authorization I received yesterday to have me removed from the account. Instead of signing, she scribbled all over the signature and date sections so I now have to reorder another form. However, she did explain that she closed the accounts.

Later on, I called the bank to confirm this. They did to a degree. Two out of the three accounts are closed. Only one more remains. They will send me the information and paperwork to try to close this account again. I told them that I tried to get Natalie to sign the authorizations previously, but she refused. Let's try this again; Round 2.

After the drop off, I went to get some gas across the street. I noticed Natalie was still in the parking lot taking pictures of the children. She called my cell phone when I was still able to see her. She explained that Aaron has severe sunburn and this is child abuse on my part. She explained that he had severe sunburn last month under my care and had welts all over his body. She threatened me saying that she "has the pictures to prove it." I told her that I always put sunblock on him and will put more if she would like.

Luckily, I took pictures of all the boys before handing them off to her to show that he did not have severe sunburn, or really any sunburn at all. I sense I know what game she is up to now.

Overall/Concluding Visitation Thoughts:
During this visitation week, Michaela and I noticed more break downs in the children's behavior and had multiple concerns. Most of these behaviors are all new (since last month). We do not know how they came about, but will have to follow up with their pediatrician.

Eric and Aaron's listening skills are diminishing. I often have to repeat myself multiple times and they either tell me "no" or claim they understand and do the exact opposite thing they are supposed to. Other times, they question everything I ask.

Aaron is exhibiting extremely high and low emotions. When he is at a high, he begins to flap his hands and arms uncontrollably. He begins to use foul language as well (like on the train ride). When he is bored or has a low, he explains that he wants to hurt himself, he wants to die, or he uses the suicide terminology. However, this talk ends when he is reengaged or entertained. I tend to think this is a tactic he is using for attention, but it is severely disturbing that a six year old would talk like this because of boredom.

All three children were constantly touching their private areas in both public and private. They could not keep their hands off of the private parts. This is a new habit they are all doing (including the baby). I spoke to a few people about this and we all have many concerns with why they may be doing this.

We thought it could relate to a new person the children were talking about. They were talking about a man named "Uncle Don" and every male adult they came across during the week they called "Uncle Don." It could correlate with this, which would be a worst case scenario, or just a nervous habit all three children picked up somewhere. Nonetheless, this is something I am going to monitor which in itself is going to be hard to do as my divorce decree states the next scheduled visitation is for their school vacation in April. A lot can happen from now until April of next year!

I also still have concerns with the children's television time while they are with their mother. It was a concern while I was married to her and still runs to this day. The children are still being babysat by the electronics. While the television was on up here during the visitation, all three children (including the baby) were completely immersed in whatever show was playing. They just turned off the world and stared blankly into the screen.

Aaron and Eric were talking about video games every chance they got and wanted to play each day. They did not know how to play outside, run around, and use their imaginations. I had to show them how to play, how to create an adventure, even how to throw rocks into a pond.

Every night, Eric wet his pants in bed. I had to put on a pull-up on him to prevent the bed from getting wet. This is completely new. He did not wet the bed before. On Tuesday afternoon, Aaron tattled on Eric when he peed in his pants. After I changed him, I noticed Aaron defecated all over the bathroom along with a full load in his pants. It was so bad; I just trashed his underwear and pants. I do not know why both boys cannot use the bathroom. They were potty trained in the past.

On another occasion, Aaron had stains in his underwear like he did not wipe himself. He explained how he does not have to wipe each time. I forced him back into the bathroom to clean him and told him how bathroom cleanup works. He began wiping standing up and did not wipe effectively (dabbing instead). I tried to show him how to wipe, but he told me he rather do it the way mommy showed him.

Even though I cannot correct the behavior as I only see them a few weeks a year, I try to do whatever I can to give them the love and support they desperately need. My children are desperate for attention. It is apparent that they do not get enough down in New Jersey. Even Michaela took Aaron to the side one day to talk with him and tell him he is loved. He broke down in tears and gave her a hug. Every night I made a point to snuggle with them, give kisses, hugs, moral support, and just saying I love you. Before the boys left, Aaron told Michaela and I that he did not want to leave. He wanted to stay with us and Eric said to me "daddy, you are my best friend."

Friday 8/26/2016: Just a few days after dropping off the children, I received notification that Natalie is still playing her old games. I received bills from the Port Authority of New York with pictures of her car claiming that on 7/9/2016 she did not pay any of her tolls when she went over various bridges. I am responsible to pay them. I called Natalie up to ask why she did not pay her tolls. She responded that there is nothing I can do to fight it and I must pay her tolls. I called the Port Authority to inform them of the dilemma (especially moving forward). They told me I have to provide a letter to them for each toll Natalie blows through along with copies of my divorce decree awarding her the vehicle. I asked them what if she does this the next couple of years (since this is not the first time she did this). They informed me that it will be the same procedure. Just wonderful, another thing to look forward to! So, as it only took Natalie a few seconds to decide not to pay her tolls, means hours of paperwork and writing letters for me.

Saturday 8/27/2016: Natalie called me several times. Despite what she and her attorney claimed to the court about the children traveling too much during visitations with me, she begged me to take the children for Labor Day, which is less than two weeks since the last visit.

My diary may be at an end, but my story is not. My saga is to be continued…

CPSIA information can be obtained at www.ICGtesting.com
Printed in the USA
BVOW05s0103160916

462228BV00004B/8/P